THE STORY OF

UNIONS
IN
CANADA

JACK WILLIAMS

J. M. DENT & SONS (CANADA) LIMITED

Printed in Canada

1 2 3 4 5 6 7 8 9 10   Alg   84 83 82 81 80 79 78 77 76 75

Contents

Appreciation is expressed to the Ontario Federation of Labour for assistance which made this book possible, as well as to Eugene Forsey and Mary Kehoe for their suggestions. Responsibility for the contents rests entirely with the author.

Cover photo courtesy The Canadian Labour Congress

1 The Earliest Days

The Canadian labour movement had a difficult birth. The first unions were the result of weak and sporadic efforts, and the most optimistic of their members can hardly have foreseen these faint stirrings as the beginning of a movement of more than two million men and women, a major economic and social force. Outside influences were strong, first from Britain and then from the United States. This has left its mark, but over the past century and a half the labour movement in Canada has developed its own characteristics, and it remains peculiarly Canadian.

From its very outset the movement has been involved in trouble. There is a story that a group of Quebec voyageurs staged the first strike in Canada, taking their paddles from the water of Lac la Pluie in 1794 in protest at low wages.

The first evidence of union organization is found in Nova Scotia, where it faced stiff opposition. In the early 1800s the Legislature of that province was told:

> Great numbers of journeymen workmen in the Town of Halifax and other parts of the province have, by unlawful meetings and combinations, endeavoured to regulate the rates of wages and effectuate illegal purposes.[1]

The Nova Scotia workers were simply uniting in an effort to improve their working conditions, but in those days the legality of such organization was questionable, and it was to be many years before it was clarified.

At about the same time there were stirrings of organization in other centres. Some New Brunswick tradesmen formed unions during the War of 1812, and in the succeeding years other labour groups came into existence, prominent among them the printers, in Quebec City in 1827 and at York (now Toronto) a few years later. A pride in their craft was a binding influence. The York printers, in a statement announcing the formation of their union, explained:

> Owing to the many innovations which have been made upon the long established wage of the professors of the art of printing, and those of a kind highly detrimental to their interests, it was deemed expedient by the Journeymen Printers of York that they should form themselves into a body, similar to societies in other parts of the world, in order to maintain that honourable station and respectability that belongs to the profession. [2]

Shoemakers also showed an early interest in organization, with one group formed in Hamilton some time before 1830 and others about the same time in Montreal and in Saint John, N.B. In various communities during the first half of the last century there were organizations of carpenters, stone cutters, cabinet-makers, foundrymen, painters, bakers, and tailors.

Many of the unions were small and their success was limited; but considering the atmosphere of the times this is hardly surprising. Slavery had only recently been abolished and, even then, in a merely technical sense. As late as 1800 the *Upper Canada Gazette* published an advertisement offering for sale 'a healthy Negro woman about 30 years of age' and going on to list among her accomplishments that she 'understands cookery, laundry and taking care of poultry. She can dress ladies' hair'. In the early part of the century there were still many who favoured slavery, and it was not until 1833 that it was finally abolished. The treatment of employees was often little different from that of slaves. It was almost unthinkable that workers should be allowed to form organizations to speak on their own behalf and to make demands on employers.

In their halting efforts to establish unions, Canadians were following an example which had already been set in both Britain and the United States. Large numbers of skilled tradesmen had come to Canada, and the British, especially, brought with them the traditions of an established trade union movement.

The growth of the early British unions had been an outcome of the Industrial Revolution. Workers shifting from farms to factories were confronted by entirely new conditions, which took a heavy toll in human suffering. They turned to union organization to protect themselves. Originally unions were outlawed by the Combination Acts; but organizational efforts continued nevertheless, and in 1824 the Acts were repealed.

Union organization grew, and by 1831 the National Union for the Protection of Labour had some 100,000 members and was engaged in trying to get the working day reduced to ten hours. Although the legal restriction had been removed, practical opposition to unions remained strong, and the National Union lasted only a few years. In 1834 there was the affair of the Tolpuddle Martyrs — a group of English agricultural workers banished to Australia for their efforts to form a union. Some of these pioneers of the British labour movement later came to Canada, settling near London, Ontario.

Factory workers saw their livelihood threatened by the introduction of new labour-saving machinery, much as today's workers regard automation. One group of English textile workers smashed the machines which they thought jeopardized their jobs. Their leader was Ned Ludd, and they won their place in history as the Luddites. Lord Byron, speaking of them in the House of Lords in 1812, said:

> These men never destroyed their machines until they became useless — worse than useless, till they became actual impediments to their exertions in obtaining their daily bread. . . .
> These men were willing to dig, but the spade was in other hands; they were not ashamed to beg, but there was none to relieve them. Their own means of subsistence were cut off; all other employments preoccupied; and their excesses, however to be deplored or condemned, can hardly be a matter of surprise.
> When a proposal is made to emancipate or relieve, you deliberate for years, you temporize and tamper with the minds of men; but a death bill [against the Luddites] must be passed off-hand, without a thought of consequences.[3]

The threat which new machines and methods presented to jobs was something that workers in Canada were to face time and again. When the Journeymen Tailors' Operative Society was formed in Toronto in 1852, its prime objective was the removal of the Singer sewing machine from the shops. On one occasion some Toronto tailors used what would now be called a public relations approach, hiring a horse and buggy carrying a sign reading 'Unfair' to follow their employer about the city.

In 1854 tailors employed in the Hamilton establishment of Lawson and Brothers struck in protest against mechanization, and the Hamilton *Spectator* reported:

> A terrible row has been going on in the city for the last eight or ten days among the sons of the goose and needle. The fiend that has come amongst us is none other than the steam engine with his sewing machines and other implements of evil, threatening extermination of the whole craft. It is no wonder, therefore, that they have come out and separated themselves from the evil, and have left the monster alone in his glory with his gussets and seams and shirts.[4]

The company tried to hire strikebreakers, advertising for men who were not afraid of machines. Some workers were imported from the United States, but when they discovered they were in the midst of a strike situation, most returned home. The Hamilton tailors won that battle, as did others in somewhat similar situations; but eventually it became apparent that smashing machines, or blocking their introduction, was no final answer to the problems of technical advance. The role of the union took on a new dimension, one that has acquired renewed importance with modern automation.

But it was not only mechanization that created a sense of insecurity among Canadian workers in the first half of the 1800s. There were wild fluctuations in the economy; employment was uncertain, and the resources the workers had available to weather periods of unemployment were meagre. Unemployment insurance was not even dreamed of, and ability to move about in search of work was limited by a lack of money. Many were hesitant to become involved in a movement which was strongly opposed by employers, while those who summoned sufficient courage to become active had to carry on their union work in secret. It was common practice for employers to 'blacklist' known union supporters, making it almost impossible for them to find employment. The bond between employers fighting union organization was sometimes stronger and more effective than that between employees.

The unions that managed to survive were completely preoccupied with economic problems. In periods of depression and recession the chief objective was to avoid pay cuts. Attitudes which still exist toward apprenticeship and the recruitment of new tradesmen had their roots in these difficult times. Abuse of the apprenticeship system was widespread. After an apprentice had finished his term, the employer would invite him to sign on for a second term in the hope of getting labour at a rate well below that paid a skilled tradesman. An overabundance of apprentices was a very real threat to the jobs of established tradesmen.

Collective bargaining as it is now practised developed gradually. At first, workers simply decided the minimum amount they were willing to work for and individually pledged not to work for less. The appointment of a committee to speak on behalf of the employees and to enter into discussions with the employer came later.

A strike of York shoemakers in 1830 tells the story of the sort of circumstances workers faced. William Lyon Mackenzie reported in *The Colonial Advocate:*

> Never did we witness so many journeymen shoemakers walking about the streets as we have done in the last two days. On enquiry some of the most intelligent and steady men, whose statements may be relied on, informed us there had been a disagreement between them and their employers; and that their employers wanted them to work for scanty wages, and board in their houses, for which they shall pay two dollars out of their hard-earned pittance, for board that positively was not worth one. In addition to this, they had to lie on beds of straw and that of the worst kind. On account of this they have, with one voice, opposed them and quit their shops, and are resolved to earn their living by hewing timber or any other useful employment, rather than submit to

> such tyrannical oppression in a land of liberty, where the light of freedom burns with the brightest lustre, and the rights of man is [sic] understood and most abundantly enjoyed by other mechanics.[5]

Some disputes involved not only the amount of wages but punctual payment of what was due the workers. In 1833 York carpenters staged a strike in an effort to force the employers to advance $5 a week on account, with the balance of money earned payable at the end of the month. A committee was appointed to present the workers' case, but the majority of employers refused such an arrangement. The carpenters then issued a public statement announcing: 'We therefore thought ourselves justified in not returning to our employment.'

Shorter working time has always been a natural desire, and this was one of the early union objectives. In 1834 Montreal carpenters announced that in future they would work no more than eleven hours a day. About the same time, the Amicable Society of Bricklayers, Plasterers and Masons set maximum hours at 6 A.M. to 6 P.M., with two hours off for meals. Their public statement reflected their Old Country background, referring in glowing terms to the freedoms enjoyed in the British Isles and comparing this with conditions in York, which were 'known to exist in few places except where Negro slavery is not yet abolished'.

As more unions were organized, competition began to develop among them, a condition which was to continue and intensify, weakening the movement then as it does now. The Montreal carpenters were apparently confronted with such a situation in their struggle for shorter hours. A statement published in the Montreal *Gazette* complained:

> We are further unanimous in declaring our opinion that the society calling itself the 'Mechanics' Protective Society' is calculated to produce the worst consequences; such a body of men cannot be considered competent to that they have undertaken, neither are they likely to confine themselves to decent and becoming order, they are, therefore, dangerous to the peace and safety of good citizens.[6]

By mid-century the number of unions had increased considerably. Organization was extensive in shipyards, including the Shipwrights' and Caulkers' Association at Kingston, Ontario; shipwrights at Victoria, B.C.; Ship Labourers' Benevolent Society at Quebec City; Shipwrights' and Caulkers' Association at Halifax; and Ship Labourers' Society at Saint John, N.B. About the same time, ships' porters and longshoremen formed unions on the Toronto and Montreal docks.

Some of the unions which were prominent in those days have since almost completely disappeared. The cigar makers, which in the 1970s had only eight members in one local in Canada, was once a powerful organization, with locals in twenty Canadian communities from Victoria to Saint John. The International Journeymen Coopers, composed of workers in the barrel-making industry, was another leading organization, and from its ranks came some of the day's labour leaders. In Toronto a Private Coachmen's Society was formed in 1854.

British Columbia, still noted for a very militant labour movement, has a history of union organization going far back. One of the first locals was that formed by bakers in Victoria. A notice published in the *Victoria Gazette* in 1859 announced:

> At a meeting of the Practical Bakers of Victoria, held at the Royal Hotel Monday, January 17th, they resolved to form themselves into a society for the protection of their trade, together with regulating the wages of journeymen so that they have just compensation for their labour, and doing away with Sunday work. They hope to merit the approbation of the public by their endeavours to do justice to the men who have served to apprenticeship in the trade. [7]

The militancy of British Columbia miners was apparent soon after coalfields were opened in that province and before there was any formal union organization. At Fort Rupert, on the northern end of Vancouver Island, there was a strike in 1849. Most of the men were Scots who had been brought to Canada to work at the mine. Two were placed in irons for six days as punishment for their part in the work stoppage.

On the other coast, Newfoundland shipyard workers had an organization shortly after the mid-century. Even before that there was an organization of some 13,000 men who worked seasonally as seal hunters. In 1845 they struck for higher wages. A union of seal skinners, along with butchers and coopers, won wage rates well above the average, though these occupations later suffered through the introduction of machinery.

In Central Canada, Toronto continued to be an important union centre in the 1850s, with organizations representing painters, bricklayers, moulders, carpenters, shoemakers, and printers. A Toronto branch of the (British) Amalgamated Society of Engineers appeared in 1858.

Quebec printers were represented by Société Typographique, a good union but one restricted by prevailing economic conditions. In 1839 the members petitioned their employers for a wage increase. Their approach was considerably different from that of present-day unions. Attention was drawn to increases which had taken place in the cost of living, but the employers were assured that no strike action was planned and that there would be a sense of indebtedness for whatever increases might be forthcoming. The union was in a far from secure position, and it suffered from periods of inactivity. Besides trying to improve the economic lot of its members, the organization sought to develop a sense of brotherhood among the craftsmen and to 'perfect them in the art of typography'. In later years it sponsored a number of educational and cultural projects, establishing a library of more than a thousand volumes and arranging lectures and dramatic programs.

Another prominent Quebec union was the Ship Labourers' Benevolent Association, formed by Quebec longshoremen in 1857. Ten years later it had become so successful that it came under attack in the House of Commons on the ground that it was too powerful, a criticism which was to be heard of many unions in succeeding years. The Association remained in operation until 1940.

But there was no centre of union activity at that time to match Saint John, New Brunswick. Senator Eugene Forsey, recognized as a foremost authority on Canadian labour history, suggests that from the late 1830s on to the late 1850s that city may have been the trade union capital of British North America, with more, bigger, stronger, and more respected unions than any other place in the North American colonies.

The union organization which had started during the War of 1812 had expanded rapidly. The Sawyers' Friendly Society of Saint John and Portland was in existence by 1835 and was a powerful organization. There was also the United and Friendly House Carpenters' and Joiners' Society and unions representing painters, cabinetmakers, and tailors.

The extent of union organization in Saint John was demonstrated by participation in parades and other public gatherings. The laying of the cornerstone of the Mechanics' Institute in 1840 was marked by a 'Trades Procession', in which 1,200 workers marched. Later that year there was a procession to welcome the new Governor-General, Poulett Thompson (afterwards Lord Sydenham), and 1,500 took part. There was an even larger turnout in 1853, when the first sod was turned for the European and North American Railway. Shipyard workers still constituted a large part of the labour movement, with shipwrights from sixteen yards marching on that occasion.

Also related to shipping was the Labourers' Benevolent Association, a union of longshoremen which flourished in the 1850-75 period. By 1874 the Saint John longshoremen had established a rate of $3 a day. This was when Toronto printers were fighting to get $13 for a six-day week. Eventually, the Labourers' Benevolent Association became part of the International Longshoremen's Association.

Gradually support for unions grew, but even those who favoured this rather novel approach to employee-employer relations were somewhat hesitant and sceptical, apparently fearful of anything resembling radicalism. William Lyon Mackenzie had attended a dinner of the Journeymen Printers of York in 1833, and his impressions were recorded in the Society's minutes:

> Since he had investigated the principles of the constitution he could find nothing therein but a consistent and moderate policy — nothing that savoured of exclusive privilege — but on the contrary arrangements that would secure respectability to journeymen

without interfering with the interests and prerogatives of the employers.[8]

When the union was reorganized in 1844, becoming the Toronto Typographical Union, it adopted the motto 'United to support, not combined to injure'.

At the middle of the century the movement was gaining some degree of stability, and during the 1850s and 1860s it enjoyed still further growth. This was when 'international unionism', as it is now called, made its appearance. The first 'internationals' were of British origin. The Amalgamated Society of Engineers, a British union, established locals at Hamilton, Toronto, and Brantford during the 1850s, and others followed. While this was a British organization, the Canadian activities were directed from a New York office. The link with Britain was maintained until 1920, when the locals were absorbed into the International Association of Machinists, a United States based union.

Another British organization, the Amalgamated Society of Carpenters and Joiners, established itself in Canada in 1871 and soon had branches in Hamilton, Toronto, Kingston, and St Catharines. These eventually merged with the United Brotherhood of Carpenters and Joiners of America, which arrived in Canada ten years after the British union.

The first United States union to organize locals in Canada was the Iron Molders, in 1861, with members in Montreal, Hamilton, Toronto, London, and Brantford. Canadian delegates attended the union's 1881 convention in Cincinnati, and the name of the organization was changed to the Iron Molders Union of North America in recognition of the inclusion of Canadians in the membership.

Printers on the two sides of the international border established ties at an early stage. In 1837 a Nova Scotia printer had attended a New York meeting of the National Typographical Society and was recognized as a fraternal delegate.

Printers belonged to an itinerant craft, and there was a good deal of movement back and forth between shops in Canadian and American cities. This was facilitated when the National Typographical Union authorized the recognition of Canadian union cards in 1854. Relations between printers' unions in the two countries were discussed at conventions, and in 1860 the American union decided to approach the Canadian unions, suggesting an alliance. The resolution adopted indicates that the purpose may not have been entirely altruistic:

> It will, if we succeed in bringing these unions under our jurisdiction, strengthen both our numbers and our finances; it will do away with the difficulties which now exist in regard to the exchange of cards . . . and it will be the means of strengthening the bonds of fellowship and good feeling that should exist between ourselves and our sister countries.[9]

In 1865 the union amended its constitution, making provisions for the acceptance of Canadian unions, and charters were then issued to the Canadian units. This marked the beginning of a relationship in printing and other industries which was to be the cause of argument for the next hundred years and longer.

The mushrooming expansion of Canadian railways during the 1880s saw the introduction and growth of union organization in what was then a new field. In 1850 there were only fifty miles of railway line in Canada; ten years later there were 2,000 miles. This expansion provided fertile ground for union organization. The Brotherhood of Locomotive Engineers, already established in the United States, came onto the Canadian scene in 1865, with its first Canadian divisions at Toronto and London, followed by others at Hamilton, Belleville, Stratford, St Thomas, Montreal, and Richmond, Quebec.

The Locomotive Firemen established a lodge at Brockville in 1877 and others at Belleville, Toronto, and Stratford. The Trainmen's Union appeared in Canada at Woodstock, New Brunswick, in 1885.

Many of the railway workers of the two countries had personal contact in their jobs, and there was little objection to establishing a union relationship on international lines. There was also an advantage for Canadians in joining a union which, in addition to its normal functions, acted as a benefit society. Railway work was considered very hazardous, and railway employees had difficulty obtaining insurance from private companies. The rail unions in the United States had established programs providing accident and death benefits.

Margaret Mackintosh, one of the first to compile information on early Canadian labour history, wrote:

> Another factor making for community of interest between American and Canadian railway employees was the influence of American methods on railway construction and operation in Canada — the gauge, rolling stock, organization of construction companies, the grant of land to promote construction, and, unfortunately, the political influence wielded by the companies.[10]

Beyond this, just as the presence of British tradesmen had its effect on union organization in Canada, so did an influx of workers from the United States. Canadian industrial development was some thirty years behind that in the United States, and many Americans looked on Canada as a land of new opportunity. They brought north a link with the unions to which they had belonged.

One organization that had a meteoric record about this time was the Knights of St Crispin — not to be confused with the Knights of Labour, which achieved prominence later. The name St Crispin commemorated a Christian martyr who had abandoned a background of nobility to serve and convert workers in Italy and France during the third century. With his brother, St Crispin earned his living as a shoemaker, and he later became the patron saint of the shoemakers.

The Knights of St Crispin was formed at Milwaukee in 1867 and grew rapidly, spreading across Canada as well as throughout the United States. Eventually there were local branches in Halifax, Montreal, Quebec City, Saint John, Guelph, Petrolia, London, Strathroy, Galt, Barrie, Brampton, Chatham, Orillia, Stratford, Toronto, Hamilton, Windsor, Prescott, St Catharines, Georgetown, Three Rivers, and St Hyacinthe.

Basically this was a protest movement, formed to oppose the practices being followed by some employers in connection with the introduction of new machines in the shoemaking industry. Here again, a union was trying to cope with the challenges of technological change.

The preamble to the constitution of the Knights of St Crispin included a statement of policy:

> Recognizing the right of the manufacturer or capitalist to control his capital, we also claim and shall exercise the right to control our labour, and to be consulted in the price paid for it — a right hitherto denied us; and we believe an international organization embracing all workers on boots and shoes in the United States and the provinces of North America is the only way in which this right can be successfully vindicated.[11]

The philosophy of the movement was extremely moderate. Strikes were permissible only as an expression of refusal to teach new hands who might replace those already employed in the industry. The Knights repeatedly made it clear that they were not opposing the introduction of machinery; their quarrel was with the use of unskilled workers to operate the machines, replacing skilled tradesmen. On this issue strikes were staged in several Canadian communities, but the locals involved suffered heavily in loss of membership and financial resources.

The Knights were strong supporters of both producer and consumer co-operatives and for a time operated a shoemaking co-operative at Saint John. Despite its lofty ambitions the movement had a short life. By the early 1870s a decline had set in, and by 1878 it was no longer an international body of any consequence, though some Canadian locals persisted for several years.

It would be misleading to suggest that all union growth during this time was attributable to international organizations. As we have seen, there was a great deal of activity by purely Canadian organizations, but one of their weaknesses was the lack of contact among them. The beginning of a national organization still lay in the future, as we shall see in the next two chapters.

2 The Toronto Printers' Strike

Organized labour has learned most of its lessons by experience, and this was certainly true of the circumstances which brought together unions in Toronto and forcefully pressed home the need for a more formal relationship among various labour organizations. The Toronto printers' strike in 1872 had this effect; there are few events in the history of the Canadian labour movement of greater significance.

While the printers were, as has been shown, among the first Canadian trade unionists, they continued for many years to meet stiff employer opposition. Peter Brown, publisher of a semireligious Toronto newspaper, the *Banner*, was among the master printers taking this position. He was a Scot who had arrived in Toronto from the United States in 1843, and he quickly made known his opinion of unions. Several *Banner* employees who were active in the typographical union were fired, and Brown used the columns of his paper to publicize his opposition to such organizations. His reactionary views covered a wide field. Free education was a subject of public discussion. Brown emerged as one of the leading opponents, declaring free schools to be a move toward socialism, communism, and other such wickedness.

The printers branded Brown's shop 'unfair' and circulated this information in Buffalo, New York, where he was attempting to hire new employees. The printers also sought public support by distributing a leaflet outlining their case and accusing Brown of employing printers at substandard rates.

Some of these attitudes were passed on to his son, George Brown, who became a prominent political figure and publisher of *The Globe*. He also clashed with the union when, in league with two other Toronto printing firms, he instituted a wage cut. The two other employers reached a compromise agreement with the union, but Brown held out. *The Globe* was declared a 'rat shop', and union members refused to work there. Brown hired replacements from rural areas.

Then, in 1869, the union made representations to all the master printers of the city, proposing a reduction in the work week from sixty to fifty-eight hours. The request was promptly rejected by the employers, but the union's minute book recorded a determination to continue the efforts:

> . . . it should not be suffered to drop, but be considered as our right to be obtained as soon as practicable, and that in the meantime a committee be appointed to wait on the employers and disabuse them of some erroneous ideas they have conceived as to the loss they will suffer by granting concessions.[12]

But the employers were adamant, refusing to meet with the printers' committee and also turning down a request from the bookbinders' union for a nine-hour day, even though the employees were prepared to accept proportionate wage cuts.

George Brown emerged as the leading spokesman for the Toronto master printers. In an editorial in September 1871 he suggested that differences should be settled by

> . . . consultation, conference, mutual concession and arbitration; not by the rough methods of strikes and lockouts which have been used and are causing so much misery, loss and heart-burning.[13]

The words were conciliatory, but Brown remained among those who refused to sit down with union representatives to discuss the differences.

Brown was a man of contradictory nature, sometimes very progressive and at other times quite reactionary. He had the strong evangelical background of his father. Together they had assisted runaway slaves escaping from the United States to

Canada; and he had lectured on prison reform at the Mechanics' Institute. As a publisher he was both capable and successful. He wrote hard-hitting editorials and displayed considerable business skill. Under his direction *The Globe* installed the first cylinder press in Toronto, capable of turning out 1,250 papers an hour compared to the 250 that came off the commonly-used flatbed presses. Brown arranged a news wire linking Toronto with Buffalo, Montreal, and New York, something previously unheard of. Yet he remained staunchly opposed to the unionization of his employees and rallied the owners of Toronto print shops in fighting the Typographical Society.

Finally the men decided to strike. They were then asking $10 for a fifty-four hour week, with 25 cents an hour overtime. The employers refused, and on 25 March 1872 the men walked out of the shops.

On 15 April a parade was arranged to mobilize public support. It was a cold day and snow was falling, but some 2,000 union members turned out and marched to the accompaniment of several bands. A listing of the unions taking part is a cross section of the Toronto labour movement in 1872: bricklayers and masons, iron moulders, cigar makers, furniture workers, bakers, coopers, Knights of St Crispin, varnishers and polishers, machinists, blacksmiths, coachmakers, and the printing trades.

The printers and bookbinders, as pioneers in the struggle for shorter hours, were the heroes of the day. They were at the rear of the parade as it wended its way to Queen's Park. There, outside the Ontario legislative building, two lines formed a guard of honour, and members of those two unions marched to the front.

The crowd had swelled to 10,000, and this being well before the days of public address systems, it was obvious that speakers were going to have difficulty being heard by everyone. A second platform was hastily erected, and those taking part in the program scurried from one platform to the other, addressing the crowd in relays. They were unanimous in declaring their support for the strikers and denouncing Brown and *The Globe*.

The demonstration must have boosted the morale of the strikers, but it also spurred action from the employers. Charges of seditious conspiracy were promptly laid against twenty-four of the union leaders.

The employers had reached far into the law books for a weapon which few union members realized existed. Almost twenty years before, some *Globe* employees had been similarly charged and found guilty, but it was a nominal conviction and they were each fined only a penny. At one time, British employers had successfully used charges of conspiracy against unions, but this practice had been brought to an end by revisions of the British statute and specific recognition of the legality of unions. In Canada the old British law remained in effect, jeopardizing the whole structure of the labour movement.

However, the Toronto employers' action backlashed. The union leaders were quickly released on bail, and when they reappeared they received demonstrations of even greater public support. Another procession was held, this time from the Trades Assembly Hall to the City Hall, where a public meeting took place. Cheers greeted a resolution declaring that:

> This meeting views with indignation the outrage that has this day been committed upon a peaceful community by the arrest of twenty-four highly respected workmen, and pledges its determination to support them under all circumstances; and further resolves to use all available means for the repeal of any law that might exist to warrant such an unjustifiable interference with the rights of the people. [14]

The position of the employers was outlined in a front-page editorial which appeared in *The Globe* two days later, expounding ideas that still have a familiar ring:

> There are few instances on record, we imagine, of a dispute between employers and employed so utterly indefensible on the part of the employed as that now existing in the printing trade of Toronto. The rates of wages are higher than in any other part of the Dominion; the duration of each man's daily labour is left to his own discretion; the wages are paid in cash weekly; and in every one of the 'closed' offices the men with but very few exceptions left declaring their satisfaction with the treatment they had received and their deep regret at being forced by the mandate of the

Toronto Typographical Society to abandon their comfortable situations. The sole end and aim of the strike is to establish the dominancy of the union over the internal administration of the Toronto printing offices, and making the employers helplessly subservient to the will of an outside influence.

The proprietors of the various offices have suffered for years from this intolerable and increasing oppression; and the effort they are now making is to free themselves entirely from it, and gain control of their own business. They have simply declined to be longer ruled by the Typographical Society; and while regretting that so many good men have thrown up excellent situations, they have proceeded to fill their places.

In the endeavour to supply those vacant places the employers complain that intimidation, coercion, personal violence and bribery have been exercised by the Typographical Society to prevent their succeeding; and these systematic efforts of the Society have been carried so far that the employers have at last been compelled to appeal to the law to put a stop to them.[15]

The whole affair took on deep political implications. Brown was one of the country's leading Liberals, and *The Globe* was looked on as the voice of the Liberal Party. Editors of some other newspapers, including the Toronto *Leader*, Hamilton *Spectator*, and Montreal *Star*, disagreed. The *Star* commented:

The one characteristic of *The Globe*'s style is the attempt to intimidate. If the printers are guilty of any offence, the managing editor of *The Globe* stands convicted on years of criminality.[16]

The Prime Minister of the day was Sir John A. Macdonald, and, astute polititian that he was, he quickly seized the issue as a means of embarrassing the Liberals. He hurriedly introduced legislation to bring the Canadian law into line with the revisions made earlier in Britain, and he also sponsored a Trade Union Act to clarify the legal status of unions. The legislation was adopted with little opposition from the Liberal benches, and the prosecutions against the Toronto union leaders were dropped.

There was an interesting aftermath, steeped in politics and with an element of mystery. Arrangements were made to honour Sir John and Lady Macdonald with a gala celebration, including a torchlight parade and presentations of an illuminated manuscript to Sir John, recording labour's appreciation for his efforts, and a gold jewel case to Lady Macdonald.

But some union members were suspicious of political motives. There was a strange secrecy about just where the gold jewel case had come from. It first appeared at a meeting of the Toronto Trades Assembly, with the explanation that it had been provided 'by an anonymous gentleman'. There were mutterings, but it was not until the next meeting that the opposition broke into the open. There was a general election in the offing, and Terence Clarke of the Bricklayers charged that efforts were being made to use the Assembly for political purposes. Nevertheless it was decided to proceed with the presentation.

Those who were suspicious were not to be silenced, and it was not long before Brown, seeing the political possibilities, joined in the discussion, with an editorial comment that:

> The testimonial to Lady Macdonald has as fishy an aspect as can be imagined. The money to buy it has apparently come from the clouds.[17]

It soon became apparent that Clarke was in close contact with Brown. A letter to the editor appeared in *The Globe*, signed by Clarke and saying:

> The testimonial in question is not the spontaneous offering of the workingmen at all. They have never been asked to subscribe anything for its purchase; and to my certain knowledge, no one has ever given a cent to the fund.[18]

Clarke also pointed out that invitations for the anonymous donor to come forward and identify himself to clarify the whole matter had been met with silence.

Meanwhile Brown kept the fire burning briskly in *The Globe's* editorial columns:

> This . . . places the whole testimonial business in an exceedingly whimsical light. . . . Here is a nice gold affair, purporting to be presented by the International Workingmen's Association, and not a workingman either gave or was asked to give a copper for its purchase. A worthy gentleman living 'beyond the city limits' and

greatly under that lively sense of favours to come which men have agreed to call gratitude, hands in the needful for a testimonial and begs the Assembly to get into hysterics and grateful admiration and praise without a moment's delay.[19]

Despite this wrangling, plans went forward. The torchlight procession was held, and the crowd then assembled in the Music Hall, where John Hewitt had the somewhat embarrassing assignment of making the presentations on behalf of the Assembly. He referred to the public discussion and, without explaining its origin, said the jewel case was as much the property of the Trades Assembly as the *Globe* building was the property of George Brown.

The *Globe* report of the gathering said it was largely composed of women, who only partly filled the hall, adding that the 'rabble' later accompanied Sir John and Lady Macdonald home. The *Ontario Workman*, a labour paper, reported the hall filled by workmen and their wives.

Hewitt, unwilling to let the affair die a natural death, wrote *The Globe*, claiming that a subscription had been taken among workers. Brown, using his editor's prerogative, published an editorial in the same issue, bitterly attacking Hewitt personally. Hewitt was a member of the Coopers' Union and one of the city's most active labour leaders. He had chaired the City Hall protest meeting. In the editorial Brown described him as

. . . an idle fellow who thinks it much nicer, every way to figure as corresponding secretary [of the Trades Assembly] and to make speeches on the rights of labour, at the expense of those who pay him, than earn a decent living by that 'honest labour' of which he prates so much but practises so little.[20]

The editorial promised further disclosures by Clarke, the whole affair having taken on a wait-for-the-next-chapter tone. But when Clarke's letter appeared, it was no more than a further criticism of Hewitt on the ground that he had moved about a good deal. It is unlikely there was much foundation to the suggestion that Hewitt was reaping a financial gain from his office in the Trades Assembly, for the resources of that body were extremely modest.

The Assembly later took a strong stand vindicating Hewitt and expelling Clarke on the ground that 'this person in the course he has been pursuing is no longer entitled to the confidence of honest men'.

The source of the funds with which Lady Macdonald's gold jewel case had been purchased was never finally revealed. If the Assembly gained anything, it was a lesson in practical politics. As the *Ontario Workman* sagely commented:

> We have seen the rights of the masses tossed to and fro between two contending political parties, the party in power nearly always proving to be the more conservative, and the party out of power taking up a few popular causes for the purpose of carrying them into power.[21]

The printers' campaign for shorter hours was eventually successful. Before the year 1872 was out, the employees in twelve of Toronto's largest print shops were working a fifty-four hour week, with overtime after that. Forsey has described the campaign as 'the first piece of successful political action by Canadian unions'.

On both sides of the Atlantic, pressure had been building for a shortening of working hours. A nine-hour day campaign was underway in Britain; and in the United States, Eight-Hour Leagues had been active since the 1860s.

Pressure for a wider adoption of the nine-hour day continued, and a convention with that end in view had been held in Hamilton in 1871. Delegates attended from as far away as Montreal, and it was decided to form a new organization, to be known as the Canadian Labour Protective and Mutual Improvement Association. The purpose was to strengthen the bonds between unions so that they could act promptly and effectively as a united force when their common interests were threatened. The organization was also to promote educational and social activities. The plans were ambitious, but the association never actually functioned.

The real significance of the Hamilton meeting was its expression of the urgent need for some more formal alliance among various unions. The basic issue in the Toronto printers' strike had become the legislation which threatened the legal rights of all unions. This was squarely in the political arena, where individual unions had limited strength and where concerted action was essential.

Unknowingly those who had struck to shorten hours (and those who had supported them) had sown the seeds for a national labour organization. The importance of the strike extended far beyond Toronto. The time had come for unions across the country to move forward.

3   A Union of Unions

The importance of having a central labour organization is obvious, but the matter by no means holds first place in the priorities of union members. This was as true in the 1800s as it is now. A member's first allegiance is to his own organization — carpenters, rubber workers, retail clerks, or whatever it may be. It is at the union level that the practical and immediate issues of wages and working conditions are foremost, because that is where actual collective bargaining takes place. The concerns of the central organizations are largely with broader matters, particularly in the areas of legislation and social problems. The average union member finds it difficult to relate personally to such matters.

Yet, particularly among the more active unionists and those in positions of leadership, it is realized that in many situations no single union, regardless of its size, is strong enough to stand alone. The old adage about unity providing strength applies to organizations as well as to individuals.

Toronto unions had moved toward a uniting of their forces even before the printers' strike. In 1871 the Coopers' Union took the initiative, calling together representatives of the city's unions. The first meeting was held on 27 March 1871 with John Hewitt as chairman and J.S. Williams of the Typographical Union as secretary. The twenty-six who attended represented three lodges of the Knights of St Crispin and the bakers, cigar makers, iron moulders, coopers, and printers.

The initial meeting was largely exploratory, as those present lacked authority to take definite action. There was agreement that some sort of central organization should be established, and reports to that effect were carried back to the various unions. The present Toronto and District Labour Council can trace its origin back to that March 1871 meeting, though the path over the next century was not a smooth one and there were times when the organization seemed to have disappeared.

A second meeting decided to proceed with a new organization, and the new body was named the Toronto Trades Assembly. A constitution was drafted, and the Assembly's records show that 400 copies were later printed at a cost of $22.

The Assembly was soon active in several areas, speaking on behalf of the working people of the community, encouraging union organization, keeping a watchful eye on working conditions, and sometimes acting as intermediary in efforts to settle disputes between employees and employers. There was also pressure for improvements in legislation, including extension of the franchise and the introduction of secrecy in the balloting for municipal elections. The enactment of a fair Mechanics' Lien Act to protect wages due tradesmen was another early objective.

But central bodies were even more vulnerable than unions in periods of high unemployment. Between 1875 and 1880 a severe depression swept the country, and the Toronto Trades Assembly was one of the victims. It had, however, established a reading room with a good collection of books, and this was extensively used by unemployed workers with time on their hands. No record remains of the Assembly after 1878. Three years later there was a successor organization, the Toronto Trades and Labour Council.

Labour in other communities was also showing interest in the establishment of central councils. This was particularly true in Ottawa, where there were strong unions in the printing and construction trades. Many union members had found employment in the construction of the parliament buildings. The Ottawa Typographers had organized in 1866 and three years later were involved in the first of several strikes. By 1873 the Ottawa Trades Council was in business. Labour councils were formed about the same time in Hamilton and St Catharines, Ontario.

The spirit of unity soon spread beyond municipal boundaries, and among Toronto labour leaders, as elsewhere, there was a growing desire to attempt to bring together unions in all parts of Canada. The Toronto Trades Assembly discussed the possibilities with the Ottawa Assembly, and invitations to a conference were sent prospective member groups. The conference, held in 1873, resulted in the formation of the Canadian Labour Union, which was in intent and spirit, if not in fact, Canada's first national labour organization. It was to be short-lived, as were some of the successor organizations.

Representation at the first meeting of the Canadian Labour Union was only from Ontario centres — Hamilton, Bowmanville, St Catharines, Cobourg, London, Ottawa, and Toronto. The unions included the Amalgamated Engineers, Coopers, Typographers, Shoemakers, Iron Molders, Carpenters, Bricklayers, Tailors, Stone Cutters, Longshoremen, Limestone Cutters, and Painters.

Messages were received from the typographical unions in Montreal and Quebec City expressing support and regret that delegates could not be sent 'owing to a lack of pecuniary resources'. There were also greetings from the Industrial Congress of the United States, which gave assurance of a welcome to 'foreign unions'.

It was a big occasion for the Toronto unionists. They spruced up their hall and hung a new sign outside. A committee was appointed to meet out-of-town delegates at the railway station.

John Carter, a painter who was president of the Toronto Assembly, chaired the opening session and was later elected president of the new organization. He was obviously impressed with the historic significance of the occasion, and his opening remarks reflected the moderation of his views:

> I think I speak your sentiments and feelings when I say that you do not meet with a view to confusing a spirit of discontent and dissatisfaction; you do not meet to create agitation for supremacy or undue power; nor to create or foster hostilities between capital and labour. But you do meet for the purpose of disseminating the true principles of unionism; to foster a spirit of common brotherhood throughout the Dominion; to seek the protection of those

laws that make no distinction of man as man. To this end, and with these objects, you are called upon, in this the first place, to establish a Canadian Labour Union. Its necessity is beyond doubt. . . .

It is also highly necessary that there should be a thorough system of organization among workingmen, so that they may raise themselves into a good moral position and enjoy the rights and privileges of citizenship. . . .

How can we fully estimate the importance of this Canadian Labour Union, where the whole body thinks and acts as one? It occurs to me that we are planting a standard this day, the influence of which will be felt by the workingmen all their lives. . . .

Workingmen are beginning to realize the fact that they are possessed of power — power to think, power to act — and with increased knowledge will come increased power. And the time is not distant when the great men of the land will find it absolutely necessary to consult with the workingmen in the matter of legislation, both political and commercial.

In conclusion I urge upon you the necessity of being wise and moderate in your deliberations and enactments, and let those who are watching your movements at this, the first Canadian Labour Congress, be compelled to admit that we are honest, earnest and prudent workers. [22]

One of the first items on the agenda was the adoption of a constitution, and its opening paragraph says:

Whereas the workingmen of the Dominion of Canada in common with the intelligent producers of the world, feel the necessity for co-operation and harmonious action to secure their mutual interests, just compensation for their toil, and such limitation of the hours of labour as may tend to promote their physical and intellectual well-being, and believing that the causes which have operated in the past to the detriment of labour may always be traced to the want of proper organization in the various branches of industry; therefore, to unite the energies of all classes of labour in this Dominion of Canada for the purpose of guarding their inherent rights, we, the representatives of the workingmen of the Dominion of Canada in convention assembled, do hereby enact . . .[23]

The convention declared its intention

. . . to agitate such questions as may be for the benefit of the working classes, in order that we may obtain the enactment of such measures by the Dominion and local Legislatures as will be beneficial to us, and the repeal of all oppressive laws which now exist.[24]

The Canadian Labour Union was to be financed by payments from supporting organizations — five cents per quarter per member from unions directly chartered by the federated body and three cents per quarter per capita from affiliated unions.

Like most labour conventions since, the founding gathering seems to have been an extremely serious affair. Sessions opened at eight in the morning, continued until noon, and then went on from two to six o'clock. The delegates worked a full eight-hour day.

There were a few lighter moments: one afternoon the visitors were taken to see the museum at the Normal School. A banquet held one evening was probably a rather more exciting affair. It was attended by about 200, and the Toronto *Mail* reported:

> On the cloth being removed the usual toasts were proposed, and drunk with tremendous enthusiasm. . . . The healths of several gentlemen present were drunk, and the company dispersed about one o'clock this morning. The proceedings were enlivened by a number of songs contributed by different delegates present.[25]

The expansion of union organization ranked high among the objectives of the new group. The delegates to the convention also outlined a procedure to be followed in providing assistance to unions involved in strikes or lockouts. It was by no means to be automatic. The president of the CLU was to be advised of all the circumstances, together with evidence that the union had endeavoured 'by arbitration, to settle the difficulty'. If the president was satisfied, then he was authorized to circulate affiliated unions, asking them to send donations to a specified appropriate person, 'so that assistance given may promptly reach those for whom it is intended'. Much more was to be heard of the use of arbitration in settling disputes, a subject on which there were sharp differences of opinion and a good deal of confusion.

Another area of interest, and one which continues to involve the Canadian labour movement, was politics. The delegates received a report from a convention committee stating:

It is essential to the recognition and establishment of the just and equitable rights of the workingmen of this country that they should have their own representatives in the Dominion Parliament, and, with this idea in view, it is the opinion of this Congress that a workingman's platform should be put before the industrial classes of the country, and that the President do appoint a committee to draw up such a platform.[26]

Among those supporting the recommendation was Daniel O'Donoghue, an Ottawa printer who, the Toronto *Mail* reported, 'dwelt at some length upon the importance of having a workingman's platform, independent of party politics'. There were differences of opinion on this point, and even O'Donoghue himself was later to become embroiled in party politics. Political, religious, and ethnic loyalties were then stronger and more evident than they are today.

The use of both immigrant and prison labour was a hot topic in the days of the Canadian Labour Union. There was vigorous opposition in labour circles to government subsidization of immigration. One delegate to the 1873 meeting complained that the country's immigration program was costing every Canadian forty cents a year and was resulting in an undercutting of established wage rates. There were charges that the government was simply financing the private interests which were the only beneficiaries of immigration at a time when Canadian workers were already suffering from unemployment. There were others — a minority — who regarded this as a selfish position and who argued that there were many Old Country people who should be welcomed to Canada but who needed assistance to pay their passage.

The views expressed about the use of prison labour would send shivers down the spines of those concerned with modern prison reform. The attitude of union members in the late 1800s resulted from the practice of contracting work done in prisons out to private interests, thus creating unfair competition for those who were dependent on employment for their living. There was also labour opposition to prison training programs, on the ground that prisoners taking part might, on their release, threaten the jobs of those already in the trade.

The CLU founding convention adopted a resolution protesting the employment of convicts 'in any other capacity than that of hewers of wood and drawers of water'. This was considered a very important subject, and at a later convention a delegate was reported by *The Globe* to have been quite forceful:

> It was entirely unjust to mechanics to have to compete with criminals under such disadvantageous circumstances. It was a system of pampering the worst class in the country.
> These men should be sent to build roads and perform such work as that, instead of being learned [sic] such good trades free of expense, and have them work in competition with those who had to pay for learning their trades.[27]

There was also talk about the employment of children, and the convention supported a resolution favouring measures to prohibit the employment of children under ten years in factories, mills, and other manufacturing establishments where machinery was used. As far as apprenticeship was concerned, the convention wanted government action to assure proper training, so that an apprentice would become 'a finished workman, and therefore a credit and benefit to the country at large'. Another objective was the establishment of a federal 'Bureau of Labour and Statistics'.

Public reaction to the establishment of a 'national' labour body appears to have been cautiously favourable. The Toronto *Leader*, in a rather class-conscious editorial, commented:

> We are pleased to see from our report of the preliminary proceedings that the assembly seems to be of an intelligent cast, and likely to conduct the proceedings in a practical common sense manner. . . .
> All over the civilized world a signal change has come over the workingman within the last ten years. This typical individual, like the English agricultural labourer, has awakened to the consciousness that he is, or ought to be, a power in the world and with this consciousness has arisen a desire and determination to make that power felt. Combinations, leagues and societies have been formed in England, in Continental Europe and in America, all aiming at the social and political elevation of this class. . . .
> But, while we allow that the days of serfdom are gone forever, we

must allow that the so-called advancement of the age is leading one class of the people into devious paths, paths of license and absurdity, and that class is the labouring one.[28]

The editor was very concerned about an international labour organization which had appeared in Switzerland and which seemed to be influenced by 'a socialist and revolutionary element'. He was, however, confident that Canadian workers were 'possessed of higher intelligence than the average European workman'.

Despite its auspicious start Canada's first 'national' labour organization was soon on the downgrade. When the second convention was held in the Parliament Buildings at Ottawa, only fourteen delegates turned up. While the iron moulders and Knights of St Crispin reported membership increases, most unions were losing members because of unemployment and were in no position to give active support to a central body. The charter fee for new unions was reduced from $5 to $2, and the basis of representation at conventions was increased to one for every fifty members instead of one for every hundred, in an attempt to encourage participation. The Ottawa convention devoted a good deal of time to discussion of economic conditions, and there were demands for higher tariffs to protect Canadian industry and jobs.

The third CLU convention was at St Catharines, with sixteen delegates. This small representation did not prevent Alfred Jury, a tailor prominent in Toronto labour circles, from speaking of the gathering as 'The Parliament of Labour', a phrase that is still applied to national labour conventions. There was continuing concern about the loss of membership. Desires were expressed for the employment of a full-time union organizer, but there were no funds. Delegates were disturbed by the effect of the law in breaches of contract. If an employee broke his contract of employment, he was subject to prosecution under the Criminal Code; but a breach of contract by an employer was a civil matter.

A highlight of the St Catharines convention was a trip by four-horse van to Niagara Falls. The convention report notes that the vehicle was provided 'with everything in abundance calculated to make the journey enjoyable'.

When the next convention was held, in Toronto in 1876, only one of the delegates was from outside the city. There was discussion about gaining voting rights for all workers, and a resolution was adopted favouring extension of the franchise to 'every man of sound mind and unconvicted of crime, or who is not a burden on the country'. A few brave souls went so far as to suggest that women should be allowed to vote, but they were obviously before their time. The next year the CLU again met in Toronto, but that occasion marked its end.

A Canadian historian and early editor of *The Labour Gazette*, R.H. Coats, later wrote:

> On the whole the Canadian Labour Union had a vitality and independence that makes its record pleasing. It defined the aims of labour in language that still requires but little modification, and, though it worked in leading strings, its position was consistently sound from a trade union standpoint.[29]

Despite its short life the Canadian Labour Union had been an important beginning. Further efforts were to be needed before a truly national organization could be established, but there were those whose determination was not to be dimmed by the initial failure. Among them was the man who later won for himself the title 'Father of the Canadian Labour Movement' and who is the subject of the next chapter.

4   Father of the Canadian Labour Movement

'Father of the Canadian Labour Movement' — the sire of an organization of more than two million men and women — may seem an exaggerated title for any individual. Scores of men and women have contributed to the labour cause, many at great sacrifice, without sharing the limelight. This was not true of Daniel O'Donoghue, who happened to be at the right place at the right time and who became well known in his day as an extremely effective spokesman for organized labour. Father or not, he was unquestionably an outstanding leader at a time when the labour movement was coming of age.

O'Donoghue has the almost unique distinction among Canadian labour leaders of having become the subject of a biography, a brightly-written book by Doris French, an Ottawa journalist, entitled *Faith, Sweat and Politics*. The Canadian labour movement has had many colourful personalities, but most have faded into history leaving behind no record of their personality or contribution. It is therefore with some justification that Mrs French has expressed doubt whether any organization anywhere can match the Canadian labour movement in having so successfully 'murdered all the excitement, all the humour, tragedy and high spirits of their own history'. Her book helps remedy this unfortunate vacuum, and for much of what follows concerning Daniel O'Donoghue, I am indebted to her research.

O'Donoghue was Irish, born at Tralee in 1844 and brought to Canada when he was eight. The family settled at what was then

Bytown, a backwoods community of 8,000 souls that was later to become Ottawa. When the O'Donoghues arrived, they found a rough-and-ready town, dominated by the Irish, with the French-Canadians a close second.

Daniel's early years strongly influenced his later career. His father died when he was only thirteen, and that marked the end of his formal education. Forced to go to work, he became an apprentice printer. He was an active lad, slight of build but fond of sports, especially boxing and lacrosse. He grew to be a distinguished-looking man, and pictures from the period show him with a pointed beard and a large-brimmed hat worn at a jaunty angle. He had inherited an Irish charm that he carried through life and that proved a valuable asset in some of the difficulties he was to face.

As soon as he completed his apprenticeship, O'Donoghue looked to greener fields and set off for the United States. He found a job in a Buffalo, New York, print shop, and it was there that he first came in contact with a union. He stayed in Buffalo only a short time, but as he moved about the United States he repeatedly found union organization a topic of discussion among printers.

When O'Donoghue returned home to Ottawa, he took with him the union message. Through his efforts, Ottawa printers formed an organization in 1866. A short time later the group affiliated with the Typographical Union in the United States.

The going rate for Ottawa printers was then $8 a week. Government contracts provided a good deal of work and were subject to bidding. In 1869 the Ottawa *Daily Citizen* bid for and won a contract with a quotation which was based on rates below the $8 level. As soon as the contract was signed, the *Citizen* instituted a wage cut.

O'Donoghue promptly wrote a letter to the editor of *The Times*, where he was employed, pointing out the unfairness of the prevailing government practice of accepting the lowest tender, regardless of wage rates involved. He was pioneering the idea of fair-wage legislation, a principle which is now firmly enshrined. The *Citizen* printers went on strike, and the rates were restored to the previous scale.

The importance of labour's relations with the government in power was always evident to O'Donoghue, and he was responsible for introducing a practice which still continues. In 1873 he led a small delegation to the Prime Minister's office to discuss matters of concern to the working people with Sir John A. Macdonald.

Records of the meeting are scanty, but it is known that the delegation argued for a law which would protect the interests of employees should their employer go into bankruptcy. As it was, companies supplying materials usually had the first claim, and the employees shared what was left over after other debts had been settled. The matter was primarily within provincial jurisdiction, and it was in Ontario that the first Mechanics' Lien Act was introduced some time later by Mowat's Liberal government. Initially it applied only when the tradesman was owed more than $50, an enormous amount at that time; but in response to pressure from labour this qualification was later removed.

This is a fairly typical example of labour's success — slow and plodding as it sometimes seems — in promoting legislation in the interests of the working people. Legislative matters continue to form a large part of representations made by organized labour to the Prime Minister and members of his Cabinet. These confrontations are now much more formal than they appear to have been in O'Donoghue's time. It has become customary to present a lengthy printed document including a recital of the government's alleged sins of omission and commission, and an exchange between government and labour spokesmen follows. Within labour circles the annual event is sometimes called the 'cap-in-hand session', but labour's attitude has seldom been subservient.

In the 1870s, however, the legislative activities of the Ottawa unions were secondary. Wages came first, and by 1873 printers had won a wage rate of $10 a week, equal to that paid in Toronto, though the Ottawa printers worked longer hours. While the men had cause for satisfaction, the owners were disturbed by the growing union strength, and they announced a rule forbidding their employees to belong to a union. Only the

Ottawa *Times* refused to go along with this management decision, and printers in all the other shops went on strike.

The employers, echoing the sentiments of George Brown, issued a statement declaring:

> We will support every employer of labour in this city in our endeavour to free ourselves from a tyranny that is insufferable.
> The Typographical Union is a combination which is swayed by dangerous men, and has tried on more than one occasion to crush us.[30]

Replacements were brought in as strikebreakers. Two *Citizen* employees were taken to court, charged with having unlawfully left their employment without giving proper notice. They were each fined $1 and given a stern warning. The strike dragged on for two months before the men had to give up and go back to work. The employers had won, and the strike had been broken.

O'Donoghue's convictions about the importance of government policy led him to become a firm believer in political action. He held the view that workers would only receive justice when they had their own representatives in the legislative halls. When a provincial by-election was called in 1874, he saw an opportunity to put his theory into practice.

Six candidates were nominated, but four withdrew, leaving in the running only Irish Dan and a wealthy Ottawa citizen, R. Nagle, who had Liberal support. In an election held only a short time before, Ottawa electors had been narrowly divided, and with O'Donoghue's appearance on the political scene the Conservatives sensed an opportunity for victory. They approached the new candidate asking him to carry the Tory banner. O'Donoghue refused, but he was still assured of Conservative support; the party had little other choice. The campaign was lively, and the young trade unionist proved well able to take care of himself in the free-swinging politics of the time. He won decisively, polling 887 votes to Nagle's 285.

There was a great celebration, including the traditional torchlight parade. When it was all over, there was a rather stunned reaction from some quarters. The Ottawa *Citizen*, its partisanship showing, commented:

> The result is remarkable. Mr. O'Donoghue is a poor mechanic who has nothing to depend upon for support but his wages. His election by an immense majority over a wealthy candidate backed by the Ministry shows how little sympathy the people of Ottawa have with the party in power.[31]

Shortly after the election Irish Dan was invited to a reception given by the Governor-General, Lord Dufferin, who, meeting the young member for the first time, inquired who he represented. O'Donoghue replied, 'Your Excellency, I represent the rag, tag and bobtail'.

There was a general election the next year, and he was returned. Apparently he was proving an acceptable member. An Ottawa and Carleton County reference book spoke favourably of him:

> Mr. O'Donoghue is a young man, a printer by trade, a sociable and agreeable gentleman, very intelligent and well informed, who, though a 'working man' has done the city for which he is the sitting member no descredit as its parliamentary representative.[32]

O'Donoghue was one of those continually pressing for extension of the franchise. If workers were to be successful in electing their own representatives, they first had to have the vote. Property requirements had been wiped out in Ontario, but there was still a qualification related to income. The Liberal government introduced a bill easing restrictions and extending the right to vote.

More and more, O'Donoghue found himself in agreement with the policies of the Reform Party, a position that was later to lead to political embarrassment. The Conservatives, who had originally supported him, began to shy away, while the Liberals were in a quandary as to whether or not to embrace him.

From faraway Toronto *The Globe* gave advice to the Ottawa electors:

> From the course Mr. O'Donoghue has pursued in the House since his election, from the sensible, practical tone of his speeches, and

the evidence his conduct has afforded of shrewd, intelligent observation, we confess to having formed a favourable opinion of him, and we would be glad to see him back again in the next Legislature. Are there any insuperable objections to his selection by the Reform Party? We have not heard of any.[33]

The Ottawa Liberals thought otherwise and chose the Mayor, Featherstone, as their candidate. The Conservatives put up Hon. John O'Connor, a man pledged to do his best for the lumber trade, which was Ottawa's main industry. The political lines were clearly drawn, and O'Donoghue had become no more than 'the workingman's candidate . . . without position, without means'. He was returned in the 1875 election, though by only fifty-three votes, and suffered defeat when the electors next went to the polls in 1879.

O'Donoghue had become a victim of the insecurity of tenure which is still prevalent in both political and labour circles. Lacking means, he was in immediate need of a job. He went to Guelph, working for a time as editor of a paper, and then he moved to Toronto, returning to his old trade and working as a printer on the Toronto *World*. It was an important move, because it again put him in contact with the labour movement.

The time was opportune. In 1881 the International Typographical Union of North America held its convention in Toronto, and this helped revive interest in the idea of a central labour body. It was at this time that the Toronto Trades and Labour Council was formed.

The depression was lifting, and the country was on the verge of a wave of expansion; the prevailing spirit was one of optimism. All of this meant great opportunities for the new Labour Council. At first O'Donoghue was in the background, then in 1883 he appeared as a Council delegate with a credential from the Typographical Union. He was also active in the Knights of Labour (see Chapter 5), and two years later he sat on the Council representing the Knights.

His interest in government affairs remained keen, and for many years he headed the Labour Council's legislative committee, keeping a watchful eye on legislative developments, writing long reports, and using every opportunity to press labour's interests. Mrs French describes him as a 'one-man research economist, public relations expert and lobbyist without peer'.

The Labour Council was inclined to be cautious in its approach to outright political involvement. The minutes noted:

> There appeared to be strong objection by all present at the appearance of politics introduced into the late Trades Assembly; and if there was any intention to introduce the same into this, their unions would have nothing to do with it.[34]

On the other hand, credit was given the former Assembly for its accomplishments in the improvement of legislation, 'these remarks being well received by the delegates generally'.

This discussion points up the difference in approach between those who favoured seeking legislative changes by representations and indirect action and those who thought labour could only succeed by direct and active political involvement. Those opposing direct action aimed their criticism particularly at O'Donoghue, whom they had come to regard as being allied with the Liberal Party. At first he suffered the criticism in silence, but by 1886 his position on the Council was firmly established and he spoke out in his own defence. It was an emotional oration. The entire text of his remarks later appeared in *The Globe*. These two paragraphs give their essence:

> I speak on a matter personal to myself. All the capital I have in the world is my character, and I value it accordingly. Members of this body have thought fit to bring my name before you in connection with my actions during the time I served in a public capacity, and have charged me with not having done my duty properly as a labour representative on the floor of the Legislature. These charges were made at such times and on such occasions that I had not the opportunity of refuting them. . . .
> During the four and a half years I was a member I was never approached, either directly or indirectly, by any member of the government to ask me to support them. All the votes I ever gave I have no apology to make for. I gave them of my own free will. There was no bargain. I never forgot how I stood with the body that sent me there, nor what was due that body.[35]

He did say, however, that he had been approached by the Conservatives, who, seeking his support in the defeat of the government, had offered him a cabinet position if they became the government. He had rejected the offer. Later O'Donoghue had the opportunity of a seat in the Senate. He was unable to meet the property requirements, and he rejected a suggestion that arrangements could be made to get around this difficulty.

Despite his critics — and they were many — O'Donoghue was a man of high principles and the most effective labour advocate of his day. He saw the responsibilities of the labour movement extending far beyond wages and working conditions. He had strong personal views on many subjects of social significance, and his union participation provided a platform for their expression.

Immigration was a pet subject. He was strongly opposed to the practice of paying immigration officials according to the number of immigrants they attracted to Canada, regardless of the conditions the people would have to face when they arrived. He successfully led a fight to have appropriations for this purpose reduced.

Coupled with a campaign to shorten working hours, in which he was active, was an effort to compel the early closing of retail stores, by which was meant by 8 P.M. There was also opposition on labour's part to the Sunday operation of streetcars, it being maintained that this should be a day of rest for all employees. A faithful Catholic and officer of the Lord's Day Alliance movement, O'Donoghue proudly claimed never to have ridden on a streetcar on the Sabbath.

He was involved in efforts to widen educational opportunities through free schools and compulsory attendance. He was also a promoter of technical education and is credited with being one of those responsible for the Toronto Technical School, one of the first institutions of its kind in the country. Some older craftsmen opposed technical education, fearing it would lead to an oversupply of tradesmen.

O'Donoghue favoured public ownership and sponsored a resolution which was adopted by the Toronto Trades and Labour Council requesting a commission to investigate:

> . . . whether it would not be desirable for the government to take under control the working of the railways, waterworks, telegraphs and gas factories for the benefit of the country.[36]

His personal interests became increasingly centred on improving working conditions. Labour had advocated special government departments at both federal and provincial levels to deal with labour matters. When the Ontario government finally established a 'Bureau of Industries' — initially as a branch of the Department of Agriculture — O'Donoghue was appointed departmental clerk.

The next year, 1886, the Ontario Factory Act was passed, the first legislation of its kind in Canada. It provided a penalty of $100 for factory owners who employed boys under twelve years of age and girls under fourteen. Women and children were not to work more than ten hours a day or sixty hours a week. Children were not to be allowed to clean machines while they were in motion. Other provisions applied to ventilation, sanitation, and fire exits.

Conditions in many of the establishments were shocking — almost beyond belief. The minutes of the Toronto Trades and Labour Council describe an accident in which a fourteen-year-old boy named Farry lost all the fingers from one hand in a factory accident. The boy had been sent out to work by his widowed mother. The Council minutes continue:

> She had arranged for him to learn the cabinet business and the first morning he started the boss placed him to work a shaper machine, the boy not having worked or had anything to do with a machine before. Such machines being dangerous to an experienced hand and more especially to a boy of no experience, within four hours of his starting work he was under chloroform having all the fingers of his left hand amputated. The boss, Mr McGuire, refused to compensate or do anything to assist the boy.[37]

There were no laws placing responsibility on the employer, and a lawyer advised Mrs Farry that she had little hope of succeeding in a legal action. The best the Council could do was to offer sympathy, pass the hat, and continue to press for legislation that would at least provide compensation.

O'Donoghue was very sensitive to the outrages suffered by industrial workers, and he used his position as a government official to investigate conditions such as those in McGuire's factory. The work of government inspectors was not easy. They reported finding boys who seemed unusually small for the age they claimed, and they knew that sometimes children were hidden in packing cases as soon as the inspectors were sighted.

A Royal Commission of the federal government investigating factory conditions in 1886 heard evidence of scores of cases of child abuse. In Nova Scotia law, there was nothing to prevent the employment of boys ten years of age in underground coal-mine operations. Montreal glassworks employed some children who worked throughout the night. Large numbers of young girls were employed in cigar factories; they were charged for any cigars which failed to pass inspection and as soon as they were old enough to claim more than a child's wage they were fired.

J. R. Booth, one of Ottawa's leading citizens and a baron of the Ottawa Valley lumber industry, told the Commission he paid no attention to the Factory Act and was not even aware of its provisions. He testified he employed boys who worked from 6 A.M. to 6:30 P.M. and he thought there were others who worked all night. Investigators for the Commission reported that some of the children they interviewed did not know how old they were, but many appeared to be about twelve. A number had missing fingers and some had missing hands.

It was his knowledge of factory conditions that led to O'Donoghue's association with Mackenzie King. King was writing a series of articles on sweatshop conditions in Toronto, and O'Donoghue proved one of his most valuable sources.

A short time later, in 1900, the federal government created a Department of Labour, and King became the first Deputy Minister. He invited O'Donoghue to become the first fair-wage officer. He promptly accepted and returned to his home town. It has been suggested, but never fully substantiated, that the post of Deputy Minister was offered to O'Donoghue before King but that he turned it down because of his limited educational background. It is interesting to speculate on the possible effect on Canada's history had he taken the post instead of King, who went on to become Prime Minister. It is believed to have been King who first called O'Donoghue 'Father of the Canadian Labour Movement'.

Daniel O'Donoghue died in 1907, his death attributed in part to overwork. The Trades and Labour Congress at its convention later that year recorded the sentiments of many Canadian trade unionists:

> Our old associate, true to the last to the principles that governed him in his lifetime, sacrificed his life for his friends, the poor, and in years to come his record will live enshrined in the hearts of the toilers of the Dominion of Canada.[38]

There is no monument to enshrine the memory of Irish Dan O'Donoghue. He was not even accorded a place in the Hall of Fame established by the Canadian Labour Congress in 1972. Perhaps his best memorial is to be found in some of his own words. In 1900 he wrote of the movement to which he had contributed so much:

> The trade unions are the legitimate outgrowth of modern society and industrial conditions. They are not the creation of any man's brain. They are organizations of necessity. They are born of the necessity of the workers to protect and defend themselves from encroachment, injustice and wrong. They are the organizations of the working class, for the working class and by the working class.[39]

5   The Noble Knights

The official name was 'The Noble and Holy Order of the Knights of Labour'. It was no coincidence that this sounded more like a fraternal organization than a trade union, for the organization had strong moral overtones and an element to secrecy. This was the same Knights of Labour which numbered Daniel O'Donoghue as one of its most active supporters.

It all started in Philadelphia, where a little group of nine garment workers decided it was time for a new kind of labour union. Their leader was Uriah Stephens, a one-time student for the Baptist ministry who had strong views about the application of the principles of Christianity to everyday working life. From that simple beginning the Knights expanded into an organization which briefly held promise of becoming a truly worldwide labour body, the like of which has never been fully realized. Just as quickly it slid into obscurity; but in the process it had provided new inspiration and a broadened outlook.

At its peak the Knights had more than 700,000 members — 12,000 of them in Canadian assemblies, as the local units were called. There were other assemblies as far afield as Great Britain, Ireland, Belgium, Australia, New Zealand, and Hawaii.

Then a single incident brought about the virtual annihilation of the organization's base in the United States. In May of 1886 a group of police charged a Chicago picket line with such force that a half-dozen people were either killed or injured. Feelings ran high, and a protest meeting was held in the city's Haymarket Square. In the midst of the proceedings someone threw a bomb. Pandemonium broke out. The police opened fire. When it was all over, seven policemen were dead and sixty or so people were injured. A number were arrested, and responsibility for the Haymarket Riot was publicly laid on the doorstep of the Knights of Labour.

It was never determined who threw the bomb, but seven men were sentenced to death. Four of the condemned were hanged, one committed suicide, and the other two had their sentences commuted. The Governor of Illinois later issued a pardon declaring that there had been a miscarriage of justice, but the affair had already been as fatal to the Knights of Labour in the United States as it had to the five who were dead.

The Haymarket Riot had less effect in Canada, where the Knights continued to take part in the affairs of local labour councils and the Trades and Labour Congress. Here the eventual downfall of the Knights resulted from conflict with other labour groups, culminating in the organization's expulsion from the Trades and Labour Congress.

In Canada the first assembly was formed at Hamilton about 1867 and others quickly sprang up in both large and small communities. Eventually there were seventy-seven in Ontario and others spread from the Atlantic to the Pacific, including in their membership a wide spectrum of occupations.

This was no ordinary union. There were elaborate rituals and, initially, strict rules of secrecy. Members were required to swear not to reveal their membership. Information was exchanged by a secret code and strange chalk marks left in appropriate places. Members identified themselves to each other by a secret handshake.

All this led to some difficulty in the province of Quebec, where the predominantly Catholic population was forbidden to join secret societies. It was suspected that the Knights were in some way connected with Freemasonry. A pastoral letter was circulated, instructing Catholics that they were not to join the Knights; those who had already joined were to resign immediately and so inform their parish priest.

Fortunately for the Knights, this was at a time when their rules of secrecy were being relaxed. Supporters in the United

States included a number of prominent Catholics, and they used their influence with church authorities in Quebec to have the ban lifted. The Knights later enjoyed considerable organizational success in the province.

The support of church people may have been related to the organization's objectives, which went well beyond purely economic matters. They were defined in somewhat lofty terms:

> . . . To make industrial and moral worth, not wealth, the true standard of individual and national greatness. To secure for the workers full enjoyment of the wealth they create, sufficient leisure in which to develop their intellectual, moral and social faculties; all the benefits, recreation and pleasure of association; in a word to enable them to share in the gains and honours of advancing civilization.[40]

Union organization up to that time was almost entirely along craft lines, with emphasis on pride of craft and the exclusive nature of membership. The Knights, on the other hand, had an open-door policy, seeking to extend the benefits of organization to all workers, regardless of their skill or craft.

They went still further and actively sought women members. Some communities — Brantford, Belleville, Thorold, and Montreal — had special 'Ladies' Assemblies'. In the United States the Knights solicited membership among black workers and encouraged the formation of joint black and white assemblies, a remarkably progressive policy. But the door was not open all the way. The constitution specified some occupations as not acceptable: 'no person who makes his living by the sale or manufacture of intoxicating drink; no lawyer, professional gambler or stockbroker' would be admitted to the union.

The Knights were active in community affairs, establishing reading rooms and arranging lectures. Their newspaper, *The Labour Advocate*, expounded the organization's program. Monetary reform had high priority. The country's economic woes were blamed on the fiscal system, and the Knights were among the first advocates of the policy which eventually led to the establishment of the Bank of Canada. They used every opportunity to press for the creation of a publicly-owned bank which would have exclusive authority to issue currency, a privilege which was then shared among private banks.

There was considerable Knights' membership in British Columbia. A foothold was established at Nanaimo in 1883, and within a year the assembly boasted 240 members and its own hall. Other assemblies were formed at Victoria, Vancouver, New Westminster, Kamloops, Rossland, and probably other centres. The members included woods workers, teamsters, miners, longshoremen, and general labourers.

But on the west coast the Knights adopted an attitude toward Orientals which was in peculiar conflict with the general philosophy. There was widespread resentment among workers at the competition of labourers brought from China to work at substandard wages. There was also public objection to the ghetto-like existence of the Chinese and their failure to fit into community life though there was little if any encouragement for them to assimilate.

In 1887 the Knights of Labour took an active part in a hate campaign directed against the Chinese in the province. A boycott against Chinese-owned businesses was extended to other firms which did business with the Chinese. Premises of those involved were marked with a large 'X'. On one occasion a camp housing a number of Chinese labourers was raided. Martial law had to be declared to restore order, and three of the attackers were arrested. With the aid of legal defence provided by the Knights, the three were acquitted.

In Winnipeg, where the Knights organized in 1894, they were instrumental in establishing the city's first central labour organization and also had a prominent part in creating the Winnipeg Building Benefit Society and a co-operative store.

The top officer of the Knights was Terence Powderly, who, with the impressive title of Grand Master Workman, was regarded as the outstanding labour orator of his time. He declared that no strike should be permitted unless

> . . . the cause is just; every reasonable means has been resorted to to avert the strike; the chances of winning were at least as good as the prospect of losing; and the means of defraying expenses of the

strike and assisting those in need were in the treasury or in sight of it.[41]

Despite these restrictions some Knights did become involved in strikes. One, in 1882, involved the Brotherhood of Telegraphers of the United States and Canada, which was part of the Knights' structure. There were 1,200 Canadians affected, from North Sydney to Winnipeg, creating what might be regarded for that time as a national strike. With members in the United States also taking part, this amounted to what Forsey has described as 'the only genuinely international strike we ever had'.

The Brotherhood was seeking wage improvements and shorter hours. It is interesting that their proposals included equal pay for men and women and parity between Canadian and United States rates. The highest-paid operators in Toronto were receiving $70 a month but few were at that rate. Most were paid about $35, and 'ladies' with six to nine months' experience were paid less than $5 a week.

The management, like many of their colleagues since, was strongly opposed to the international ties of the Canadian employees. Erastus Wiman, president of the Great North-Western Telegraph Company, described the union's position as

> . . . a most extravagant demand, made in an offensive manner; which, if acceded to, would have the effect of placing the entire telegraphic communications of the Dominion in the hands of an organized mob, governed by regulations emanating from a band of agitators in a foreign country, enforced by intimidation and coercion in some cases almost bordering on brutality.[42]

Wiman was applying a double standard; his own company was under the control of Western Union, an American corporation. Forsey points out that Wiman himself later moved to the United States and became an advocate of commercial union between the two countries. Actually, Canadians were well represented on the executive of the Brotherhood.

The management of the telegraph companies flatly refused to negotiate, and the strikers were soon in trouble. There were defections from the union ranks, and after a month the leaders had to admit defeat and advise their members to go back to work. This was not enough for the companies; in a number of instances they forced returning employees to sign 'ironclads', or 'yellow dog contracts', pledging not to join any form of union. That was the end of the Brotherhood of Telegraphers.

The circumstances were somewhat similar in a dispute at the Toronto Street Railway in 1886. Three men had been fired because of their membership in the Knights of Labour, and other employees were told they must sign an undertaking not to join the organization. The men not only refused but promptly lined up to pay their dollar and join. Their names were immediately removed from the work assignment lists. They were locked out.

The company tried to keep the horsedrawn cars moving by hiring non-union people; but the employees had considerable public support, and many people refused to ride in the 'scab cars'. There were a number of incidents disrupting the service, and the Mayor, who had declared his sympathy for the strikers, issued a proclamation calling for an end to attempts to interfere with the cars.

A temporary settlement was reached on the basis of those originally dismissed being taken back. A few weeks later there were other firings, and the men struck. This time the disruption went on for several weeks, during which time the strikers attempted to operate a service of their own. Because they had no licence, fares had to be paid on a voluntary basis. The scheme collapsed, as did the strike.

As an economic force the Knights were weak, lacking ability to rally effective strength on behalf of those they represented. The mixed nature of the assemblies and the scattered and diversified membership did not lend itself to effective collective bargaining. This may have been one of the reasons that leaders of the movement were strongly opposed to strike action. When members did find themselves in strike situations, there was little leadership.

The Noble and Holy Order of the Knights of Labour was noticeably stronger on rhetoric and peaceful pursuits than on economic action. O'Donoghue is quoted as saying:

The tendency of the principle and methods of the Knights of Labour is in the direction of intellectual development, peaceful and lawful agitation, and an intelligent and united use of the ballot as a remedy for many of the grievances of which wage earners complain.[43]

And the editor of *Palladium of Labour* wrote:

While advocating trade unionism we have striven to take a broader view of the entire subject of labour reform than is embodied in mere unionism, and to grasp and apply those great underlying principles of equity and justice between men which alone can permanently and satisfactorily solve the issues between capital and labour.

We have in season and out of season striven to impress upon workers that great truth that men are in reality born free and equal so far as rights are concerned, and that all wrong and injustice of the social system arise out of the denial to the many of the opportunities and joys monopolized by the privileged few.

We have endeavoured to enforce the doctrine that as labour is the source of all wealth, no man is of right entitled to what he does not earn in the sense of giving positive value for it, and that the plea of acquiring something for nothing, by which so many speculators, usurers, landgrabbers and other classes of idlers live on the labour of other classes is a fraud and a wrong to those by whose toil they subsist.[44]

That was all very well, but most trade unionists were more vitally concerned with their immediate and personal needs, and the restructuring of society was something for the future.

Conditions in the labour movement were changing, and international unions were gaining strength. Behind them was the considerable force of the American Federation of Labor, which was taking a growing interest in Canadian affairs. Many of the Knights held dual membership, belonging also to a craft union. This was a practice which was regarded with disfavour by most craft unionists and even more so by the international headquarters of their organizations in the United States. Even before the founding of the AFL there had been demands from the crafts for dissolution of the Knights and an end to dual membership.

Now, thanks to the Haymarket Riot, that had been accomplished south of the border.

One ground for objection to the situation still existing in Canada was that through their association with the Knights some individuals gained a voice in labour meetings which would otherwise be denied them. This was true of O'Donoghue, who while a government official, continued to be active and vocal in labour affairs, with full status as a delegate from the Knights of Labour.

Clashes between the Knights and the craft unionists became increasingly frequent. The Knights sponsored resolutions which were sharply critical of the Trades and Labour Congress, particularly demanding the undertaking of organizational campaigns which would go beyond the craft boundaries. Coupled with this were objections to the influence being exerted on Canadian union affairs from the United States.

At the TLC's 1901 convention there was open opposition to O'Donoghue and others who were using their Knights membership to gain access to the inner circles of the labour movement. A motion for their expulsion was defeated, 47 to 20. But by the time the next convention was held, the gap had widened, and a motion to expel the Knights was carried.

Andy Andras, a long-time student of the labour movement in Canada, concluded in his booklet *Labour Unions in Canada*:

> The Knights had started out as a workingman's organization, had been diluted by farm and middle-class elements; had attempted unsuccessfully to combine skilled and unskilled workers alike and had finally ended up as a happy hunting ground for believers in an assortment of social and political cure-alls.[45]

Martin Robin, in *Radical Politics and Canadian Labour*, is even more outspoken, referring to the Knights' organization as 'a haven for discredited politicians and wire pullers expelled from trade unions'.

There is ground for such criticisms, but the fact remains that the original aspirations of the Knights were commendable and in some respects more far-sighted than those of the craft unions.

But in practical terms the Knights failed because of a seeming lack of desire, and certainly a lack of ability, to function as an economic force. That was then, as it is now, the fundamental purpose of the union movement. Without it there is a lack of strength to attain the broader social objectives.

6   The Solid Foundations

While the Knights of Labour were preoccupied with attaining social justice, other unions were concentrating on increasing wages, shortening hours, and bettering working conditions. As a result, between 1880 and the turn of the century there was vigorous and healthy growth in the labour movement in Canada, despite very strong employer resistance.

It was in this period that the solid basis of the movement was laid. While most of the activity was centred in particular unions, the way was being paved for the organizational structure which was to develop into today's labour movement.

The effects of the depression of the 1870s were wearing off, and the country was emerging into a period of brisk economic growth. Yet this was a relatively early stage of Canada's development. It was not until the latter part of the 1880s that Winnipeg became much more than a Hudson's Bay trading post; the Second Riel Rebellion took place in 1885; and in 1891 British Columbia had a population of barely 100,000. (In terms of trade union recruitment, it is worth noting that almost half of B.C.'s population were native Indians or Chinese, who at that time were unlikely to be candidates for union membership.) Against this background the labour movement was expanding, especially on the railways and among building trades.

The United Brotherhood of Carpenters and Joiners, originally a purely American union, started organizing in Canada in 1881, first at Hamilton, Toronto, and St Catharines. Membership grew rapidly, and the union was in the forefront of the struggle for shorter hours and other improvements. Ten years later the Carpenters Union had eighteen locals in Ontario and others in Montreal, Saint John, Yarmouth, Winnipeg, Victoria, New Westminster, and Vancouver.

Canadian bricklayers had become part of the international union movement. The Hamilton local, 'Ontario No. 1', sent five delegates to an 1882 convention in Buffalo, New York. Other locals were organized in Toronto, Guelph, London, and St Catharines.

The growth of the Bricklayers was indicative of what was happening in union circles. By 1889 the Toronto local had 700 members, and its president, Alex McCormick, was a vice-president of the international union. It was becoming a common practice for international unions to name a Canadian as vice-president. The bricklayers and others regarded the international ties as valuable in providing assistance in strike situations. When the Hamilton bricklayers had stopped work in 1883, for example, money from the international headquarters had helped them win a four-week struggle. In 1890 the Toronto local was involved in a six-week strike, during which $11,523 was received in assistance. They won the strike.

The bricklayers' union had a total membership in 1892 of 22,000, of whom 1,240 were in Canada. There were eight locals in Ontario, three in British Columbia, and one in Nova Scotia. The per capita dues paid by locals to the international headquarters varied according to needs. During the 1880s they were never above twenty-five cents a year and at one time were as low as twelve cents. Strike benefits were financed by special assessments. In the case of the Toronto strike this amounted to fifty-two cents per member.

Union growth was healthy throughout the building trades. The plumbers were beginning to emerge as a specialized trade. The International Brotherhood of Electrical Workers, formed in the United States in 1891, had added 'International' to its name in 1899 and sent an organizer to Canada. He soon had five locals established, and H. S. Hurd of Hamilton had become an international vice-president.

Trades councils were emerging as a means of establishing closer co-operation among unions with interests in particular industries, most of them in the construction field. The Federated Council of Building Trades was established in Toronto in 1886. Vancouver had a Building Trades Federation in 1891, with a card system to enforce closed shop conditions and thus restrict employment to union members. Building trades councils were also established at Ottawa and Kingston, Ontario. An Allied Building Trades Council was organized in Toronto in 1895, and councils of woodworkers and the metal trades followed a few years later.

Community labour councils, bringing together unions of various trades and industries, were also springing up. The Toronto Trades and Labour Council was actively attempting to spread unionism and employed one of its delegates, Tom Moor, as an organizer. Moor was having difficulty getting a job because of his reputation as a union man. One of the objectives of the Toronto Council was the organization of women employees. In 1883 the Council welcomed its first women delegates, members of the Female Shoe-Fitters.

In other centres labour councils which had disappeared during the time of heavy unemployment were revived. Among the earlier councils were those at London, Montreal, Hamilton, St Catharines, Ottawa, Vancouver, Brantford, Victoria, and Halifax. The greatest concentration was in Ontario, where there were twenty-five councils functioning by 1901.

All this growth was in the face of management opposition, which became more obvious with the threat of union strength. This applied in both Canada and the United States, and the opinion expressed by an owner of railway and mining interests during an American strike was no doubt echoed by many of his counterparts in this country:

> The rights and interests of the labouring men are best protected, not by the labour agitator, but by the Christian men to whom God has given the property rights of the country.[46]

On the other hand, the effectiveness of union organization was recognized by the Royal Commission on Capital and Labour which, reporting in 1889, said:

> Among other matters brought out . . . is the interesting and important bearing on the labour question of the influence of workingmen's organizations. Nothing could be more striking than the contrast furnished between organized districts and others where as yet the principles of a trade organization are little known and still less acted upon. And if the progress that has been made toward uniting capital and labour in cities that are comparatively well represented in the ranks of labour bodies is to be taken as a criterion to the usefulness of such societies, we may well believe they are destined to be a very important factor in the solution of this labour problem.[47]

At another point in its report the Commission commented:

> No one can become a member who is not sober, and as a consequence, union men and women are temperate, industrious in their habits. The universal testimony of wage earners is that the money spent by them to support their societies is as good an investment as they ever made.[48]

The Ontario Bureau of Industries was also favourably inclined toward unions, stating in its 1890 report:

> Despite the imputation of thoughtless radicalism, the organized labour element in its unity has always been conservative in the broadest sense of that term.[49]

The word 'conservative' was, however, hardly applicable to all the workers of the time. There were, for instance, the Irishmen, who provided much of the labour for canal construction as well as other public works. They were noted for their fiery disposition, and they rebelled under disciplinary measures that were likely to be accepted by the English and Scottish immigrants.

And at both ends of the country there were developments in the latter part of the century that demonstrated the militancy of an expanding labour movement. In Nova Scotia much attention had centred on the Provincial Workmen's Association (PWA), which had come into being in 1879 and which has been described as

> . . . the first organization of workmen in Canada which extended beyond local bounds and held its own for many years. . . . For almost thirty-eight years it held the miners of Nova Scotia together in a notably successful campaign for legislation, for safety measures and other matters of vital concern to working people.[50]

However, there were times when the PWA came under criticism for what appeared to be an unduly close association with management. There was a reluctance on the part of the Association to become involved in strikes, though it was in fact responsible for some major work stoppages.

It was a wage cut imposed by the Springhill Mining Company that had led to the formation of the Provincial Workmen's Association in 1879. During the night a group of miners had met secretly in the woods on the outskirts of Springhill and decided to form a union and strike. The first minutes recorded:

> At a largely attended meeting of miners held at Springhill . . . on the 29th day of August, 1879, it was unanimously resolved to form an association to defend and protect the interests of the miners and other workers about the [collieries].[51]

Pioneer Lodge No. 1 at Springhill was soon followed by other branches, and later in the year, delegates from five lodges met at Truro to form a provincial organization.

The constitution spelled out various objectives: to shorten the hours of labour and assure fair practices in the weighing of coal; to improve wages 'as the state of the trade shall warrant or allow'; 'to strive in obtaining better legislation whereby the more efficient management of the mines . . . may be effected . . . thereby securing the health and safety of the workman'; 'to secure compensation for injuries received while at work . . . where the employer may be liable'; and to support members locked out by employers or 'forced to discontinue work on account of insufficient wages or from any unjust cause whatsoever'. There was also reference to the fostering of virtuous habits to improve the condition of members morally, mentally, and socially.

The Association was headed by a 'Grand Council', which, while it did not have authority to call strikes, could provide advice and sanction strike action or withhold support from strikes which had not received formal approval. The Council had power to impose a levy to finance strikes, that not to exceed a dollar a member.

Membership in the PWA fluctuated seasonally with varying employment conditions and was at times related to interest in political affairs. Organizing campaigns in occupations outside coalmining were undertaken to meet the competition presented by the Knights of Labour. Efforts were made to recruit members among garment workers, railway employees, boot and shoe workers, longshoremen, and retail clerks; but all met with limited success.

The PWA placed great emphasis on safety in underground operations, a matter naturally of vital importance to the miners, but one in which they were denied a voice. Such safety inspection as there was involved only a government inspector and company officials. The union was denied the opportunity to appear at coroners' inquests inquiring into mine fatalities. Likewise, the men had no means of pursuing complaints about the short-weighing of the coal they mined or excessively high prices for the dynamite they had to buy from the employers.

By going on strike the union finally gained a limited form of recognition, with the management agreeing to meet a committee of miners. Then in 1887 the Provincial Workmen's Association became involved in a strike which lasted throughout the winter, accompanied by widespread suffering among the miners and their families. In this and almost every other stoppage, the company had the militia called out to protect property interests.

Still the PWA was opposed in principle to strike action, explaining that:

> As an association we do not believe much in strikes, but we are forced to look upon them, for want of something better, as a necessary evil.[52]

In common with other sections of the labour movement, the Association was inclined toward arbitration, with a willingness to accept the decision of a third party. This was a matter which would be debated for many years to come. In Nova Scotia, legislation providing for the arbitration of labour disputes was supported by the PWA but was opposed by mine managements.

The PWA's greatest activity was in the legislative field. One bone of contention between the companies and the union was the company-owned stores, dubbed 'Pluck Me's'. As part of their compensation the miners received credit at the stores, and they were thus trapped into making purchases at unduly high prices. It is true that when there was unemployment, credit was still available, and in the absence of any other form of assistance, this was considered to be an advantage. Others recognized the system as a snare allowing the accumulation of debts which had to be paid once there was work.

The Provincial Workmen's Association eventually disappeared as the result of a jurisdictional fight with the United Mine Workers, a story which is told in more detail in Chapter 8.

It was also miners who provided much of the initiative for union growth in British Columbia. There was activity among other groups, but it was in the rough-and-tumble of the mining camps that some of the toughest and most significant battles took place.

In the strikes which followed so closely on the opening of Vancouver Island coal mines in the mid-century, Robert Dunsmuir emerged as a key personality on the management side and went on to found a vast industrial empire. As an employee Dunsmuir had refused to join Fort Rupert miners who struck in 1855 in protest at working conditions. He was said to have been rewarded with a grant of the coal rights on 1,000 acres in the Nanaimo fields. However acquired, the holdings were unquestionably valuable, and they were rapidly expanded.

When the men at the Wellington Mine struck in 1877, protesting wage cuts and short-weighing practices, it was Dunsmuir they faced. The miners' union was the Miners' Mutual Protective Association. Dunsmuir tried to import strikebreakers, and when this was not successful, he ordered the miners' families out of the company houses they occupied. They refused to move, and Dunsmuir arranged to bring in the militia, backed by a British naval vessel. The families were evicted, and after a four-month struggle the strike was lost.

The Miners' Mutual Protective Association managed to remain above water for a time, but it finally succumbed in another strike in 1883. The major issue in that dispute was the employment of Chinese in the mines. The Occidentals objected on the grounds that the Chinese were ready to work longer hours for lower wages and that they disregarded safety regulations. Unable to read or write, and in most cases barely able to understand English, they had little or no knowledge of what was involved in safety and were prepared to work under hazardous conditions.

Opposition to the employment of Chinese had reached such a point that the organization known as the Workingman's Protective Association was formed primarily to combat Chinese immigration. It lasted for only a short time, but the bitterness remained. In 1892 the Victoria Labour Council reported to the Trades and Labour Congress:

> Thousands of young men on the Coast, who are now wrecks, physically and mentally, can lay their ruin to the Chinese who taught them the terrible habit of opium smoking.[53]

One of the more successful organizational efforts among the miners was at Nanaimo, where 1,000 men attended a meeting in 1890, forming the Miners' and Mine Labourers' Protective Association. This soon became involved in a hard-fought but unsuccessful struggle for the eight-hour day.

Other mining operations were opening in the interior of British Columbia, largely on the initiative of American companies, with the ore being shipped out of the country. Before long the Canadian Pacific Railway became active in the area, buying up a short line and smelter at Trail. Later, with financial support obtained through the Crow's Nest Pass subsidy plan, the CPR's mining operations spread into other territory.

In the United States the Western Federation of Miners had become prominent. This was a rough, tough organization, which at one time seriously considered forming a rifle corps to enforce its programs. Quickly tagged 'radical', it was of a very different character from the conservative American Federation of Labor or, in Canada, the Trades and Labour Congress. The Federation was led by activists who had little regard for the ordinary bread-and-butter trade unionism and who ridiculed the lobbying tactics of union leaders in the East.

The first Canadian branch of the Federation was formed at Rossland, British Columbia, in 1895. Further growth was slow until a wage cut, following a reduction in hours, resulted in a strike. The strike was lost, but a stronger and more united organization had been established.

In 1901 the Federation engaged in another strike at Rossland, one which had an important effect on labour legislation. Some of the mines were under an ownership which was involved in a strike with the Federation in the United States. Eventually, more than 1,000 men in the Rossland area walked out.

William Lyon Mackenzie King, then Deputy Minister of Labour, went to Rossland and conducted an investigation. He reported that, while wages were an issue, the miners 'had reason to believe that the mining companies had decided to break up their organization, if possible', and this was the basic cause of the strike.

The companies imported strikebreakers, and some operations were resumed. Then the companies obtained an injunction to prohibit picketing, and the strike was broken. Not satisfied with this, the management took legal action against the Federation. Rossland thereby became a Canadian parallel to the famous British Taff Vale case, in which unions were ruled subject to suit for damages. In British Columbia the litigation dragged on for two years, and eventually the courts found against the Federation, holding it liable for damages of $12,500. The union hall and some funds were seized, although action by union officials had moved other resources beyond the reach of the law. The important outcome was the adoption of legislation to protect unions against liability in such situations, a policy still challenged by many on the management side.

Fishermen on the west coast were also showing an interest in union organization. At first they were chiefly concerned with trying to limit the number of licences. This was opposed by the canning companies, which favoured a large number of licences in the hope that more intensive competition among fishermen would bring down prices. There were serious divisions among those employed in the industry; nearly half the licences were held by Japanese. A strike over prices in 1900 brought new unity and marked the beginning of a continuous organization.

Much of the union expansion in the West was related to railway construction. Work on extending the Canadian Pacific to the coast started in 1880 and was completed seven years later. Again, many of those employed were Chinese who had been brought to Canada to provide a source of cheap labour. But with the new rail lines there was a healthy growth in union organization. These were the days of the 'boomers' — union organizers who rode the rails from one centre to another, preaching the union gospel. Highly significant, from a long-term point of view, was the opening of vast new areas of the Prairies, with new opportunities for industrial growth and accompanying union organization.

There was a growing spirit of national unity in the labour movement. It was evident in a strike of London, Ontario, street railway workers toward the end of the century. Support for the strikers was solicited by the Trades and Labour Congress, and more than half the funds raised came from British Columbia.

Even government employees decided it was time to organize. The Federated Association of Letter Carriers was formed in 1891, marking the beginning of union organization in the public service.

Formal recognition of the importance of organized labour came with the institution of a general holiday to honour working people. There has been a great deal of controversy about the origin of Labour Day. Americans claim to have initiated it, while Canadian unionists maintain it started in this country. In any event there was a labour-sponsored celebration in Toronto in 1882 and even before that there was a public gathering at the time of the 1872 Toronto printers' strike. The holiday became official in 1894 when, following a request from the Trades and Labour Congress, the first Monday in September was designated Labour Day.

7 The Trades and Labour Congress

The Canadian labour movement came of age when the Trades and Labour Congress was formed in 1886. There had been earlier efforts (see Chapter 3), and still another abortive attempt was made in 1883. But finally the Trades and Labour Congress became a fact. It was the foundation on which a continuous national organization would be built; it was the source to which the present Canadian Labour Congress directly traces its lineage. The path of development was to prove rough, but a start had been made.

In 1883 it was again the Toronto Trades and Labour Council which sparked the attempt. Co-operation among unions in Toronto, as in other communities, had proven worthwhile, and officers of the Toronto Council were convinced the principle should be extended, regardless of previous failures. Invitations were sent out for a convention to be held in Toronto during the 1883 Christmas holiday period.

The timing might have been expected to restrict attendance to the most dedicated, but the promoters had some misgivings and suggested that delegates should be chosen with regard to their sobriety. The invitation explained:

> As practical work, and as much of it as possible within the time specified, will be one of the main topics on this occasion, there will be no time for holiday enjoyment, and, as a consequence, it is to be hoped that all organizations will honour themselves in the ability and judgment of those whom they elect to represent them.[54]

The forty-eight delegates who responded were apparently both serious and sober. 'With hearty approval' they declared their support for 'any practical legislation tending to reduce the consumption of intoxicating liquor'.

Charles March, president of the Toronto Council, speaking at the opening session, outlined the interests and concerns of Canadian trade unionists in the early 1880s. March said:

> While I may find it somewhat difficult to define minutely the many reasons that urged the Toronto Trades Council to call together representatives of labour in its various phases throughout the Dominion, yet I feel justified in saying that the disturbed conditions of trade matters, coupled with strikes always detrimental under any phase, occurring from time to time, and the apparent need for a closer cementing of all classes of labour for common defence and protection, has been not a small factor in the determination.
>
> That the Council was not governed by narrow-mindedness in the premises is best evidenced by the call embracing not only trade unionists, but also Knights of Labour. That this is right in principle I know you will all agree, as between the two bodies antagonism should not, and I am glad to find does not, exist, and between them no section or class of wage-earners need be without organization, and consequently protection. In the perfection of an organization lies education and a consequent raising of the masses to a thorough realization of their own power under our present advanced system of government, although a system capable of many improvements.
>
> Although no program has been provided as to the measures that ought to receive your earnest attention, still, speaking for myself, I think you should not overlook in your deliberations such questions as the extension of the franchise to a much greater degree than now prevails, the Chinese immigration curse, pauper and assisted passage from Europe, the necessity for factory and sanitary legislation, such legislation by the Dominion Parliament as would protect the wages of mechanics and labourers involved in insolvent estates, a protest against placing the product of convict labour in competition with the product of labour of honest men, and the liability of employers when employees suffer disability through unprotected machinery and so forth.
>
> It appears to me, too, that some action will be necessary with a view to devising ways and means for the better prosecution of efforts toward securing such legislation as may be required in repealing such unjust laws, as well as securing the passage of such

measures as may be deemed requisite in justice to the working class from time to time.[55]

Then the convention got down to business. The very first resolution was directed to the bugbear of Chinese immigration, calling for a complete ban. It got unanimous support. The convention also recorded its opposition to the practice of subsidizing European immigrants. These positions were related to prevailing unemployment, and the delegates also advocated shorter working hours to spread available work. Other resolutions sought improvements in working conditions, as March had suggested.

Education has always been a subject of interest to the labour movement, though the nature of proposals has changed with the times. In 1883 the unions opposed government grants to universities; today they favour general increases in expenditures on education. In the 1880s university education was available only to young people whose families were quite able to look after their educational needs on their own. This meant the virtual exclusion of children from working-class families. Delegates at the 1883 conference were more interested in having textbooks made available without charge to students in lower grades.

The political situation was discussed, and there was a consensus that working people had to be elected to legislative bodies if the interests of the working class were to be protected. There was a good deal of discussion about methods of dealing with disputes between employees and employers, a topic explored later in this chapter.

Then the delegates, who had sacrificed a good deal of their Christmas holidays, went home. They must have been discouraged when a year later there was insufficient response to justify holding another convention.

But in 1886 there was another try, and that time interest ran high, with 109 delegates turning out. For the first time representation went beyond Ontario's boundaries: one of the delegates was from the Quebec City Assembly of the Knights of Labour. Some progress was being made toward an organization that was national in more than name.

It was unanimously agreed to form a new central body to be called the Canadian Trades and Labour Congress. Later there was some juggling of the name — Trades and Labour Congress of the Dominion of Canada in 1887, Dominion Trades and Labour Congress in 1888, and finally Trades and Labour Congress of Canada in 1892. That was the way it was to remain until the TLC became part of the Canadian Labour Congress in 1956.

It was decided that membership in the new Congress should be open to both craft unions and the Knights of Labour, and the primary purpose was defined as

> . . . the uniting of all labour organizations in order to work for the passage of new laws or amendments to existing laws, in the interests of those who have to earn their living, as well as to insure at the same time the well-being of the working class.[56]

Clearly the emphasis was to be on legislative activities, as there was no mention of any program to extend union organization. But it was not long before there was disagreement between the craft unions and the Knights on this point. In 1894 some of the Knights' delegates introduced a sharply-worded resolution:

> It being proven that this Congress has outlived its usefulness, through its incapacity to obtain even a fraction of justice from the federal and provincial governments; be it resolved that before its adjournment this Congress be reconstructed on a system in accord with the ideas of the age, and which may permit it to grant charters for the organization of workers' societies in no matter what branch of workers, to the end that at all times we may be in a position to concentrate our forces for the political battle, being convinced that to petition governments for reform is a loss of time, and that it is only by independent political action, like that of the Socialist Workers' Party, that we will obtain the measure of justice that we have so long sought.[57]

This was a highly contentious position. Organizationally the delegates were almost evenly divided — twenty-seven from the craft unions and twenty-six from the Knights. But the resolution passed, and the constitution was amended giving the Congress authority to charter:

. . . organizations in localities where they do not now exist, whether of local unions or Assemblies of the Knights of Labour; but in no case may they grant charters to any body of workers belonging to any trade or profession having a national or international union now in existence.[58]

This pointed up the sanctity of union jurisdictions, a matter which has continued to bedevil the labour movement ever since. Established unions were not going to have some other organization attempting to supplant them. Neither would they allow other organizations to invade territory which was regarded as the home of potential members, regardless of whether or not the original union was prepared to undertake their organization at the moment. In other words, they wanted the right to sit firmly on their jurisdiction.

The policy which was adopted gave the central body power to take in miscellaneous groups which did not immediately fit into the framework of affiliated national or international unions. Even with this restriction, every effort was to be made to have them become part of one of the established unions later.

Organizing the unorganized was definitely to be a secondary role for the Congress. Its main function was lobbying. There was an executive body, known as the Parliamentary Committee, with regional representation. When Parliament was in session, the president or some other designated person was stationed in Ottawa to attend sessions and keep an eye on the proceedings. Information concerning legislation was circulated, and Congress affiliates were encouraged to petition and lobby their local member, seeking support for labour's policies.

The legislative interests remained largely unchanged: voting rights, shorter hours, methods of settling disputes, safety, employee rights, fair-wage clauses in government contracts, employer responsibilities, use of prison labour, taxation, and immigration.

The Chinese question was still prominent. The 1885 Parliament had imposed a $50 tax on every Chinese immigrant entering the country. The Trades and Labour Congress took the position, as did the British Columbia Legislature, that this was entirely inadequate. The Vancouver Trades and Labour Council wanted a $500 entry tax and a continuing tax of $200 a year. The argument continued, and in 1900 the federal admittance tax was increased to $100.

But there were much more positive concerns, such as factory acts, safety regulations, and compensation for time lost through industrial accidents. Many of these were consolidated when the Congress drew up a *Platform of Principles*. Some of the objectives are still relevant. The platform sought:

1. Free compulsory education.
2. Legal working day of eight hours, and six days a week.
3. Government inspection of all industries.
4. Abolition of the contract system on all public works.
5. A minimum living wage, based on local conditions.
6. Public ownership of all franchises, such as railways, telegraphs, waterworks, lighting, etc.
7. Tax reform, lessening taxation on industry and increasing it on land values.
8. Abolition of the Senate.
9. Exclusion of the Chinese.
10. Placing of the union label on all manufactured goods.
11. Abolition of child labour by children under fourteen and of female labour in all branches of industry such as mines, workshops, factories, etc.
12. Abolition of property qualifications for all public offices.
13. Compulsory arbitration of labour disputes.
14. Proportional representation and the cumulative vote.
15. Prohibition of prison labour in competition with 'free labour'.

Slowly but surely, the Congress was becoming national. In 1889 the convention was held in Montreal, the first time outside Ontario. The following year, at Ottawa, there was the first participation from British Columbia, in the person of Ralph Smith, a Member of Parliament representing a British Columbia constituency. More was to be heard of him when he held the presidency of the TLC from 1898 to 1902.

New Brunswick was represented at the 1897 convention, and when the Congress met in Winnipeg the following year there were delegates from what was then the North West Territories — now Saskatchewan and Alberta. By 1901 delegates from Prince Edward Island and Nova Scotia were taking part in Congress deliberations.

Membership was growing. In 1901 the TLC boasted 8,381 members and had an annual budget of $809.98. It reached such a stage of affluence that it was able to afford 'a stenographer and a typewriter'.

While it was the individual unions that were directly involved in collective bargaining, the central Congress spoke on their behalf concerning legislation which affected bargaining. The accounts of these earlier discussions tend to become confusing because of various interpretations placed on such words as 'arbitration' and 'conciliation'. In present-day terminology 'arbitration' is generally taken to mean the intervention of a third party clothed with the right to make a final and binding settlement. Such intervention may be on a voluntary basis, by agreement of the parties, or compulsory, a method of settlement imposed by higher authorities. 'Conciliation', on the other hand, is a process through which efforts are made to reach an agreement which, it is hoped, will be accepted by both parties, without any degree of compulsion or prior commitment.

In the 1890s and early 1900s the words were subject to various interpretations and were often used interchangeably. There was a strong body of union opinion quite ready to accept automatic government intervention in employee-employer disputes, amounting to compulsory arbitration. Today's labour leaders look on the idea with horror, as do most management people.

The Canadian Labour Union (see Chapter 3), at its final convention in 1877, had adopted a resolution which appeared to touch all bases, stating:

> This convention is of the opinion that the application of the principle of arbitration and conciliation in labour disputes is one well calculated to advance the prosperity of the trades and to promote amicable relations between employers and employed; and urges

upon all branches of trade the desirability of establishing such boards wherever possible.[59]

The sponsor of the resolution, J. S. Williams, editor of the *Ontario Workman*, indicated he was advocating a form of voluntary arbitration when he spoke of the procedure being adopted by mutual consent. Other delegates were quite prepared to accept a government board which would be free to act on its own initiative.

O'Donoghue was among those advocating some form of arbitration, expressing the view that:

> Arbitration will ultimately remedy the necessity for strikes and . . . co-operation, productive as well as distributive, will in course of time take the place of the present wage system.[60]

The idea of government intervention gained ground, and delegates to the 1883 convention favoured 'the appointment of a board of arbitration to which all disputes between workmen and their employers should be submitted'. Presumably the decision of such a board would be binding.

When the TLC founding convention was held three years later, the delegates took a position advocating voluntary settlement if at all possible or, failing that, binding arbitration. The resolution, which was adopted by a vote of 137 to 17, read:

> That this convention affirm the principle of arbitration in all cases in which difficulties arise between employers and employees that cannot be otherwise settled, and that this Congress further requests that a law be passed making it binding that in all cases where disputes arise, each party must proceed to arbitrate, and making the decision of such arbitration in all cases binding.[61]

The subject came up time and again, and the position of some delegates, including O'Donoghue, swung back and forth. One opinion, still widely held, was that arbitration should be imposed only in situations involving essential services, such as transportation, communications, and the protection of life and property. In 1892 the TLC appointed a special committee to study the matter. The committee's report proposed the creation of conciliation boards on a community basis, composed of representatives of labour and management with an 'outside' chairman. Delegates to the convention which received the report preferred a straight government-appointed committee which would be available to those who wished to use its services.

'Compulsory arbitration of labour disputes', as has been mentioned, was included in the 1898 *Platform of Principles*. The next year the Congress asked the Dominion government 'to establish a Board of Arbitration to adjust all disputes between employers and employees'.

The government's response was the adoption of a Conciliation Act in 1900. This gave the minister authority to investigate labour disputes, bringing the parties together and appointing a conciliator or conciliation board to attempt to effect a settlement. The Act specified:

> It shall be the duty of the conciliator to promote conditions favourable to a settlement by endeavouring to allay distrust, to remove causes of friction, to promote good feeling, to restore confidence, and to encourage the parties to come together and themselves effect a settlement, and also to promote agreements between employers and employees with a view to the submission of differences to conciliation or arbitration before resorting to strikes or lockouts.[62]

While the conciliator had the authority of a commissioner in conducting the inquiry, there was no power to impose a settlement. This principle of conciliation — essentially an effort to influence the parties toward agreement — was to pervade Canadian labour legislation for many years to follow.

But in the early 1900s there were those in labour's ranks who thought something more was needed, and Ralph Smith, the TLC president, was among them. His address to the 1901 convention was a flat endorsement of compulsory arbitration in essential services. Smith said:

> Both capital and labour have a legal right to insist upon what each considers its due; but when the enforcement of these claims brings

stagnation and danger to the public, they ought to be compelled to submit to the decision of impartial arbitrators appointed by the government. I am convinced that this would be a great advantage to the country, and I am persuaded that there is not a single question that labour unions ought to concentrate their energies to bring about of so vast importance as this.[63]

The convention committee which considered the officers' reports disagreed, stating it was 'not prepared to recommend a dogmatic pronouncement in favour of . . . compulsory arbitration'. The committee did, however, support the idea of 'compulsory conciliation'. There has always been a school of thought within labour that compulsory arbitration, once applied generally to so-called 'essential services' would soon spread to other disputes, eventually negating the right to strike.

Discussion of the theories of dispute settlement procedures is one thing; being confronted by an actual situation in which the theories may be applied is something else. This was the situation in 1902 when Canadian railway workers were faced with the prospect of compulsory arbitration. Legislation had been drafted, and the railway employees saw it as a threat to their interests. They voiced their opposition at the annual TLC convention and won support of the delegates for a resolution attacking the principle of compulsory arbitration on the ground that it would

. . . rob the employees of their constitutional rights, destroy their organizations, and place them absolutely in the hands of the railway companies, at the same time depriving them of that citizenship which is so dearly prized and which is the inherent right of all free-born British subjects.[64]

From that moment on, the labour movement in Canada has remained ardently opposed to the idea of compulsory arbitration.

But regardless of the form of labour legislation, government was assuming a more active role in employee-employer relations. A federal Department of Labour was created in 1900, though legislative provision for the new department was little more than an appendage to the Conciliation Act. It directed that the Department

> . . . shall collect, digest and publish in suitable form statistical and other information relating to the conditions of labour, shall institute and conduct inquiries into important industrial questions upon which adequate information may not at present be available and issue at least once a month a publication to be known as *The Labour Gazette*.[65]

The new publication appeared in September 1900 and was available to the public at three cents a copy. The first copies were distributed at the Trades and Labour Congress convention, which was being held in Ottawa, as they came off the press. The editor was W. L. Mackenzie King. *The Labour Gazette* now ranks as one of Canada's oldest magazines.

At the same time, steps were being taken to assure the payment of fair wages under government contracts — an issue which had aroused O'Donoghue and resulted in a strike of Ottawa printers in 1869. The first fair-wage legislation, adopted in 1900, required that on projects financed or subsidized by the government every effort should be made to ensure wage schedules equivalent to those prevalent for the trade in the area. Similar legislation was adopted in Ontario a short time later.

All this new attention from official quarters must have given encouragement to Canadian unionists, but some of their more serious difficulties were yet to come, and many of those from within their own movement.

8 Growth and Conflict — The East

History gives a good deal of support to those who suggest that there are times when unionists spend as much time fighting among themselves as they do fighting with management. While conflicts with management continued in the early 1900s, and were at times extremely sharp, there were inter-union jealousies and struggles for control within the labour movement which had lasting effects. The events between the beginning of the century and World War I did much to mould the nature and form of the labour movement in Canada.

Economic conditions in the earlier part of the period continued favourable to union organization. Business was good, and expansion meant jobs. But as unions grew, they attracted more unfavourable attention from employers. Small and weak labour organizations, lacking in economic clout, could be ignored; stable organizations which were increasingly effective in representing employees could not. Many employers denied the right of their employees to organize and refused to recognize the unions which purported to speak for them. Some of the most bitter and violent disputes in the history of Canadian industrial relations were the result.

Time and again there were situations in which the Riot Act was read, calling for the dispersal of crowds to restore order. The practice became so common that it can be questioned whether such extreme measures were always justified. Little more than a request from management was necessary to have the militia called out, and troops appeared at picket lines with great regularity. Government intervention in disputes was frequent but of little help to the unions.

Yet the strength of unions increased; in the years 1899-1903 the number of unions doubled. More than half of the thousand or so locals were in Ontario; 150 were in Quebec. By 1913 the labour movement in Canada was composed of 175,800 members in 2,000 local unions.

Some of the locals were in the clothing industry, where sweatshop conditions were prevalent, and it was there that the first efforts were made to establish fair-wage schedules in government contracts. The government was a major purchaser of uniforms, and cut-throat competition for contracts had a disastrous effect on wages.

Tailoring was largely on a custom basis, and many of the skilled craftsmen employed in the trade turned to unions. In 1900 the United Garment Workers of America had a Canadian membership of 3,000, and by 1902 there were thirteen locals in Canada and some additional membership among tanners and curriers in the fur shops. The union was financing itself partially by the sale of union labels to manufacturers. These were sewn into garments to identify them as the product of union labour. Another 1,500 Canadians belonged to the Journeymen Tailors of America.

The International Ladies' Garment Workers' Union, founded in the United States in 1900, organized its first Canadian local at Toronto in 1905, but this failed to survive. It was not until some time later that the ILGWU became firmly established in Canada. In 1912 a strike involving 4,500 Montreal members followed the employers' rejection of a reduction in the work week from fifty-five to forty-nine hours. There was a compromise settlement.

In the textile industry, mule spinners in Hochelaga and Valleyfield, Quebec, organized about 1905. A Quebec federation of textile workers was formed later and affiliated with the United Textile Workers of America. This was one of a series of switches in affiliation, accompanied by internal conflicts which divided the leadership and seriously weakened the effectiveness of the unions. A number of textile workers were involved in Quebec strikes between 1900 and 1908.

A dispute in the Quebec boot and shoe industry in 1900 took on historic significance with the intervention of the Roman Catholic Church, setting a pattern which was later to affect many aspects of organized labour in the province.

The situation was sparked by the dismissal of an employee, resulting in a protest strike. Other employers saw this as a union challenge to their authority, and the gates of twenty-one establishments were locked. The employees were told they would not be allowed to return to work until they signed 'yellow dog contracts', signifying that they would not hold membership in any union. The workers suggested the dispute go to arbitration, but the employers refused. Eventually it was agreed to have Archbishop Bégin intervene as a mediator, in the hope that he could bring the parties together. Operations were resumed in the meantime.

The Archbishop was critical of the constitutions of the three unions involved — Lasters, Cutters, and Machine Shoemakers — on the ground that, if applied literally, they would be 'sure to greatly injure personal liberty, freedom of conscience and justice'. He insisted the constitutions be amended and also proposed a plan of conciliation and arbitration which would, in effect, make it impossible for the workers to strike. His letter, directing revision of the contracts or, failing that, the resignation of Catholic members was read to congregations by parish priests. Two of the unions immediately agreed, while the third held out for a time but finally gave in.

There was a violent strike in 1906 at a small sawmill operation at Buckingham, Quebec, on the Ottawa River. The 400 employees struck in an attempt to increase the wage rate of 12½ cents an hour. The company refused to negotiate or even to take part in government mediation, objecting to the international union to which the men belonged. Under the protection of private company police, efforts were made to move some logs, and violence erupted. Two strikers and a detective were killed and a number of others injured. The strike was lost.

There was considerable industrial strife on the railways. Bad conditions in the camps were at the root of some of the trouble; but there was also the fundamental objection of the Canadian Pacific Railway to the formation of unions. Whenever there was a work stoppage, the CPR was quick to obtain injunctions restricting activities of the strikers and, at the same time, to import strikebreakers. The railway had its own private police force, and if this was not considered adequate, the assistance of the army was usually available to the company.

On the Grand Trunk Railway an early strike involved the International Association of Machinists and affected operations from Montreal to Sarnia, Ontario. Later, in another strike, the entire Grand Trunk system was tied up, and some associated lines in the United States were affected. Troops were used at Brockville, Ontario, where several people were injured in a riot.

Then, in 1908, the CPR's efforts to curb union activities resulted in a strike of machinists and carmen, which interfered with operations in all provinces except Nova Scotia and Prince Edward Island. The company served notice that it was terminating the collective agreement and instituting a wage cut. It proposed to 'remove the rights of committees of employees to meet company officers on behalf of the men' and also to 'remove restrictions on rules governing the advancement of apprentices'. A government-appointed conciliation board supported the company's position, and the strike was lost. There had been no violence.

But there was violence when 700 Fort William freight handlers struck in 1909. The issue was wages. The prevailing rate was 17½ cents an hour for day work and 20 cents for night work, with a bonus of a cent an hour for those who worked the entire season. There were rumours that some of the strikers were armed, and an intensive police search disclosed one man with a pistol. The company then called in thirty armed guards from Winnipeg. Several guards, as well as some strikers, were injured in a subsequent clash. The Riot Act was read and troops appeared. There were no further outbreaks, and the strike was settled by a three-cent increase and discontinuance of the bonus.

There is considerable argument as to the value and wisdom of using large forces of special police or the army in labour disputes. Obviously, situations differ; but there are many occasions in which the presence of an armed force only serves to exacerbate the conflict. In the Fort William case a subsequent government inquiry was mildly critical of the company's use of its private police force. The report stated:

> It would seem possible . . . that a less prominent display of force might have been dictated by prudence, and might have helped avert the calamity that followed, and it is at least arguable whether the public interests do not demand such an amendment of the law as would require that the consent of the public officers responsible for the peace of the community should be procured before so large a body of armed men is brought within the limits of the municipality concerned.[66]

Dr Stuart Jamieson of the University of British Columbia, an authority on industrial relations in Canada, made a detailed study of strikes in the 1900-1966 period for the Federal Task Force on Industrial Relations. He concluded that in the earlier part of the period Canadian workers were far from being as docile as they have often been pictured. In both Canada and the United States, violent and illegal work stoppages were far more prevalent than in other countries, as was the use of police and the army in industrial disputes.

Jamieson expressed the view that:

> Aggressive or violent action by various labour groups has often been provoked by resentment against the use of armed forces, or the discriminatory and one-sided support by governments to employers. . . .
> Violence was much more common on the industrial scene during the first three decades of this century and its incidence appears to have declined considerably since World War II. The traditions, attitudes and behaviour patterns engendered by events of the earlier decades, however, have carried over and influenced the industrial relations climate on this continent in recent years and have created special problems of legislation and law enforcement.[67]

He referred particularly to the Royal Canadian Mounted Police, which he described as 'a highly pervasive force in Canadian society', and added that:

> Its presence has been felt with enough force to tip the scales of battle in hundreds of strikes and labour demonstrations. The particular image of the RCMP, and of the federal government itself, which this situation has generated in the eyes of so many in the ranks of organized labour, in all probability has had a profound effect on the climate of industrial relations in this country.[68]

Initially the army was more visible than the RCMP. Soldiers were prominent in a major strike of the Provincial Workmen's Association of Nova Scotia in 1904. The Sydney Steel Mill had cut wages, and the Knights of Labour, seeking an organizational foothold in the area, exploited the situation. This pushed the PWA into a strike which affected not only the 1,500 employees but the entire community which was dependent on the mill's operations. The company attempted to continue work and had the militia brought in. After a seven-week struggle, the strike collapsed, and the Provincial Workmen's Association was left in desperate financial straits, with its prestige badly shattered. It had proven no match for a large company backed by the army. The Knights failed to become a significant movement in Nova Scotia.

The PWA ran into further difficulties when the United Mine Workers appeared on the Nova Scotia scene. The international union had been active in western Canada, and its first approach to the PWA was in the form of an invitation to the provincial organization to affiliate to the international. When this was rejected, the UMW started an organizational campaign to entice miners from their old union. A jurisdictional dispute followed.

The UMW was capitalizing on the miners' dissatisfaction with their union. But the PWA had a closed shop contract, with the check-off of union dues, and miners who deserted the PWA were subject to dismissal. There were clashes at Glace Bay and Springhill, resulting in the appointment of a government conciliation board. This brought down a report favouring the positions of the employers and the PWA, who were united in their opposition to the UMW. The Board was opposed to international unions, speaking of the UMW as 'a foreign organization' and expressing a fear that its power to call sympathetic strikes might endanger the marketing of Cape Breton coal.

But the miners were lining up behind the new union, and 2,500 Glace Bay miners struck in an effort to force the company to recognize the UMW. Miners at Springhill also stopped work. That 1909 strike lasted ten months but the operators managed to keep the mines going, and the strikes were lost. The cost to the men and their union was high. A detachment of 600 soldiers had been stationed at Glace Bay to break up meetings and demonstrations. Scores of union men were arrested, and several hundred families were evicted from company-owned houses. The United Mine Workers spent $1,000,000 before finally admitting defeat. The PWA had retained its position but in the succeeding years did little to improve conditions for the men.

It was some time before the UMW recovered sufficiently to make a new attempt to recruit Cape Breton miners; and then the approach was very different. Silby Barrett, a Newfoundlander who became one of Canada's most colourful labour personalities, was the key to the situation. A stocky individual with the rugged look of the Newfoundland coast, he traded heavily on his Newfoundland background and an ability to meet workers on their own level. Some of his quips have outlived him but fail to do justice to his shrewdness as a union organizer: 'Them oral agreements ain't worth the paper they're written on'; and, in an address to a group of somewhat incredulous university students, 'What did we do about them "Pluck Me Stores"? We burns 'em'.

Barrett assumed a position of leadership among the Cape Breton miners and promoted the idea of a new provincial union, which was to be 'free from entanglement or connection with any union whose officers and headquarters are outside the province'. The idea was encouraged by a Royal Commission, which saw it as an effective method of ending the PWA-UMW conflict.

The new union took over, and the Provincial Workmen's Association was dissolved. But the executive of the new union was dominated by UMW supporters, and it was only a short time before there was an overwhelming vote to affiliate to the international union. Only then did it become known that Barrett had been on the UMW payroll for some time. Cape Breton miners are still represented by the UMW, though their numbers have been reduced considerably from the 11,000 of the PWA-UMW days.

In Newfoundland, then a British colony and not for some time to become part of Canada, there had been an unsuccessful effort to establish a central labour organization in 1896. In 1907 a Trades and Labour Council was formed in St John's, 'to promote the welfare of workmen and to adjust differences whenever they arise between employer and employed'. Among the occupations involved were shipwrights, drapers, longshoremen, and clerks. The council carried on for a few years and then disappeared. It was not until after World War I that a Newfoundland organization representative of unions on the Island was established on a permanent basis.

Despite the time and energy devoted to both internal wrangling and the running battle with employers, the labour movement in the early 1900s was still able, largely through the TLC, to press on toward a number of legislative objectives.

There was continuing concern over unemployment, and the Congress urged the establishment of employment bureaus, as well as the restriction of immigration. The struggle for adoption of the eight-hour day went on; and in the provinces there was progress in the introduction of compensation for workmen injured in industrial accidents, though initially the protection was weak and peppered with loopholes. Ontario had adopted the pattern of British legislation in 1889, and other provinces followed.

Efforts to establish minimum wages date from about 1909, though it was to be many years before such provisions became law and even then they were on a restricted basis, usually applying only to female employees.

Organized labour can justifiably take credit for leadership in efforts to establish the principle of old age pensions. At the 1905 convention of the Trades and Labour Congress a resolution was adopted declaring:

> In our opinion the time is opportune to introduce legislation making provision for the maintenance of deserving poor, old or disabled citizens who are unable to maintain themselves.[69]

Pension plans were discussed with great regularity at every convention, and progress was reported in 1912 when the House of Commons appointed a committee to look into the possibilities.

There were repeated demands for legislation to clarify the right of workers to organize, to strike, and to engage in picketing. There was considerable doubt at that time about the legality of such activities. A report to the 1905 TLC convention complained:

> Notwithstanding all the litigation during the past few years dealing with the rights and duties of labour and capital, it is impossible for anyone, layman or lawyer, to say with any degree of definiteness what the law is upon these relations. The time is undoubtedly opportune to ask the Dominion government, and the various provincial governments, so far as their respective jurisdictions extend, to pass laws stating clearly and unequivocally the rights and duties of all parties concerned. We assume that we have the right to strike and to bring pressure upon our enemies to recognize our claims.
> We prate a lot about the right of free speech, but this right does not at times seem to include the right to peaceably persuade the public to give their patronage to others than those who oppose our just claims; and we find ourselves denied the right to inform workmen of the existence of a strike, or of the reasons for the cessation of work; and finally when we surmount all these difficulties we are confronted with that bogey known as conspiracy which is ever present, all inclusive, and whose confines are beyond mortal ken. Organized labour desires to observe the law, but that observance is impossible where no one can say what the law is.[70]

The most important labour legislation of the time was the Industrial Disputes Investigation Act, which became law in 1907. While it fell short of answering all the questions raised in the TLC's earlier report, it did establish a pattern for dealing with certain disputes. While the Act affected only the limited number of employees in industries under federal jurisdiction — coal-mining, transportation, and communications — it provided a model for consideration by the provinces in drafting their labour legislation.

The Act required disputes within its jurisdiction to be submitted to a Board of Conciliation and Investigation. Compulsory conciliation was to apply in situations regarded as being of public importance. Either party could apply for intervention of such a board. During the investigation the workers could not strike nor could the employer lock out. The decision of the board, while not binding, was to be made public in the hope that this would generate pressure for a settlement. The parties could, by prior agreement, accept the board's decision as binding, thus opening the door to a form of voluntary arbitration.

Labour was not quite sure whether or not it liked the new legislation. It was endorsed at the TLC's 1907 convention, but a year later there were criticisms and demands for amendments. Regardless of such weaknesses as it may have had, the Industrial Disputes Investigations Act marked the beginning of federal labour legislation which, through various forms and amendments, has now become the Canada Labour Code.

The slow pace of change sometimes leads to the conclusion that the legislative and political activities of organized labour are of doubtful effectiveness. The eventual introduction of pensions and the formulation of labour legislation demonstrated the value of such efforts, even though these efforts have often been muddied by the intricacies of politics, the subject of Chapter 10.

9 Growth and Conflict — The West

The period preceding World War I was even more hectic on the west coast. Economic conditions on the two coasts differed sharply, but unrest and a sense of insecurity were general.

The Western Federation of Miners, which had crossed into Canada to organize miners in the new operations in the interior of British Columbia, tried unsuccessfully to win bargaining rights on behalf of the coalminers employed by the Dunsmuir interests on Vancouver Island.

On the mainland the Western Federation had a new ally in the United Brotherhood of Railroad Employees, an organization which had been formed to organize railroad employees on an industrial basis in competition with the craft unions of the American Federation of Labor. There were close ties between the Federation and the UBRE in the United States. In Canada the railway union undertook to organize CPR employees and soon found itself embroiled in a strike.

There was sympathetic support from other groups, including longshoremen and coalminers. Walkouts occurred as far east as Montreal. There were outbreaks of violence, and in one incident a picketer, Frank Rogers, was killed by gunshot. The labour publication *Western Clarion* charged that the shots had been fired 'by a gang of thugs employed by the Canadian Pacific Railway Company'. Two men were charged, but only one was taken to trial, and he was acquitted. Labour groups staged demonstrations of protest, claiming the trial had been a farce. Rogers became known as 'the first of British Columbia's labour martyrs'.

All this led to demands by management and some politicians for legislation to control international unions. Some of the proposals advanced make more recent suggestions look tame. An extraordinary bill was introduced in the Senate providing for an amendment to the Criminal Code which would have made non-Canadians subject to imprisonment should they

> . . . counsel, incite, urge or induce any strike or lockout, or a rise or fall in wages, or the imposition of additional or differential conditions on terms of employment, or impairing the exercise of industry.[71]

The Bill received second reading but died without reaching the House of Commons.

The attacks on international unionism were strongly supported by a Royal Commission which was appointed in 1903 to look into British Columbia's labour troubles. The Minister of Labour, Sir William Mulock, had proposed the commission in a letter to the Prime Minister, Sir Wilfrid Laurier, in which he said:

> The working people of Canada have to a large extent come under the domination of the American Federation of Labor, whom they recognize as their friends. Perhaps it would assist to disillusion them if an intelligent Commission, one in which the working people have confidence, were to point out the injuries that have come to them because of the interference of American unions. Such a pronouncement would have an educational effect.[72]

The Commission was composed of Chief Justice Gordon Hunter of the Supreme Court of British Columbia and the Rev. Elliott Rowe, a Methodist minister from Victoria, neither of whom had any experience in industrial relations. The secretary was Mackenzie King, then Deputy Minister of Labour and right-hand man to Mulock. At the outset the chairman explained that the fundamental issue to be decided was whether or not British Columbia coalminers were to be allowed to join the Western Federation of Miners. Meantime, it was suggested, the men should immediately return to work and sever their union relationship. The 'educational' process suggested by Mulock had begun.

James Dunsmuir, who had succeeded his father as head of the vast enterprise including Vancouver Island coal mines, had no hesitation in telling the Commission that it was company policy to forbid union organization and to promptly fire any employees found to be active in union affairs. It was obvious that many Dunsmuir employees were afraid to provide information, much less testify before the Commission. Nevertheless, evidence was brought out of company interference with free speech and other civil rights and of the cheating of company employees of their earnings.

The Commission drew a distinction between legitimate' unions and those it described as 'revolutionary socialist'. Both the Western Federation of Miners and the United Brotherhood of Railroad Employees fell into the latter category; and it was the opinion of the Commission that they had been engaged in a conspiracy 'to sweep all employees of the Canadian Pacific Railway into the United Brotherhood and all coalminers into the Western Federation'.

The Commission regarded the UBRE as a secret organization directed from San Francisco, and it said the miners' work stoppage had been ordered by the WFM headquarters in Denver, Colorado. The Commission went on:

> It is obviously against the public interest that any body of Canadian workers should be subject to be called out on strike by a foreign authority over whom neither our legislatures or courts can exercise control, and that whether they have any grievances against their employer or not.[73]

To meet the situation, legislation was advocated which would have gone even beyond the terms of the earlier Senate bill. It would have made it an offence for any non-British subject:

> . . . to procure, or incite any employee in Canada to quit the employment without the consent of the employer, or for any person within Canada to exhibit or publish, or in any way communicate to an employee the content of any order, request, suggestion, or recommendation . . . by any person or persons ordinarily resident without Canada that he quit their employment.[74]

The Commission also wanted unions incorporated and made subject to civil damage actions and recommended the prohibition of boycotts and the elimination of picketing.

The Trades and Labour Congress, despite its deep differences with both the Western Federation and the United Brotherhood, was vigorously opposed to the report, describing it as 'biased and partial'. The TLC claimed that irresponsible action by a few was being used as an excuse to impose laws 'which if carried into effect, would strike a severe blow at all labour organizations'. The matter was raised at a convention of the American Federation of Labor, and the president, Samuel Gompers, vehemently denied any United States control of Canadians. He took the position that when AFL unions became involved in a strike, in either the United States or Canada, the initiative rested with the workers concerned.

The TLC's criticism of the Royal Commission report has since been shared by many labour historians. Jamieson has described it as 'a highly partisan and conservative report in which the findings and recommendations were in contradiction to most of the evidence'.

Despite pressure by the Canadian Manufacturers' Association and others, the government took no immediate action on the recommendations. However, legislation was not needed to break the United Brotherhood of Railroad Employees. Its ranks had been infiltrated by spies who, the Commission found, were in the employ of the CPR. Among them was Harold Poore, the senior UBRE organizer in Canada, who was revealed by the Commission's investigators to have sold union correspondence to the company 'for valuable consideration'.

Organizational breakthroughs by the United Mine Workers in British Columbia and Alberta were accompanied by a good deal of trouble. When British Columbia legislation imposed an eight-hour day for underground work, Vancouver coal mine operators instituted a wage cut. Those who objected were locked out. Despite government mediation efforts the company refused to deal with the UMW, and the dispute dragged on for four months, until it was finally settled by the intervention of Mackenzie King. King's solution was recognition of an 'Employee Representation Committee', which had the ultimate effect of short-circuiting normal union relationships. This was a favourite tactic of King's and won for him the dubious title 'Father of Company Unionism'.

On Vancouver Island, as elsewhere, King's solution was no answer, and in 1911 the lid blew off with a violent strike that lasted almost two years. The Dunsmuir mines had been taken over by another company, and the UMW was making a new effort to organize. Several men were fired, and 3,000 walked off the job. The company hired non-union and Oriental labour to keep operating. After a few months the strike spread to other collieries, finally involving a total of almost 7,000 men.

Despite outbreaks of violence the company was able to continue some mining. There were proclamations of the Riot Act and use of both provincial police and soldiers. There were a number of injuries and extensive property damage. Arrests were frequent, and at one time more than 250 miners were in custody, many remaining in jail for months without trial. This has been properly described as 'one of the bitterest and most expensive strikes in the history of Canada'.

Labour throughout British Columbia rallied behind the miners, and there was talk of a general strike, though it never materialized. The UMW provided $1,500,000 to the men and their families before finally calling it quits. The companies eventually agreed to the principle of allowing employees to belong to a union but still refused to recognize or deal with the union. After the strike there were persistent reports that workers who showed any interest in union organization were being blacklisted — refused employment by any coal company.

A subsequent investigation resulted in condemnation of the violent and intimidating tactics used by the miners but endorsation of the principle of collective bargaining. There was also a recommendation for the legal enforcement of collective agreements, with provisions to prevent discrimination against employees for union membership.

While union strength was growing in British Columbia, so was co-operation among employers. By 1905 there were some twenty-six employer associations in the province, where this type of organization has continued to be far more popular and successful than in other provinces.

The British Columbia logging industry was an important source of new union membership, despite the handicap of small and scattered operations and the employment of Orientals. An early but short-lived effort was made about 1900 by the British Columbia Woodworkers' Union, which had the backing of the Vancouver Trades and Labour Council.

A short time later the International Workers of the World — the 'Wobblies' — appeared. The IWW had been formed in Chicago in 1905, taking under its wing most of those who were ideologically opposed to the American Federation of Labor. Prominent among the original leaders were the American socialist Eugene Debs, and William Haywood, who had been prominent in the Western Federation of Miners. But there was soon a parting of the ways between Debs and his followers, who favoured political action, and those, including Haywood, who wanted more direct and forceful action. Haywood's group emerged in control of the IWW.

Haywood visited Canada on many occasions, and on one trip he addressed twenty British Columbia meetings. He remains one of the legendary characters of the labour movement in North America. When he was accused of instigating the assassination of the Governor of Idaho, he was successfully defended by Clarence Darrow in what came to be regarded as a classic trial. During World War I Haywood was found guilty of sedition and sentenced to twenty years' imprisonment. He appealed and while on bail escaped to Russia, where he ended his days.

It was in British Columbia and Alberta that the Wobblies gained their greatest Canadian support. Paul Phillips, a British Columbia labour historian, has described their 'spectacular strikes, flaming oratory, and moving hymns'. Those were the days of Joe Hill, a young union organizer who was executed by a firing squad at Salt Lake City after being found guilty of murder in a verdict about which there was considerable doubt. He became a legendary character and the subject of a song which unionists in Canada as well as the United States still sing.

The *British Columbia Federationist* in January 1913 published a letter from a worker describing the conditions new employees found on their arrival at one of the railway camps:

> They are told that there is no work for them at their trade or on the conditions which they were originally hired, and they will have to work as common labourers with pick and shovel or any other work they may be set at. The wages run from $1.75 to $2.25. One dollar per day is charged for board, 25¢ per month is charged for mail they never get, and $1 per month for a doctor they never see. The price of boots is $12 to $18, and other things in proportion.[75]

The men were trapped; there was no way they could get out, even if they were prepared to pay their own transportation. The correspondent told of the discovery of the bodies of sixty-four men who had tried to escape by raft down the Fraser River. It is hardly surprising that there were strikes and riots — which, of course, contributed to the IWW's reputation for violence.

The Wobblies favoured industrial unionism and had a special appeal to unskilled workers. The first Canadian chapter was the Vancouver Industrial Mixed Union, No. 322, formed in 1906. At first the organization made relatively little impact in other parts of the province, perhaps because of the already militant nature of British Columbia unions. The IWW made even less impression in eastern Canada, probably because of the extreme conservatism of most of the labour movement there. An exception was the clothing trades, where the Wobblies were welcomed by Europeans who had a revolutionary background. Membership reached a peak of some 10,000 in Canada in 1911, then a decline set in. The organization fell into disrepute during World War I, when it was among the organizations declared illegal.

While they left few traces, the Wobblies are deserving of considerable credit for their efforts to organize workers who were being largely ignored by the unions of skilled tradesmen. This was particularly true in the British Columbia logging camps and in railway construction. Though organizational success in the formal sense was limited, the presence of the IWW brought much-needed improvements in living and working conditions.

The militancy of British Columbia unions and their ardent desire for political action became major factors in differences which developed with the Trades and Labour Congress. At the same time, the TLC was running into difficulty in eastern Canada because of a growing dissatisfaction with the influence being exerted by the American Federation of Labor.

At the 1901 TLC convention, Ralph Smith, while not opposing international unions, spoke in his opening address of the need for a stronger Canadian structure:

> A federation of American unions, represented by a national union, and a federation of Canadian unions, represented by a national union, each working with the other in special cases, would be a great advantage over having local unions in Canada connected with the national unions in America.
>
> Greater success would be accomplished in the settlement of disputes in each country if the leaders were representatives of their own national grievances. . . . There are such distinctive differences in the condition of each that a presentment of Canadian matters by Canadian leaders, and vice versa by the American leaders, would lead to a greater success and would not in any way prevent a federation of the national bodies.[76]

This section of the address was not approved by the convention but was referred to a special committee for later consideration. Among the Quebec delegates, especially, there was growing opposition to the international union ties.

Western delegates continued voicing their criticism of the Congress for its failure to undertake a vigorous organizational campaign. Actually the organizational picture was badly blurred. In recruiting new members the TLC remained under the restrictions imposed to protect the jurisdiction of established unions; but the American Federation of Labor was actively organizing groups of Canadian employees, not only into unions affiliated to the AFL, but into separate unions. The jurisdictional lines had become so confused that some members were unable to determine the relationship of their union to the central bodies.

The top organizer for the American Federation of Labor in Canada held the office of first vice-president in the TLC. Backed by the far superior financial resources of the AFL, he was busily engaged in recruiting members into the American organization rather than into the Congress. The dominance of the international unions, which had been firmly established with the expulsion of the Knights of Labour, continued undiminished.

The dissatisfaction of the British Columbia unions reached a climax in 1903, when the Vancouver Trades and Labour Council decided to withhold its dues from the Congress, a first step toward severing the relationship. The national body was accused of being ' part of the Liberal machine' and 'an appendage of the capitalist party'.

Differences reached such proportions that Sam Gompers, AFL president, journeyed from Washington to Vancouver in an effort to raise the prestige of the Federation and of international unions generally. He was given a rough reception. A majority of those attending the meeting he addressed were socialists, and they were extremely vocal in making their views known.

In his autobiography, *Seventy Years of Life and Labour*, Gompers described events following the meeting:

> The men who had tried to interrupt the meeting had gone down the street, got a box, and had commenced a street corner harangue in which they attacked all trade unionists, the trade union movement and me in particular. They denounced me in the vilest language I ever heard. They gathered about them a mob of about fifty, and when I came into the street all joined in howling and booing after me. I lit my cigar and with the committee walked forward to the hotel. Others joined in the howling mob that followed me. I walked more slowly.[77]

The TLC, through both its own structure and its close relationship with the AFL, remained predominantly a craft organization. Mounting demands for a form of industrial unionism extending beyond the skilled trades became the basis of a conflict which was to go on for years.

At the TLC's 1911 convention a Vancouver delegate, Victor Midgley, presented a resolution endorsing the principle of industrial unionism and criticizing craft unions as being 'inadequate to successfully combat the present-day aggregations of capital'. Supporters of industrial unionism maintained that the craft structure contributed to jurisdictional conflicts between unions, to the detriment of the labour movement.

Midgley's resolution was adopted by a 70-52 vote; but the convention was in Calgary, and the presence of a large number of western delegates undoubtedly contributed to its success. The resolution did not reflect the policies favoured by the administration of the Trades and Labour Congress.

The next year, with the convention back in eastern Canada, at Galt, Ontario, the matter was revived. A similar resolution was adopted, but on that occasion with the clear understanding that it was not to be regarded as permitting any interference with the affairs of the craft unions and its effect was to be 'only of an educative, permissive' nature. In other words, the teeth were drawn.

One of the beneficial effects of the western separatist movement was the encouragement of central organizations on a provincial basis. The British Columbia Federation of Labour was formed in 1911 and the Alberta Federation a short time later. Previously the provincial executive of the Trades and Labour Congress had filled the role that was to be occupied more efficiently by provincial federations of labour.

10 Early Political Activities

Politics has always been a hot issue in labour circles. In the early days there were loud and long debates as to whether unions should concentrate on lobbying the party in power or try to gain political power on their own. Those favouring the latter course were divided between advocates of a straight labour party and those who favoured endorsing individual candidates or one of the existing parties.

Political lines were sharply drawn, with strong party alliances among a large part of the membership. Over the years Canadian labour leadership has leaned heavily toward supporting a moderately leftish party — first the CCF and then the NDP — but the membership has been slow to follow.

The question of whether labour should dabble in politics at all has been raised from time to time and has been the cause of some serious divisions. One factor has been the policy of the labour movement in the United States, once considerably more influential in Canada than it is today. This policy dates back to the philosophy of Samuel Gompers and his belief that 'pure and simple unionism' could bring about reformation of the economic and social systems and provide justice for all. This was the basis of his advice to 'stand faithfully by our friends and reward them; oppose our enemies and defeat them'.

Gompers' theory of non-participation remains the basic principle behind the political attitude of the major part of the trade union movement in the United States. While it may make sense there, its application in Canada fails to take into account the fundamental differences between the two political systems. In the United States, politicians enjoy much greater freedom of action than do the elected representatives in Canada, where the British parliamentary system of strict party discipline applies. Individual Members of Parliament have little power on their own and can only be really effective by influencing their party. It is also significant that the political system in Canada has provided greater opportunity for small parties. These have given a voice to farm and labour groups which have found themselves in disagreement with the two major parties.

The weakness of applying the Gompers theory in Canada has been proven by the relative ineffectiveness of labour representatives who have been elected as individuals. At the same time, the labour movement has always been faced with the impracticality of a purely labour party. The nature of the Canadian electorate and the division of ballot-box strength, particularly as between farmers and urban voters, together with public attitudes toward organized labour, still militate strongly against a labour party.

The oft-expressed view that labour people should elect one of their own came into conflict with the strong party loyalties of many of the early unionists. These were recognized to such a degree that, for a time, the presidency of the Toronto Trades and Labour Council was rotated regularly between persons known to be Grits and those identified as Tories. Even the seating of delegates at Council meetings was on a partisan basis. The Conservatives sat on one side of the room and the Liberals on the other, with a small group of socialists relegated to the rear of the hall.

Labour's publication, the *Ontario Workman*, was staunchly Conservative and blamed political differences for the collapse of the Canadian Labour Union (see Chapter 3). The paper complained that delegates had attended meetings 'as party representatives rather than in the spirit of working men'. Later, when the *Workman* folded, its critics said it was because of the Conservative partisanship of the paper.

At the 1887 convention of the Trades and Labour Congress one delegate declared with a measure of truth that most workingmen voted 'the way they have been educated from the cradle', and he added:

> It would be just as easy to move Hamilton Bay and put it on the Mountain as to get a Conservative workingman to vote for a Reform-Labour candidate, or a Reform workingman to vote for a Conservative-Labour candidate.[78]

The two established parties were keenly alert to any threat from outside, and both were quick and successful in luring political newcomers into their fold.

There was, for example, the case of H. B. Witton, an employee in the Great Western Railway shop at Hamilton. In 1872, following the Toronto printers' strike, he ran under the 'Liberal-Conservative' banner. He won a seat and thereby gained credit for being 'the first artisan' elected to the House of Commons.

Witton was an interesting person; self-educated, he had a broad range of interests — geology, astronomy, microscopy, and the French language. He was a man of moderate social views and gave public recognition to those he identified as his 'natural superiors'. He regarded both employees and employers as capitalists, maintaining that the man whose capital was in a strong right arm and the man whose capital was in his money should work together for a common end. The promotion of greater harmony between capital and labour was prominent in his election platform.

Once elected he found little difficulty in fitting into his new surroundings. Lady Dufferin, wife of the Governor-General, noted in her diary:

> In the evening we had a large parliamentary dinner. One of my neighbours was very interesting. He is a 'working man' member. We had him soon after his election when he dined in a rough coat, but now he wears evening clothes. He talked so pleasantly and was full of information.[79]

Some of Witton's fellow unionists were less enthusiastic. At a Trades and Labour Congress convention a few years later a delegate complained:

> They had a man in Hamilton named Witton who was sent to Parliament. What did he do? The first situation that was offered him he took, and went to Vienna on some sort of government exhibition business.[80]

While the victories of labour candidates were not numerous, politicians had cause to be aware of labour's potential political power. In 1883 the first candidate to run on a 'Labour' ticket was elected to the House of Commons when A. T. Levine carried Montreal East. It was in 1898 that Ralph Smith was elected to the British Columbia Legislature; four years later he went to Ottawa as a member. Winnipeg electors chose Arthur W. Putee, a typographer, as their Member of Parliament in 1900. During the next few years successful labour and socialist candidates in British Columbia included J. H. Hawthornthwaite, Parker Williams, William Davidson, and John McInnis. In 1906 Alphonse Verville, then president of the Trades and Labour Congress, ran as a labour candidate and won the Montreal riding of Maisonneuve in a federal election.

These were, however, essentially independents, lacking in political power but under constant pressure from their labour electors, whose expectations ran high. Their only real hope for accomplishment was in some form of alliance with one of the parties, and this left them open to charges of collusion from suspicious supporters. As Desmond Morton put it in his book *NDP – The Dream of Power*, some of them 'found it impossible to reconcile parliamentary responsibilities and the demands of their doctrinaire supporters'.

The same sort of criticism was directed at those who accepted civil service positions. There was a natural desire on the part of labour to have factory acts and similar legislation administered by individuals who were understanding and sympathetic toward the workers; but those who took government positions found themselves highly vulnerable, as Daniel O'Donoghue discovered.

In an 1885 editorial the *Palladium of Labour* commented:

> The man who accepts a government position binds himself, if not to openly throw his influence for the party of the administration, at least to refrain from opposing them or denouncing wrongs perpetrated under their auspices. Ought a Liberal Reformer to place himself in such a false position? Ought a free citizen who professes to have at heart labour's enfranchisement, and to devote himself to that work, to wear a muzzle of partyism on his mouth and put his conscience in the keeping of politicians who seek only to delude and befool the workingman, with his assistance if possible? No — a thousand times — no.[81]

Labour's experience with its elected representatives gave cause for such doubts. The Montreal labour politician Levine, once elected, was quick to become a Conservative supporter. In British Columbia, Ralph Smith's political alliances came under question. The electors who had sent him to the Legislature included a large number of miners from Wales, England, and Scotland who had strong political convictions and who looked on him as a spokesman for labour. When he successfully contested a federal seat in 1902, it was as a Liberal.

Although Smith was president of the Trades and Labour Congress, feelings among the Nanaimo miners ran so high that they refused to support him as a delegate to the TLC's annual convention. He obtained a credential from a Vancouver union; but once at the convention he faced sharp attacks, both for his political ties with the Liberal party and for his alleged friendliness with the management of the Canadian Pacific Railway. He decided not to seek re-election as president of the TLC and in his farewell address spoke of the tyranny of the masses over their leaders as being 'worse than the tyranny of capital over labour'. He continued his political career, eventually becoming Minister of Finance in a Liberal administration.

While there were differences of opinion as to the best approach, there was agreement within the movement on the need for legislative action. The Toronto Trades and Labour Council formulated a comprehensive legislative program as early as 1882, preceding the TLC's *Platform of Principles*. The Toronto unionists wanted legislation for shorter hours, equal pay for equal work regardless of sex, extension of the franchise, compulsory education, a factory act, employer liability in industrial accidents, an apprenticeship act, letting of public contracts by public tender, and 'the prohibition of Chinamen on all public contracts and the limitation of Chinese immigration'.

The Council waged a continuing campaign for the extension of public ownership, with Toronto's street railway system as the top target. The streetcars were being operated by private interests and, according to *The Labour Advocate*, were reaping an annual profit of a quarter of a million dollars. The Council also wanted public ownership of the telephone service, gasworks, electric power, and the city's fire brigade.

Despite the strong influence of both Grits and Tories within the Council, the legislative committee report introducing the program made a strongly class-oriented attack on the existing system:

> While capitalists have amassed riches, the condition of the toiler has remained little changed. While one class lives in luxury, and the other exists in comparative poverty, there can be no harmony between capital and labour; for capital in its modern character too often consists of unpaid labour in the form of profits, legally though unjustly taken from the producer who is compelled to sell his labour and skill at such a price as the grasping employer may choose to offer. The only hope for changing this state of affairs is the working classes themselves. The wage earners represent the majority of the people, and in their hands rests their own future.[82]

The arguments for and against a labour party raged on. At the 1894 TLC convention the committee reporting on the opening address of the president, P. J. Jobin, disagreed with his recommendation that active lobbying should be continued. The committee reported:

> We believe that the time has come to stop knocking at the government doors and that the time has now arrived to take such

> independent political action as will leave the doors open to us all the time through the formation of an independent labour party.[83]

The delegates turned down the committee's report, but a resolution was promptly introduced declaring that:

> Petitioning the government is a mere waste of time, and . . . only by independent political action similar to the Socialist Labour Party shall we obtain the justice we have so long been seeking.[84]

The resolution was effectively killed by having it referred to a committee, where it disappeared.

There was an upsurge of interest in socialist ideas, and new organizations sprang up in various places. Among the first were offshoots of the Socialist Labour Party, which was formed in the United States in 1894. There were branches at Hamilton and Toronto a few months later, but the organization never became a national entity in Canada.

The Socialist Labour Party of Canada was more successful. It started in British Columbia in 1894 and soon established ties with socialist sympathizers in Manitoba, later spreading to Ontario. Its more ardent supporters looked with disfavour on political action by unions, which they considered to be purely economic organizations operating solely in the interests of their own members.

The Canadian Socialist League, started in Toronto in 1895, had a different attitude and actively sought union support. Socialism, in one form or another, was proving more attractive than before, but there was a notable lack of cohesion among the various groups trying to promote it.

In 1895 the TLC delegates voted by a narrow margin to admit the Socialist Party of Canada to the Congress, but the decision was revoked the following year. A few years later the Toronto Trades and Labour Council endorsed the Canadian Socialist League, gave a $5 donation and decided to put up two candidates in a provincial election. Both were soundly defeated. One of them was the Council president, James Simpson, who was also defeated when he next ran for that office. He attributed his Council defeat to his political activities.

By 1898 the advocates of direct political action were successful in having the Ontario executive of the TLC adopt a resolution which declared:

> The time has arrived, if labour is to be protected and its rights respected, we must be independent at the ballot box, irrespective of whatever political party is in power. As the capitalistic lobbyist controls and corrupts our government it is imperative that more attention be given by the toilers to the selection of representatives who will at least voice their rights on the floors of our legislative halls.[85]

The next year, reports from both Ontario and Manitoba executives urged direct political action, and the national convention adopted a resolution recommending that

> . . . various bodies . . . take some steps to form themselves into political organizations on independent lines from the old capitalistic political parties, and wherever, in the opinion of our central bodies they are in sufficient numbers to warrant placing candidates in the field, that we endeavour to have direct representation in the various houses of parliament on lines similar to the organized workers of Great Britain, British Columbia, New Zealand and Australia . . . and that this be submitted to a referendum vote of all organizations in affiliation with this Congress, and should such a vote be in the affirmative, then immediately proceed on the above lines.[86]

The referendum resulted in a vote 1,424 to 167 in favour of such action.

In Nova Scotia, unionists displayed considerable interest in politics. The Provincial Workmen's Association had supported Conservative candidates in the 1882 election on the ground that the Liberal candidates were company officials. In 1885 three 'workingman' candidates were put up, and one was successful. In the succeeding years several labour candidates were nominated and other candidates were endorsed.

Later, interest in politics was further sharpened by visits from Keir Hardie, a well-known Scottish labour Member of the British House of Commons. His first trip to Nova Scotia was in

1904. That year Stephen McNeil, Grand Master of the PWA, contested a federal seat, running as an independent labour candidate, but he made such a poor showing he lost his deposit.

In Winnipeg there were several false starts before the Labour Party of Winnipeg was established in 1896. The purpose was

> . . . to study economic subjects affecting the welfare of labour and the promulgation of information regarding same; and also to secure for labour a just share of the wealth it produces, by such means as obtaining representation from our own ranks in the parliamentary and municipal bodies of the country.[87]

While the party included various occupations in its membership, the constitution required that three-quarters be wage-earners. The organization shied away from using the word 'socialist',

> . . . because in this new movement there are great numbers here who are yet so timid as to become greatly alarmed if they found themselves branded with the awful term 'socialist'.[88]

But not all were so timid, for in 1902 a Socialist Party of Manitoba was formed to attain

> . . . the socialization of the means of production, distribution and exchange, to be controlled by a democratic state in the interests of the entire community and the complete emancipation of labour from the domination of capitalism.[89]

The gap between the traditional trade unionists and the pure socialists widened and was to plague both groups for years to come. Many of the socialists favoured the dual union membership which had been accepted by the Knights of Labour but rejected by other unionists, and this placed them in opposition to the TLC administration. Some purists on the socialist side looked on any form of union organization as an obstacle in the way of the true cause of socialism.

The chief trouble was still in the West, where the movement was most highly politicized, and in 1906 the Trades and Labour

Congress undertook to mend its fences and gain strength there. New labour councils were established in Regina, Brandon, Fernie, Cranbrooke, and Revelstoke. The choice of Victoria as the site for the national convention was part of the program.

The British Labour Party had scored a victory by winning 29 seats only a short time before, and there was a lively political awareness among union people. A resolution was placed before the convention calling for the formation of a Canadian Labour Party, while another resolution sought endorsation of the already existing Socialist Party of Canada.

James Simpson, the Toronto typographical worker who was a Congress vice-president, was one of the few able to communicate with both the pure socialists and the pure trade unionists. He put forward a compromise resolution which, while it failed to pass, aired an interesting point of view. The resolution proposed

> . . . that this Congress affirm it is the individual right of the wage workers of Canada to organize themselves into either a Socialist or Independent Labour Party, separate and distinct from this Congress, and that in our opinion the highest interests of this Congress can be served if we continue as a legislative body entirely, looking to either the Socialist or Independent Labour Party to promote such legislation as this Congress shall determine in convention and through our executive committee from time to time; and that we further express our conviction that it will be in the best interests of the wage earners of Canada if they will voluntarily sever their connection with all parties not organized in the interests of the proletarian class. [90]

The resolution which the convention finally adopted was introduced by the Congress secretary, P. M. Draper, and represented the position of the administration. It focused attention on the Congress's legislative program as 'the epitome of the best thought and effort of organized labour', and called for the election of labour candidates 'for the direct purpose of conserving the interests of the working people of this country'. The resolution was supported by sixty-two delegates, while seven voted against and fourteen abstained. Supporters heralded this as a victory for the trade unionists and a defeat for the socialists, but the struggle was by no means over.

It was the TLC's intention to have provincial meetings to consider political action at that level, giving support, if feasible, to the new Canadian Labour Party, which would put forward 'straight labour' candidates. In Ontario and Manitoba, where the socialists were less effective than on the west coast, the more traditional unionists looked on the idea of the Canadian Labour Party as a counterpart of the British Labour Party, and provincial branches were established. In British Columbia the socialists, though numerically a minority, displayed superior strategy, which left the branch formed there little more than a token gesture toward straight labour candidates.

When the Trades and Labour Congress met in convention later in 1907, there was a move to grant autonomy to the provincial groups in determining the political course they would follow. This would have given the British Columbia socialists a cloak of legitimacy for their defiance of previous TLC policy. The resolution was defeated, 51 to 39. While the position of the straight unionists had been upheld, it was clear the division was of serious proportions.

The same year a political gathering in Alberta supported the socialist position, putting two western provinces in conflict with the Congress. In Saskatchewan, organization was still weak, and no political position had been established.

These differences were, to say the least, a serious handicap to effective political action by any section of the labour movement. In the 1908 election the Canadian Labour Party ran four candidates, all of whom were opposed by socialists.

When the TLC convened in Halifax in 1908, a federal election was only a few weeks away. Keir Hardie was present, and he made an ardent plea for labour unity in the political sphere. But the convention resulted in an impasse. There was agreement on a proposal for a later meeting to attempt to resolve the differences, but the meeting was never held. The socialists were in a minority in the TLC, but the trade unionists were unable to control the policies of the Socialist Labour Party. The Canadian Socialist League maintained a more friendly relationship with organized labour and declared its recognition of the importance of economic strength through union organization, but the League made little impact.

The attitude of the Socialist Labour Party became increasingly anti-union, with the complaint that the economic objectives of such groups 'diverted workingmen from the true cause of revolution'. The Ontario section of the party went so far as to prohibit its members from voting for straight labour candidates.

The *Western Clarion*, voice of the socialists in British Columbia, attacked unions as 'ridiculous commodity combinations', which displayed an ignorance of the true principles governing the prevailing system. The *Clarion* showed more interest in theory than in the practical day-to-day issues confronting the unions, and commented:

> The term 'scab' applied to a fellow victim of the wage system will not fall from the lips of a working man who has anything like a clear conception of capitalist production and its inhuman and merciless labour market. It is a hateful term and as a rule has no place in the vocabulary of the revolution. It has been born of a lamentable ignorance that makes the so-called labour movement a stench in the nostrils of decency.[91]

At the time of the great Vancouver Island coal strike in 1913 the Socialist Labour Party of Vancouver refused to support the miners. The party also remained aloof from municipal politics as being hardly worthy of attention. The serious differences between the 'pure socialists' and others restricted the party's election successes.

As has been pointed out, those socialists who did manage to get elected soon found themselves under attack, particularly from the purists. Hawthornthwaite left politics for a private business career. John Place and Parker Williams, the other two socialists in the British Columbia Legislature at the time, joined the Liberal party.

Even Simpson, the socialists' most valuable supporter in labour ranks, fell into disrepute among his political colleagues. In 1910 he was appointed a member of the Royal Commission on Technical Education. The pure socialists regarded technical education as a capitalist tool, and Simpson was expelled from the party.

Despite the considerable disruption it caused, the Socialist Party of Canada was never much more than a sect with limited political strength, and it operated in isolation from the established labour movement. Those union members who finally found themselves ready to abandon one or other of the old parties had little in the way of practical alternatives.

In 1917 a group of dissidents calling themselves the Social Democrats adopted a more moderate course than the Socialist Party. They contested municipal and provincial elections as well as seeking a working relationship with the labour movement, but the organization amounted to little.

In Alberta the Socialist Party had its greatest strength in the mining camps. But factional fighting was also prevalent in that province, and the Alberta Federation of Labour, which had been founded largely in opposition to the conservative policies of the TLC, decided to take no firm political position. In both Ontario and Manitoba the existing socialist factions splintered into even smaller groups.

An unusually large western delegation at the Calgary convention in 1911 resulted in the defeat of several Congress officers who were Liberal supporters, including the president, William Glocking. Socialists were elected in their place, one of them, J. C. Watters, holding the post of president until 1917. The delegates defeated a motion to endorse the Reciprocity Agreement with the United States, thereby rebuffing the Liberal Party. The principle of industrial unionism was supported.

Organized labour was far from finding an effective political role for itself; but soon the country was to be engaged in a conflict which would make new demands on labour and all other sectors of Canadian society.

11   Labour in World War I

Labour shared in the traumatic experience of Canada's participation in World War I. Economic, political, and social effects created new problems and left a lasting mark on the labour movement.

A period of serious unemployment preceded the war, and much of the Trades and Labour Congress's attention had been directed to seeking methods of finding jobs. The outbreak of hostilities brought a dramatic end to that problem. Manpower needs of the armed forces drained men from civilian occupations at the very time when the material needs of war made new demands on a relatively young Canadian industry. There were jobs for both men and women, and rising employment opened new opportunities for union organization. In the period 1914 to 1919 union membership more than doubled, going from 166,163 to 378,047.

But jobs alone did not solve the workers' problems. Prices were rising faster than wages. Cost-of-living clauses were introduced to maintain some sort of balance between wages and prices; but there was always a time lag, and as the war went on the cost of living went up and up.

Knowledge that the economic activity was artificially created and was sure to be followed by new difficulties contributed to unrest. Wartime regulations which affected living patterns were an entirely new experience and had their effect on people who were working long hours, often under strange conditions. Some of the regulations were directed at maintaining industrial peace, but labour saw them as an infringement on the rights of unions.

All this fed a growing conviction that working people were being asked to bear an undue share of wartime sacrifice, while others reaped a harvest of profits. In the labour movement this sentiment had been building up well before the first shot was fired. At its 1911 convention the Trades and Labour Congress blamed gathering war clouds on capitalist policies and suggested capitalists should be left to fight their own wars. A resolution was adopted calling for a general strike in the event of war. A similar sentiment ran through the 1912 convention, which passed a resolution stating that 'the only result war between Germany and Great Britain would achieve would be the degradation of the toilers'.

But by 1913, as the danger of hostilities grew closer, there was a softening of this position and some indication of a spirit of patriotism, with the declaration that Britain could not be held responsible, should war come. The Congress, expressing man's eternal optimism, added the opinion that:

> Despotism in Europe will be hurled to its final destruction, to make way for constitutional freedom in all the countries of Europe, in preparation for the last and great struggle of the working class to their own actual freedom.[92]

No sooner had war broken out than the matter of compulsory military service became a hot issue. Labour was opposed. At the 1915 convention, which was held in Vancouver, some delegates took the position that, while they were opposed to war in principle, every encouragement should be given to voluntary participation, 'to secure early and final victory for the cause of freedom and democracy'. Those politically oriented to the left, a minority, still maintained that the war was no concern of the working class and its outcome was largely immaterial.

The likelihood of conscription became more evident when the government established a National Service Board to undertake an inventory of the country's manpower resources with a view to their more efficient use. Opposition to conscription remained strong within the labour movement, and there were rumbles of a general strike, should the government initiate such a policy.

Governments in Canada have always had a knack for mishandling their relations with organized labour, and the wartime administration of Sir Robert Borden was no exception. There was no discussion, much less consultation, with labour people on matters which were to have a great impact on union members. It was a long time before Borden agreed, and then with reluctance, to meet with a small deputation from the Trades and Labour Congress. He abruptly rejected any suggestion that workers were being asked to carry an undue burden, and he refused to give any assurances with regard to conscription.

The National Service Board had undertaken a national registration, and this was seen as a prelude to compulsory service. The TLC had recommended that union members co-operate by filling out the registration forms, despite considerable objection, particularly from British Columbia.

Discussions led to new demands for independent political action. One suggestion was that an organization known as the Labour Educational Association should be converted into the Independent Labour Party. This idea was rejected after a brisk debate, in which Tom Moore, a Niagara Falls carpenter, led the opposition. Moore, a Yorkshireman who had come to Canada as a young man, was a leading exponent of the moderate position and supported the Gompers theory of non-participation in politics. He was to become president of the Congress.

But the position adopted by the TLC did not prevent the Labour Educational Association and a labour publication, *The Industrial Banner*, from being used for political purposes. The proponents of independent political action found an unexpected ally in Laura Hughes, niece of a prominent political figure, Sir Sam Hughes. She became one of the first Canadian women to take an active role associated with labour. After a tour of munitions factories, where many women were employed, she used every opportunity to publicly denounce working conditions.

Small groups such as the Greater Toronto Labour Party were formed in several communities and joined in a convention of the Independent Labour Party of Ontario. Its purpose was:

> . . . to promote the political, economic and social interests of the people who live by their labour, mental or manual, as distinguished from those who live by profit upon the labour of others.[93]

Opposition to the manpower registration continued, and labour councils in Winnipeg, Vancouver, New Westminster, and Victoria advised union members to defy the law and refuse to fill out the cards. The British Columbia Federation of Labour adopted a resolution censuring the TLC for its acceptance of the registration.

A climax was reached on 18 May 1917, when Borden announced that, in the view of the government, conscription was inevitable if Canada was to meet its commitment of 500,000 men. There was an uproar among union leaders, with demands for the conscription of capital resources, and there was renewed talk of a general strike. The TLC's president, J. C. Watters, who had supported the registration, declared his opposition to conscription.

Borden agreed to another meeting with the labour leaders and told them he had already given labour a voice in the government through the appointment to the Senate of Gideon Robertson, a vice-president of the Order of Railroad Telegraphers.

This was far from enough to satisfy labour, and attacks on the government went on. *The Industrial Banner* accused Borden of conducting the country's affairs 'with the Bible under one arm and complete plans and specifications for the robbery of the country under the other'. There were demands for the nationalization of railways, armament factories, mines, and banks. Watters had joined those who favoured a general strike, but he qualified his position by saying there should be no interference with direct war production.

When the Congress held its 1917 convention, conscription was in effect and a federal election was near. The TLC's executive had accepted conscription, but without any enthusiasm, stating:

> It is not decreed either right, patriotic, or in the best interests of the Dominion or of the labour classes, to say or do aught that might

prevent the powers that be from obtaining all the results they can anticipate from the enactment of the [conscription] law.[94]

The executive's report was adopted; but the western delegates, with support from Quebec, remained adamant in their opposition. The East-West split had become very clear. The *British Columbia Federationist*, in a biting editorial, commented:

> There is nothing at present in common between the labour movement of the east and that of the west. . . . The labour movement of the east is reactionary and servile to the core. Its vision has never reached beyond the matter of work and wages, the gospel and philosophy of slavery. If there has been any advance and progressive thought it has, as a rule, come forth from the west. The 106 who at the [Quebec] convention voted against the reactionary policies of the Congress were almost entirely from Winnipeg and west thereof.[95]

Support for independent political action had strengthened, and there were efforts to bring together groups formerly separated by divisions which had now come to be considered of lesser importance. The centre of political initiative shifted from British Columbia to Ontario, where demands for political action had become very strong.

There was a new move to form a Canadian Labour Party in the hope that it could prove to be a unifying force. With an election only three months away it was not considered practical to hold a founding convention, but a number of labour people contested seats in opposition to candidates of the Borden Unionist Party. In some areas they had considerable support, but the strong spirit of patriotism was against them, and all were defeated.

Belatedly the government decided to try to develop a better understanding with organized labour. Senator Robertson was taken into the Cabinet as Minister of Labour, and union representatives were invited to sit on various boards and commissions. With typical ineptness the government even turned to the American Federation of Labor for support. With Borden's endorsation, Gompers was invited to Ottawa to address the prestigious Canadian Club. The occasion was then used as an opportunity to have him address Parliament, an extraordinary honour never before or since accorded a labour leader.

Gompers later found time to make a brief appearance at an Ottawa labour meeting. He used the opportunity to express disagreement with suggestions for political action which were being put before the meeting by James Simpson. Then the AFL president hurried off to catch a train back to Washington. His contribution to the development of harmony between the government and organized labour had been purely negative. The government had again exhibited its ignorance of the sentiments of organized labour, a condition not peculiar to the Borden administration.

There was a more practical approach when acceptance of the principle that workers should have the right to organize and bargain collectively became part of the government's wartime policy; but there was no provision to enforce union recognition. At the same time the terms of the Industrial Disputes Investigation Act were extended to cover all war production.

Discontent was spreading. Prices had climbed by 18 per cent in 1917; the psychological pressures of war were being felt. The government's efforts to establish a liaison with labour had failed to dampen the determination to form a new party. The founding convention of the Ontario branch of the Canadian Labour Party attracted 400 delegates. There was a difference of opinion as to whether the party should be confined to labour or whether other groups, such as farmers, should be eligible for membership. It was decided not to be restrictive. The old conflict arose between those who regarded themselves as true socialists and those who saw themselves as primarily trade unionists.

The party was slow in getting off the ground. The political attention of some was focused on the 1917 Russian Revolution and later the founding of the Communist Third International. The more radical political groups saw new hope in a revolution which was expected to destroy the capitalist system. Their willingness to co-operate with others in a much paler program waned. They regarded Bolshevism and socialism as one and the same and concentrated on trying to consolidate far-left groups rather than becoming involved with the larger group, which shied away from the idea of a revolution.

As the war moved to a close, there was growing concern with the problems which were expected to come with the end of a wartime economy. Stresses within the labour movement complicated the approach to such questions. There was a prolonged debate about the preparation of a manifesto which would outline a national program for postwar reconstruction. The discussion became bogged down in a wrangle as to who should be responsible for the document.

Underlying such difficulties was the conflict between the East and the West. In British Columbia, objection to conscription had remained at a high level, and the situation worsened in 1918 with the shooting of a draft dodger. The victim was Albert ('Ginger') Goodwin, a vice-president of the British Columbia Federation of Labour, who had gone into hiding to avoid being drafted under the Military Service Act. The exact circumstances of the shooting were never clearly established, but his death aroused the labour movement, and there were a number of work stoppages in protest.

The Vancouver Metal Trades Council called for a twenty-four hour 'holiday'. That evening a party of several hundred returned soldiers smashed their way into the Vancouver Labour Temple, destroyed documents, and caused other extensive damage. Victor Midgley, secretary of the Council, was in his office at the time. He was taken out onto the street and forced to publicly kiss the Union Jack. Relations between British Columbia labour and other sectors of the community, as well as the TLC, deteriorated.

It was at the TLC's 1918 convention in Quebec City that the conservative elements in the Congress elected Tom Moore to the presidency. He defeated J. C. Watters, who had strong support from the West. A Winnipeg delegate, Robert Russell, was soundly defeated when he ran against P. M. Draper for the position of secretary-treasurer. The westerners lost on every issue and felt rejected.

The government's clumsiness in its dealings with organized labour was once again demonstrated in 1918 when, in a flurry of alarm, drastic legislation affecting unions was brought in. The government had instructed the Royal North-West Mounted Police, as well as other police forces and private detective agencies, to conduct an intensive investigation into the activities of the Wobblies, the Social Democratic Party, and a number of other groups and individuals. Reports now in the Public Archives at Ottawa disclose that little was found to support the suspicion of subversive plots.

A prominent Montreal corporation lawyer, C. H. Cahan, was then commissioned to look into the whole situation. He reported:

> I am convinced that the unrest now prevalent in Canada is due to the weakening of the moral purpose of the people to prosecute the war to a successful end; to the fact that the people are becoming daily more conscious of the bloody sacrifices and irritating burdens entailed by carrying on the war; and to the growing belief that the Union Government is failing to deal effectively with the financial, industrial and economic problems growing out of the war which are, perhaps, incapable of an early satisfactory solution.[96]

This may have failed to allay the government's fears, or it may have served to encourage a search for a scapegoat; in any event there were new restrictions prohibiting the use of certain languages in meetings, outlawing organizations, and banning publications suspected of having left-wing tendencies.

A number of unions were directly affected, but of still wider effect was an Order-in-Council imposing a blanket prohibition on strikes in war industries and on the railways. The measure was a complete surprise to labour. There had been no consultation with Congress officers and they protested vigorously. Moore warned:

> The government should heed the ominous signs of a coming real industrial storm and remove some of these objectionable injustices before it is too late.[97]

Threats of general strike action were heard across the country. Five Calgary railway workers made a point of defying the no-strike order; charges were laid against them but later dropped. Then, barely a month after it had been passed, the order was rescinded, with the explanation that the military situation was 'greatly altered'.

But the revolt in the West was coming to a boil, and events were taking shape for one of the most dramatic and tragic events in the history of the Canadian labour movement — the Winnipeg General Strike.

12 The Revolt in the West

Before the western delegates left Quebec City at the conclusion of the 1918 TLC convention, they held a caucus and decided to call a conference of western union representatives to consider what course they should follow. The invitation which went out for the gathering, to be held in Calgary, carefully explained that the move was in no way to be interpreted as a breakaway from the Trades and Labour Congress. The notice said:

> It must be fully understood that the idea of holding this conference is not a secessionist movement, but a movement to give expression to the aims and objects of organized labour in the West. . . . Some means must be provided for the western movement, which is so different to that of the East, to give expression to its sentiments. This is most important in view of the serious situation that is likely to develop in the near future as a result of the cessation of hostilities in Europe, and the period of reconstruction that must follow. [98]

The British Columbia Federation of Labour was the main driving force behind the idea of the conference. It took the very unusual step of postponing its own convention and then holding it in Calgary immediately prior to the western meeting.

For three days the British Columbia delegates conferred in what was little more than a dress rehearsal for the general conference. The moderate tone of the original conference call was totally ignored when, with evangelical enthusiasm, the delegates demanded the creation of an entirely new industrial-type labour movement and abandonment of the old lobbying techniques of the TLC. Speakers suggested that if labour in other provinces was not prepared to move, then British Columbia should be prepared to go it alone to win such objectives as the thirty-hour week, acceptance of the general strike weapon, and severance of the ties with international unions.

When 239 delegates trooped into the Calgary Labour Temple for the western conference, a course of action had already been carefully charted. The eighty-five British Columbians were the largest delegation, and with the exception of two from Ontario, all the other delegates were from the West. There was general acceptance, at least among the more vocal delegates, of the need for an entirely new and separate structure, outside of and opposed to the Trades and Labour Congress and modelled on industrial rather than craft lines. This was the conception of the One Big Union.

Political differences had shifted to the left. One group, which included a number of Alberta delegates, renewed arguments for a labour political movement, but they were snowed under by those who considered such an approach outdated and far too moderate. It was British Columbia's political resolution that received the approval of the conference. It declared:

> The legitimate aspirations of the labour movement are repeatedly obstructed by existing political forms. . . . ,
> This convention expresses its open conviction that the system of industrial soviet control by selection of representatives from industries is more efficient and of greater political value than the present system of government by selection from districts.
> This convention declares its full acceptance of the Proletarian Dictatorship as being absolute and efficient for the transformation of capitalist private property to communal wealth.[99]

Fraternal greetings were sent to the new Communist regime in Russia.

The wartime restrictions rankled among the delegates, and it was decided to conduct a referendum to measure support for a general strike to force their termination. The resolution complained of federal censorship as interference with free speech and called for 'the release of all political prisoners and the removal of all disabilities and restrictions now upon working-class organizations'.

June 1 was set as the date for the protest strike, should it be approved. The delegates little knew that before that time Canadians would be witnessing, for the first time in their history, a general strike within the nation's borders.

There was also to be a referendum to determine the view of Canadian workers with regard to an industrial union structure. While the vote was to be taken nationally, the returned ballots were to be divided between the East and the West, with Port Arthur, Ontario, the division point. It is doubtful how many ballots were distributed in the East; in any case, no returns from there were ever announced.

The western vote was reported to be overwhelmingly in favour of the new structure, and another conference was called for the fourth of June to implement the decision. That meeting was postponed for a week because of the Winnipeg General Strike; but the One Big Union did come into being, largely the child of the militants of the Socialist Party of Canada. The Winnipeg Strike, while not a direct result of the western conference, was a reflection of the strong opinions which dominated it and which were prevalent in the labour movement in western Canada.

Moore's prediction of 'a real industrial storm' was proving well founded. In time lost through strikes, Alberta and British Columbia far outstripped all the other provinces. In the coalfields there was one strike after another. In Vancouver, work stoppages began to approach the proportions of a general strike. While essential services were maintained, almost all industrial activities were affected, some for a period of several weeks. Workers in a number of other centres, including the firefighters in Edmonton, staged walkouts.

But the rumblings had become loudest in Winnipeg, where there were a number of incidents, including a strike of civic workers. This raised the fundamental question of the right of public employees to strike. The City Council attempted to get an undertaking that all future differences would be submitted to final settlement by an arbitrator. Meanwhile, the Winnipeg Trades and Labour Council appointed a special committee to organize strikes in support of the civic workers, should they be considered necessary.

When metal trades workers employed in contract shops struck in an effort to get wage equality with metalworkers in the railway shops, they were confronted with a back-to-work injunction. Again the Labour Council indicated it was prepared to call for a city-wide walkout. Some metal trades apprentices were getting as little as ten cents an hour and working a ten-hour day. Winnipeg citizens, in common with all Canadians, were bitter about prices, the cost of staple goods having almost doubled during the war.

The experience of the metalworkers was not unique. Winnipeg was being called 'Injunction City', as the same legal device was used against meat cutters, machinists, and retail clerks.

On 22 December 1919 a meeting was held in the Walker Theatre to give the 'progressive' section of the Winnipeg labour movement an opportunity to vent their views. The meeting was sponsored jointly by the Socialist Party of Canada and the Winnipeg Trades and Labour Council, though there were later suggestions that the Council had been led down a rather naive path in becoming involved.

Bob Russell, the unsuccessful contender for the TLC secretary-treasurership, was one of the leading speakers. Russell was a former Glasgow shipyard worker who had become business agent for the Machinists' Union and a prominent member of the Socialist Party. An effective speaker of the old spellbinder school, he was expressing the sentiments of many of his associates when his broad Scottish voice roared: 'Capitalism has come to a point where she is defunct and must disappear.'

The Walker Theatre meeting adopted resolutions protesting the continued use of wartime orders-in-council and demanding the release of those interned under these provisions. It also called for the removal of all Allied troops from Russia. In the audience, taking copious notes, was Sergeant F. E. Langdale of Military Intelligence.

On the platform with Russell were R. J. ('Dick') Johns, also a machinist; William Ivens, a former Methodist minister, who was editing the *Western Labor News*; John Queen, an alderman; Fred Dixon, a member of the Legislature; and George Armstrong, a member of the Carpenters' Union and one of the founders of the Socialist Party of Canada. They were the Winnipeg 'radicals', though their radicalism was more of the British than of the Russian variety.

Three weeks later there was another meeting, with more attacks on the Canadian government and expressions of support for Russia's Communist regime.

Members of both the metal trades and building trades unions were attempting to get wage increases. The metal trades people, having lost their earlier strike, were pressing hard for recognition of their Metal Trades Council. The three major employers — Vulcan Iron Works, Manitoba Bridge, and Dominion Bridge — refused to deal with the central organization.

On 1 May 1919 the employees walked out of the contract shops, and the possibility of a general sympathy strike again came before the Trades and Labour Council. Those in the Council were not unanimous; Russell was among those opposed, though he was later to bear the brunt of legal action. The Council president, F. G. Tipping, was also opposed. He had been a member of a commission which had investigated the metal trades dispute, and he had signed a report which the membership rejected. He was later suspended as president of the Council and eventually resigned.

When the Council met to consider strike action, it had a telegram from TLC President Tom Moore offering to address a meeting. The offer was turned down. Members of the building trades were smarting under the refusal of their international union headquarters to authorize strike action. They struck despite this.

The Council decided to conduct a vote of Winnipeg union members to determine whether or not a general strike should be called. A number of those who were opposed, among them

Russell, indicated they would be prepared to go along with the majority decision. There was no doubt about the decision — 11,000 in favour of a general strike and only 500 opposed. The strike deadline was set for 11 A.M. on 15 May.

Mayor Charles Gray and Premier T. C. Norris were desperately making last-minute attempts to get a settlement; but they failed. When eleven o'clock struck on that fateful Thursday morning, thousands of Winnipeg workers left their work places and walked out on the streets. Retail stores were abandoned, milk and bread deliveries stopped, streetcars came to a halt, and later, telephone operators left their switchboards. Winnipeg's population was just under 200,000, and it was estimated some 30,000 men and women participated in the strike. As many as 12,000 were not union members but acted in sympathy.

Winnipeg was at a standstill, and Canada had its first general strike.

13 The Winnipeg General Strike

Everything was orderly at first. The strike committee had done a good job of preparation, and administration was in the hands of this five-member committee. Later there was an 'Outer Committee' of 300, representing all the unions in the city, and an 'Inner Committee' of fifteen, as well as a number of subcommittees. Policemen had voted to join the strike, but at the request of the committee they remained on duty. The firefighters joined the strikers but were replaced by volunteers. Water pressure was maintained, though at a reduced level.

When milk and bread deliveries stopped, there were public outcries. Arrangements were made to have deliveries resumed on a restricted basis and with the carts carrying signs which read: 'By Authority of the Strike Committee'. This led to protests that the committee had taken over control of the city, which to a large extent it had. When thermometers climbed, ice deliveries were resumed. Theatre owners were asked by the committee to remain open so that people would be kept off the streets.

An organization calling itself the Committee of One Thousand quickly became prominent. The committee identified itself as a group of concerned citizens, ready to play a third-party role in helping to get a settlement in the dispute; however, it was soon evident that the committee's main efforts were directed against the strikers. Headquarters were in the Board of Trade Building, and the members were largely employers, businessmen, and professional people.

The committee considered itself the bulwark of British Empire tradition, defending Winnipeg against the Bolshevik revolution. About a third of the city's population were Europeans, many of whom had been in Canada only a short time, and much of the anti-strike propaganda was directed against them. In one of its public statements the Committee of One Thousand asked:

> How much longer is the alien to run amuk, to insult our flag, take it by force from Canadian-born citizens in our streets, continue his threatening attitude toward law and order? . . .
> There are some 27,000 registered alien enemies in the Winnipeg District. The same 'Reds' who are prominent leaders in this strike, led them during the war to hamper and block in every conceivable way, recruiting our reinforcements and supplies from going forward to the front.[100]

The strike soon took on national significance. There were work stoppages in other cities, some accompanied by threats of general strike action. Toronto metalworkers were involved in a dispute which led to the Toronto Trades and Labour Council giving authority for a city-wide strike in sympathetic support, but the response was far from general. More extensive tie-ups occurred in Edmonton and Saskatoon, with widespread disruption in Vancouver.

In Ottawa the politicians became jittery. Sir Robert Borden's government was in a shaky position. He faced hostility from Quebec over the conscription issue, and he had failed to alleviate the unrest which was so prevalent across the land. There were increasing demands for an end to the coalition which had been formed to meet wartime conditions.

Borden assured the House of Commons that the government would take steps to maintain law and order in Winnipeg and restore federal services to normal. The government was relying heavily on Gideon Robertson as Minister of Labour. Despite his trade union background, however, he had little in common with those responsible for the strike, and his conservative views were at wide variance with those of most of the unionists involved. He was sent to Winnipeg to see what he could do, and with him went Arthur Meighen, the acting Minister of Justice. Meighen's presence was seen as an indication that the government intended to use legal pressure to end the strike.

Robertson's first act was to order the postal workers back on the job, threatening them with dismissal and loss of their pension rights if they did not comply. A minority went back, and some new employees were taken on.

Robertson held back from becoming openly involved in the actual negotiations for a strike settlement. He considered that his participation would be regarded as formal recognition of the strike committee, and this he was not prepared to give. Nevertheless a good deal of behind-the-scenes discussion and manoeuvring went on in an attempt to find some face-saving formula which would settle the metalworkers' dispute and bring an end to the general strike.

There were three basic issues:

1. Firm recognition of the right of workers to bargain collectively through an agency of their choice.
2. Wage increases to meet higher living costs.
3. Reinstatement of all strikers without prejudice.

By the end of May there had been a partial resumption of public services. Daily papers were again publishing. The Committee of One Thousand had meantime been putting out a bulletin, *The Winnipeg Citizen*, mainly composed of anti-strike propaganda. An equally prejudiced position on the other side was to be found in the *Western Labor News*, which was eventually banned.

On the roof of the *Manitoba Free Press* building there was a new wireless station, which the paper boasted had restored Winnipeg's communications with the outside world. There was still little in the way of objective reporting of what was going on in the city. Newspaper reports were sprinkled with such words as 'aliens', 'Bohunks', and 'foreigners'. Cartoons depicted wild-eyed and bearded Bolsheviks with the city in their grasp.

Most of the workers were still out on strike, and almost all aspects of life were affected to some extent. Still, despite the intensity of feeling, there were comparatively few open conflicts.

Both sides actively sought an alliance with returned soldiers. No sooner had the strike started than the Great War Veterans' Association held a meeting with other veterans' groups. While there were divisions of opinion, there is no doubt that a majority supported the unions throughout the strike.

Parades became the most popular form of demonstration and were staged with such frequency that on more than one occasion people found themselves marching with the wrong group. On 31 May a large assembly of veterans marched to the Legislative Building to demand recognition of collective bargaining and then went on to the City Hall, where they disrupted a meeting of the City Council.

As the strike dragged on, tension built up in official quarters. The City Council voted to prohibit firemen from belonging to a union and to require them to sign an undertaking to this effect — a 'yellow dog contract'. The firemen were also to be required to pledge not to take part in any form of strike. Another resolution called for the dismissal of all civic employees who were on strike.

A few days later the Mayor announced that these conditions applied to the police force. The policemen refused to comply and were promptly dismissed. To replace them the City Council hired special constables at the attractive rate of $6 a day. The T. Eaton Company made its delivery horses available to the new constables. D. C. Masters, in his book *The Winnipeg General Strike*, attributes the violence which eventually broke out largely to the City Council's use of volunteer policemen.

Emotions began to run high. One incident attracted considerable attention because of the involvement of a local hero, Sergeant-Major F. G. Copping, who had been awarded the Victoria Cross in The Great War. He was a member of the volunteer police force, and as he rode down the sidewalk to break up a crowd, he was dragged from his horse and badly bruised.

Fear was mounting in Ottawa's officialdom. An amendment to the Immigration Act was introduced providing authority for the immediate deportation, without trial or hearing, of any immigrant, including British subjects and regardless of the length of time they had resided in Canada. The legislation went through the House of Commons and the Senate and was given Royal Assent, all within an hour. In addition, Section 98 of the Criminal Code, originally adopted to meet wartime conditions, was broadened to provide for arrest on suspicion, with the accused bearing the onus of proving innocence. The maximum penalty under the section was increased from two to twenty years.

Then, in Winnipeg, the authorities began to move. During the night of 16-17 June they arrested and locked up a number of the strike leaders. Those taken into custody included Russell; Alderman Queen, who was business manager of the *Western Labor News*; Rev. William Ivens, the editor; George Armstrong, the union leader; Roger Bray, leader of the veterans who were supporting the strike; and Alderman A. A. Heaps. In view of the type of propaganda that had flooded the city, it is significant that these were all men with Anglo-Saxon names.

Four men with European names were also arrested: Moses Alamazoff, Mike Verenchuk, S. Choppelrei, and F. Charitonoff. The last named was editor of the Russian-language newspaper *Working People*. Verenchuk was apparently arrested by mistake. He was taking care of a friend's house when he was dragged out of bed at pistol point and taken to the police station. His name was not on the original warrant, but it was added the next day. Verenchuk was a returned soldier who had been twice wounded and honourably discharged. He was released after being subjected to a sanity test.

Dick Johns had been away from Winnipeg throughout the strike, but he was arrested in Montreal. William Pritchard, a Vancouver unionist who had been sent to Winnipeg as an observer, was on his way home when he was taken off the train and arrested at Calgary. Those with Anglo-Saxon names were released on bail; the others remained in custody.

Meighen was anxious to settle the matter as quickly as possible and suggested the immediate deportation of all who had not been born in Canada, which meant all except Armstrong. A. J.

Andrews, a Winnipeg lawyer who was a member of the Committee of One Thousand, had been appointed as special agent for the Department of Justice. Within hours of the arrests he received a telegram from Meighen stating:

> Notwithstanding any doubt I have as to the technical legality of the arrests and detention at Stony Mountain [Penitentiary] I feel rapid deportation is the best course now that the arrests have been made, and later we can consider ratification.[101]

Meighen's sympathies had been made clear in a Commons speech in which, while recognizing the extent of organization among the employers, he expressed shock at the possibility of a similar movement on the part of workers. He asked:

> Can anyone contemplate such an event? Are we to have on the one hand a concentration of employers, and on the other a concentration of all the labour interests of the Dominion fighting it out for supremacy?[102]

There was no suggestion that the employers' organization should be broken up.

In Winnipeg those under arrest faced a number of charges, with most of the alleged offences centred around conspiracy

> . . . to incite divers liege subjects of the King, to resist laws and resist persons, some being part of the police force of the City Of Winnipeg . . . and to procure unlawful meetings and to cause divers liege subjects of the King to believe that the laws of the Dominion were being unduly administered.[103]

A few days after the wave of arrests, J. S. Woodsworth, later the first leader of the Co-operative Commonwealth Federation (CCF), was taken into custody, charged with sedition for articles he had published in the *Western Labor News*. Woodsworth, whose home was in Vancouver, had gone to Winnipeg to try to assist the strikers and had become editor of the paper after Ivens's arrest.

One of the articles which offended the authorities was a quotation from Isaiah:

> And they shall build houses and inhabit them; and they shall plant
> vineyards and eat the fruit of them. They shall not build and
> another inhabit; they shall not plant and another eat; for as the
> days of the trees are the days of my people, and mine elect shall
> enjoy the work of their hands.[104]

Fred Dixon, who was assisting in the publication of the paper,
was also arrested. The charges against Woodsworth were later
dropped, and Dixon was acquitted.

But before the trials there was 'Bloody Saturday'. The Mayor
had ordered an end to the parades; however, the group of veterans whose sympathies were with the strikers announced their
intention of proceeding with a 'silent march' on Saturday afternoon, 21 June. Robertson was still in Winnipeg, and it was
known that he had arranged a meeting in the Alexandra Hotel
for the same day. Crowds who gathered downtown to see what
was happening saw a good deal more than they expected. Before the day was over, one man was dead and thirty people
seriously injured. Heavily armed soldiers were patrolling
Winnipeg's business area.

As the crowds gathered, Mayor Gray became alarmed and
asked the Royal North-West Mounted Police to take responsibility for patrolling the streets, which had become crowded with
several thousand onlookers. A party of some fifty RNWMP appeared on Main Street, mounted and carrying clubs. They rode
into a crowd, and as they emerged two of their horses were
without riders. The police re-formed their ranks and made
another foray. This time they had their revolvers out, and shots
were fired. The police later claimed that the first shots came
from the crowd; witnesses denied this. Stones were hurled at
the police, who then fired at least two volleys. One of the bystanders, Mike Sokolowski, fell dead, shot through the heart.

People scrambled for safety down the side streets. One group
of about 200 found themselves trapped in a dead-end alley,
facing a squad of special constables. There was a ten-minute
melee. Some shots were fired, but the fighting was mainly a
matter of the police using clubs and people fighting back with
whatever they could lay their hands on. A number were injured.

Earlier, Mayor Gray, standing on the steps of the City Hall, had read the Riot Act ordering the dispersal of the crowd, and he had then called out the militia. Soon soldiers were on the streets, carrying rifles with fixed bayonets and backed up by machine guns. Peace was quickly restored, but the bruises, mental as well as physical, remained. Of the thirty who received hospital attention on Bloody Saturday, twenty-four were civilians and six were police officers. One of the civilians, Steve Scherbanques, had suffered bullet wounds in both legs and later died of gangrene.

The strike leaders who were under arrest had been released on their undertaking not to participate in any gathering. They had kept their promise. The strike committee had, in fact, asked the veterans to abandon the idea of a parade, but they had persisted. A subsequent Royal Commission report stated:

> It should be said that the leaders who had brought about the general strike were not responsible for the parade or riots which took place, and, in fact, tried to prevent them. The leaders' policy was one of peaceful idleness.[105]

After Bloody Saturday the strike was doomed. It was obvious that some form of settlement had to be reached without further delay. Union funds were running low, and families were feeling the financial pinch. On 25 June the strike committee notified Premier Norris that the sympathy strike was being ended. The next day those not directly involved in the metal or building trades disputes went back to work. The strike of metal and construction workers went on somewhat longer, but the six-week general work stoppage that had made labour history was at an end.

The terms on which the general strike was terminated were unsatisfactory to many. The document which was signed by representatives of the three metal companies recognized collective bargaining rights by quoting from an Order-in-Council on this subject. The agreement further provided that:

1. There would be no discrimination against any employee for membership or non-membership in a union.

2. Members of various organizations would 'have the right to present and negotiate schedules covering wages, hours and working conditions, with individual employers or collectively with employers of the metal trades'.
3. The employees in the contract shops, not including the railways, would have the right to elect representatives from among the employees of the firms involved.
4. A grievance procedure would be established.

The dissatisfaction was expressed in a statement issued by the Defence Committee, which had been set up to raise funds for the defence of those facing charges. It stated:

> The reasons given for their action by the Strike Committee were to the effect that as funds had run out, owing to meetings being banned, thus closing them as a source of revenue for the relief fund, many workers were finding it impossible to stay out any longer, as their families were suffering from near starvation. Then the publication of what purported to be acceptance of the Metal Trades Employers of collective bargaining, had the desired results and provided an excuse for some of the waverers to go back to work, and it was feared that there was the possibility of a stampede unless the strike was officially cut off. This and the undertaking of the provincial government to appoint a Commission to go into the causes of the strike and effect the reinstatement of all strikers, had much influence in leading the Strike Committee to its final decision. . . .
>
> It demonstrated the nature of the class struggle, the ruthlessness and brutality of Imperial capitalism. . . . It proved the futility of craft unionism and the need for industrial organization to meet the changes brought about by machine production.[106]

Following the strike, there were trials facing the Winnipeg strike leaders. The Defence Committee sold 'Workers' Liberty Bonds' to help finance the legal expenses. There had been a storm of protest across the country, and Meighen's suggestion of quick deportation had been dropped.

The authorities regarded Russell as the chief culprit, and he was tried first and separately. He was found guilty and sentenced to two years in the penitentiary. An appeal was dismissed.

Seven of Russell's colleagues were tried jointly. The mere reading of the indictment against them took an hour. Several of them used their platform experience to conduct their own defence. Pritchard's address to the jury took two whole days, but he, with four others, was convicted and sentenced to a year's imprisonment. Bray, leader of the veterans, received a six-month sentence. Heaps addressed the court for a full day and won acquittal.

Jamieson gives it as his opinion that

> . . . the convictions were all based on the dubious assumption that the strike was the result of a conspiracy to overthrow the government, rather than a concerted struggle by organized labour in Winnipeg to secure the basic rights of recognition and collective bargaining.[107]

The normal open-court procedure was followed in the trials of those with Anglo-Saxon names, but this was not the case with the others. It is believed that those whose names indicated a European origin were deported, but this was never clearly established.

All those whose trials were open were released within a year, and most went on to distinguished careers. In 1961 a dinner was held honouring Robert Russell on the occasion of his fiftieth anniversary as a union member. Among the speakers was the Hon. Justice Joseph Thorsen, then president of the Exchequer Court of Canada, who had journeyed to Winnipeg for the occasion. As a young barrister, Thorsen had been associated with the Crown in the trials. He disclosed that all the prospective jurors had been carefully screened by the RNWMP and the final jury was 'hand picked'. In the joint trial all twelve members of the jury were from rural areas. Most farmers had been strongly opposed to the strike, and a number had enrolled in the $6-a-day police force.

Some years after the trials, J. S. Woodsworth gave his personal assessment of the whole affair in these words:

> That strike has been entirely misrepresented. I know the details intimately. Without hesitation I say that there was not a single

> foreigner in a position of leadership, though foreigners were falsely arrested to give colour to the charge. . . .
>
> There was absolutely no attempt to set up a Soviet government. The money which was said to be coming from Russia in large quantities was a collection of $250 raised by some miners in Alberta to bring a lecturer from Winnipeg. It was charged that there was an attempt to overthrow the government by force, yet not a single gun was discovered from Nova Scotia to Prince Rupert.
>
> In short, it was the biggest hoax ever put over any people! Government officials and the press were largely responsible. Of course some were quite sincere, but absolutely hysterical. [108]

Allowing for Woodsworth's personal involvement, his evaluation cannot be discounted. It was later supported by many others, including Kenneth McNaught, a distinguished Canadian historian. In his biography of Woodsworth, *A Prophet in Politics*, McNaught attributed the government's actions largely to a hysteria related to the rise of Communism in Russia and a belief that constitutional authority in Canada was in jeopardy.

The Robson Commission, which conducted an investigation on behalf of the Manitoba government, suggested that high prices, low wages, resentment at 'undue war profiteering', and a desire for collective bargaining were responsible for the strike.

Both employers and union leaders had seen collective bargaining as a key issue. Many of those who have studied the strike in retrospect have come to the conclusion that it was really the One Big Union that was on trial, rather than a small group of union leaders who, despite their colourful oratory, showed little inclination to become involved in a blood-letting revolution.

Unionists could claim that a degree of recognition had been won from obstinate employers, but it was meagre recognition bought at tremendous cost. Canada had gone through the experience of a general strike, and this had been found to be no solution to labour-management differences.

14 The Twenties

A troublesome time followed the Winnipeg Strike. Organized labour was having difficulty holding its own. Membership dropped, and despite some serious strikes there was a decline in militancy. *The Labour Gazette* reported that of 132 strikes in 1921 no fewer than 87 revolved around proposed wage cuts.

The situation was not helped by factional fighting within the movement, particularly between Communists and those who opposed that philosophy. The differences had been sharpened by the Winnipeg Strike and a questioning of the practicality of the general strike as a means of attaining labour's aims.

The strike had done nothing to unify the labour movement. Most of the officers of international unions had been opposed to it. Officers of the railway unions had participated in efforts to get a settlement for the metalworkers, but at the same time they had done their best to keep the trains running. The Trades and Labour Congress had remained aloof, laying down as conditions for its support a declaration of allegiance to the TLC, repudiation of the OBU, and assurance of adherence to the constitutions of international unions. These terms were quite unacceptable to the Winnipeg strikers.

When the TLC was asked to provide support in efforts to obtain the release of those who had been arrested, Tom Moore, in a letter to the Winnipeg Trades and Labour Council, reviewed the relationship which had developed between the two bodies.

He recalled that when he had visited Winnipeg early in May the Council had refused to meet with him, and he said he had later been refused information concerning the strike.

Moore charged the Labour Council with

> . . . repudiation of the control of the international executives to grant or withhold sanction for a strike to their Winnipeg locals, and slurring attacks and repudiation of the Trades Congress and its executives.[109]

At the TLC convention later in the year Moore further explained:

> Winnipeg was determined upon its course of action, which harmonized strongly with the policies laid down in the propaganda of the OBU, and by the usurpation of the power of the international union executives by the Winnipeg Trades Council in the calling of the strike made it very plain that Winnipeg was determined to demonstrate the efficiency of the principle of massed action, sympathetic strikes and economic dictatorship as superior in achieving results to the policies of international trade unions, the Trades and Labour Congress of Canada and the American Federation of Labor, which are, and have been, a policy of negotiation and the using of the strike weapon as a last resort only.[110]

The convention adopted a resolution deploring misrepresentation by the press and calling for a fair trial for the accused strikers.

The strike had seriously weakened efforts toward the establishment of a new structure of industrial unionism. Alarm was being expressed about the radicalism of the OBU, but it was hardly justified. The philosophy expressed in the preamble to its constitution was quite moderate:

> Modern industrial society is divided into two classes, those who possess and do not produce, and those who do produce and do not possess. Alongside this main division all other classifications fade into insignificance. Between these two classes a continual struggle must take place. As with buyers and sellers of any commodity there exists a struggle on the one hand of the buyer to buy

as cheaply as possible, and on the other, for the seller to sell for as much as possible, so with the buyers and sellers of labour power. In the struggle over the purchase and sale of labour power, the buyers are always the masters, the sellers always the workers. From this fact arises the inevitable class struggle. As industry develops and ownership becomes concentrated more and more into fewer hands; as the control of the economic forces of society becomes more and more the sole property of imperialistic finance, it becomes apparent that the workers, in order to sell their labour power with any degree of success, must extend their forms of organization in accordance with changing industrial methods. Compelled to organize for self-defence, they are further compelled to educate themselves in preparation for the social change which economic developments will produce whether they seek it or not. The One Big Union, therefore, seeks to organize the wage worker not according to craft, but according to industry; according to class and class needs; and calls upon all workers to organize irrespective of nationality, sex or craft, into workers' organizations so that they may be enabled to more successfully carry on the every day fight over wages, hours of work, etc., and prepare themselves for the day when production for profit shall be replaced by production for use. [111]

This was a watered-down version of the sentiments which had been expressed with such force at the Calgary conference, but the Trades and Labour Congress was still having none of it. Essentially, of course, the TLC saw the OBU as a competitor for membership. Plans were laid to strengthen the position of the TLC and its affiliates in the hope of wiping out the OBU.

Meanwhile, the One Big Union still had support in British Columbia, largely among loggers and miners, but it was meeting opposition in Alberta. Winnipeg remained the major stronghold.

At its 1919 convention in Hamilton the TLC made plans to take advantage of these unsettled conditions in combatting the threat presented by the OBU. Taking a lesson from its Winnipeg experience, the Congress decided to tighten its control of local labour councils. A constitutional amendment was adopted giving the executive the authority to take over councils and other subordinate bodies. The British Columbia Federation rebelled, returning its charter and declaring that it could not accept 'such autocratic methods'.

In the Crow's Nest Pass area a lengthy OBU coal strike in 1919 had rallied both the operators and the government on the side of the United Mine Workers. This, with the defection of the British Columbia loggers in 1920, left the OBU greatly weakened. The organization's headquarters, which had been in Vancouver, were moved to Winnipeg.

Accurate figures of OBU membership are difficult to determine. A reasonable estimate puts the peak at about 50,000, but this declined rapidly, leaving little more than the hard core in Winnipeg. When the Trades and Labour Congress merged with the Canadian Congress of Labour in 1956, the remaining 3,000 OBU members became part of the new Canadian Labour Congress, with the understanding that they would join one of the established unions.

The days of the OBU, dramatic as they had been, were ended. Russell died in 1966, and his name is commemorated in the R. B. Russell Vocational School in Winnipeg. This is one of the very few instances in which a labour leader has been accorded such honour.

In the Nova Scotia coalfields, labour turbulence continued in the 1920s. A British company had taken over, and a three-week strike followed a 35 per cent wage cut. At the same time, the United Mine Workers were experiencing internal strife. A more militant faction had gained control of the Nova Scotia district, and when they proposed affiliating with the Red International of Labour Unions in Moscow, the UMW headquarters in Washington threatened to suspend the district charter. The idea of affiliation was dropped.

Then in 1923 came a series of strikes affecting as many as 13,000 coal and steel mill employees. Homes and offices of UMW leaders were raided and searched for seditious material. When a Sydney magistrate tried to read the Riot Act, he was knocked unconscious by a stone thrown from the crowd. The army was called in, and 2,000 troops were stationed in the area, with special police reinforcements. There were protests at the use of military force and allegations of police brutality.

New controversies arose between the UMW's district officers and the international headquarters. The strike was in violation of an existing agreement, and the established UMW policy of keeping maintenance men on the job to prevent flooding of the mines had been ignored. The union's president, John L. Lewis, revoked the district's charter and removed the local officers, appointing provisional officers in their place. The strike ended.

But the peace was not to last. In the next election, left-wing candidates were returned. Economic conditions were bad and unemployment was high. Early in 1925 the company announced a 10 per cent wage cut and termination of credit at the company stores. Once again there was a work stoppage. Forsey, who made an intensive study of industrial disputes in the eastern coalfields, has called it a lockout. Work was halted for five months. Conditions became desperate for the miners' families, but there was unusually generous support in very tangible forms: the Trades and Labour Congress raised money from unions; the Nova Scotia government provided aid; the assistance of the Red Cross was enlisted; the Great War Veterans Association started a special fund; and the Canadian National Railways provided free transportation for relief supplies.

The company asked for help from the militia, but this time the government did not immediately respond, and private guards were hired. One guard was killed in a fight with pickets, and the province then sent special police in. Serious rioting broke out; warehouses were burned and two mines were flooded. The company's attitude stiffened, and it added to its demands the elimination of the union dues check-off and the creation of a blacklist to block the re-employment of some of the strikers. Eventually there was a compromise settlement.

Within the Canadian labour movement at that time there were important developments which would have a lasting effect. They centred around a railway union, the Canadian Brotherhood of Railway Employees, which had been organized by employees of the Intercolonial Railway at Moncton in 1908. The president was Aaron R. Mosher, who later became the first and only president of the Canadian Congress of Labour (see page 163). Mosher was a freight checker. One of those associated with him was Malcolm M. Maclean, a dining car steward, who later headed the Conciliation Branch in the Canada Department of Labour.

The CBRE was organized on industrial lines and included in its membership clerks, roundhouse workers, baggagemen, and various other occupations in the non-operating categories. The union grew rapidly and at a convention held in Quebec City in 1911 was able to report divisions established from coast to coast. The CBRE soon lost a number of its members in western Canada following a CPR strike, but there were membership gains through the affiliation of groups of express employees and sleeping car porters.

The union affiliated with the TLC in 1917 but became entangled in jurisdictional difficulties with the Brotherhood of Railway and Steamship Clerks, Freight Handlers, Express and Station Employees, an international union with overlapping membership. It was suggested the CBRE should turn over some of its members to the international union, and when it refused, it was expelled from the TLC. This split later influenced the entire structure of the labour movement in Canada.

For several years the CBRE carried on alone; then, in 1927, it initiated the formation of a new central body, the All-Canadian Congress of Labour, bringing together miscellaneous groups outside the TLC. Several developments facilitated the move. For one thing, the Canadian Federation of Labour, the one-time, but always weak, competitor to the TLC, had almost disappeared. Also, many of the Quebec opponents of international unionism had become part of the Catholic union structure in that province.

The founding convention of the All-Canadian Congress attracted about a hundred delegates, half of them from the CBRE. Others included what was left of the Canadian Federation and the One Big Union, as well as the Mine Workers' Union of Canada and various small national unions, most of them groups which had broken away from international unions.

In contrast to the TLC the new congress regarded organization as its most important function. While the ACCL leaned toward industrial unionism, its position was not dogmatic. Some of the affiliates had a craft background, which they preserved. Politically the new body favoured moderate socialism, with the extension of public ownership. This did not go far enough for some of its affiliates, particularly the OBU and the mineworkers, who over a period of years were in and out of the ACCL.

By 1927 the new congress claimed a membership of 46,000 but was suffering from the divergent views of its affiliates and the energetic efforts of Communist factions to gain control. The ACCL had limited financial resources and was far from being capable of tackling the organization of the rapidly expanding mass-production industries. Its strength was further reduced when a group of electrical workers withdrew in 1936. Nevertheless, the ACCL pointed the way to a new form of national labour body, and it survived to play an important part in the founding of the Canadian Congress of Labour in 1940.

There were other important developments on the political scene. One of the effects of the Winnipeg Strike had been a class polarization in Manitoba. Disillusioned with the effectiveness of the general strike, Woodsworth and others pressed with renewed vigour for political activity, and they made considerable progress in the Winnipeg municipal election of 1920.

As far as politics were concerned, there was an uneasy peace between the OBU and the international unions, as well as new hopes, which were later proven unjustified, of farmer-labour co-operation. In the June 1920 provincial election both labour and farmers scored major victories. Labour elected eleven members to the Legislature. Of the four who won seats in the city of Winnipeg, three were still in jail serving sentences for their part in the strike. The victory was particularly surprising in view of the record of the Norris government, which had been generally friendly toward labour and had avoided the extreme position adopted by the federal government during the strike. Even the *Free Press* admitted, '. . . labour has now taken its place as a definite party in this country'.

But no party had a majority, and there was a frantic jockeying for position. Labour and farmers have always had difficulty in establishing and maintaining a working relationship, and in this instance the farmers were quick to reject suggestions of an alliance with the labour politicians. The gap widened, and in the 1922 election labour candidates were snowed under while the candidates of the United Farmers of Manitoba formed the government.

For a time things were better in Ontario, where the Independent Labour Party (ILP) was working with the United Farmers of Ontario. The provincial election of 1919 had been a major upset, with the Conservative strength cut from seventy-eight to twenty-five seats. The farmers increased the number of seats they held from two to thirty-five. The ILP, which had no previous representation, elected eleven trade unionists.

The labour members were faced with the choice of becoming part of a coalition or exercising a balance of power. The farmers issued a general invitation to other groups to help form a government, and a modified agreement was reached with the labour bloc. E. C. Drury, a former Liberal and then member of the farm group, was chosen to head the new government. During the first session, considerable legislation in line with the labour program was adopted. This included removal of the property qualification in municipal elections, establishment of a minimum wage for women, and increased workmen's compensation benefits.

But all was not harmonious. There was soon a rift between the farmers and union members on the matter of tariffs. The farmers favoured low duties to hold down the cost of imported goods, while the unions wanted tariff protection for the industries employing their members. Trades and Labour Congress support for the ILP had cooled. At the same time the TLC became involved in a dispute with the Drury government over the application of the eight-hour day to workers on a Hydro project. At the TLC's 1920 convention there was a reaffirmation of the political independence of the Congress.

The philosophical differences between farm and labour groups became increasingly apparent. The farmers were highly suspicious of the Independent Labour Party's socialist inclinations, which were seen as a threat to the farmers' position as private operators and, in a sense, capitalists. Labour members of the Legislature were at variance with their supposed allies in the legislative chamber and simultaneously involved in bickering within the labour movement. The first flush of legislation had passed, and there was criticism in union ranks over a failure to implement other measures which were part of the labour program.

In the 1923 election labour support was unenthusiastic and disorganized. The UFO-Labour government was badly beaten. Not only was the farm-labour alliance dissolved, but the ILP itself was in poor shape.

Within the labour movement, open conflict had broken out over the Communist issue. Then, as now, the majority of labour leaders resented what they regarded as efforts of the Communists to make use of their association with the labour movement and to gain control of unions. In their opinion the bread-and-butter issues and the relatively short-term objectives of the movement had low priority in the Communist efforts, which were directed essentially to the overthrow of the existing system.

A Communist party in Canada had taken formal shape in 1922, when the Workers' Party of Canada was formed. A manifesto declared its purpose to be

> . . . to consolidate the existing labour organizations and develop them into organizations of militant struggle against capitalism, to permeate the labour unions and strive to replace the present reactionary leadership by revolutionary leadership.[112]

The second item in the manifesto called for participation in elections, and the third had as its objective,

> . . . to lead the fight for the immediate needs of the workers, broaden and deepen their demands, organize and develop out of their everyday struggles a force for the abolition of capitalism.[113]

Earl Browder, a leading American Communist, attended the founding meeting in Toronto and attacked the American Federation of Labor as 'the most reactionary body in the world'. He said the success of Communism had been limited by a failure to get control of the unions.

In essence Browder was advocating the 'boring from within' tactic. Through the history of Communist activities in the labour movement this has alternated with the 'smashing from without' approach of establishing and supporting competitive unions. Not all the delegates were in agreement with Browder. Russell was shocked by the suggestion that independent industrial unionism should be abandoned in favour of an effort to become part of the international union structure. He was denounced by avowed Communists as a reactionary.

The Trades and Labour Congress was disturbed by the fact that the Communists had gained control of the Canadian Labour Party, and in 1921 it was decided to publish a monthly Congress journal to

> . . . cope with persistent and continued propaganda against trade union policies and methods, carried on by those who desire to continue the exploitation of the wage earners of this country, and also by those who would bring about the disintegration of the organized labour movement and the substitution of a 'dictatorship of the proletariat'. [114]

It had become the practice for Communist supporters to run a slate against the 'establishment' candidates for office at TLC conventions. In 1924 Tim Buck, who later became leader of the Communist Party in Canada, opposed Moore for the presidency but was defeated 156-54. The next year Buck got only 29 votes.

The Trade Union Education League, a Communist front organization patterned after one of similar name in the United States, was formed in 1922 and was a useful vehicle for Workers' Party propaganda. In 1922 the TLC warned against both the party and the TUEL, which, it said,

> . . . acting under the subterfuge of education, aims to poison the minds of the workers against the present trade union and political organizations and ultimately make them instruments for the establishment of communism. [115]

These differences extended into individual unions. In the United States the International Ladies' Garment Workers'

Union expelled a number of members for Communist activities in 1920. Four years later the union took similar action in Canada. There were also expulsions from the Amalgamated Clothing Workers. In 1928 Buck was expelled from the International Association of Machinists on the ground that he was a paid organizer for the Communist Party, promoting dual unionism in opposition to his own union, the Machinists.

Opposition to the Communist influences became so strong that the 'boring from within' method proved ineffective. The party then reversed its policy, encouraging defections and backing the newly-formed All-Canadian Congress. The TLC had dubbed this the 'All-Red Congress of Labour', adding 'credit must be given to the Communist Party of Canada for bringing into being a new Canadian Congress'.

The charge was not well founded. It was not long before the Communists found they were as unwelcome in the ACCL as they were in the TLC, and they began denouncing it as a reactionary organization. Politically the TLC had withdrawn to the safety of its traditional position, favouring a few labour candidates and emphasizing its legislative program.

But there were other events, which offered new hope to those who might best be described as 'social democrats'. In the December 1921 election, Woodsworth, with labour support, won a resounding victory and went to Ottawa as the member for Winnipeg Centre. He became labour's chief spokesman in the House of Commons. In Winnipeg North, Jacob Penner was elected as a Workers' Party candidate, narrowly defeating Bob Russell, who ran on behalf of the Socialist Party. It was ironic that Russell, having served a penitentiary term for supposedly advocating a Communist form of government, should be defeated at the polls by a declared Communist.

Woodsworth proved a highly effective member and remained firm in his determination to be free of entanglement with either of the major parties. He refused Prime Minister King's invitation to become Minister of Labour. With him in Parliament was William Irvine, the member from East Calgary, who in his maiden speech in the House explained:

I wish to state that the honourable member for Centre Winnipeg is the leader of the labour group — and I am the group.[116]

Before long the two were joined by others, those who found their position in the Progressive Party* untenable. The 'Ginger Group' came into being under Woodsworth's leadership, expressing views which were largely those of organized labour. Thus the basis was laid for the formation of the Co-operative Commonwealth Federation, which will be discussed later (see pages 153-5).

It was during the 1920s that the Catholic unions in Quebec formed the Canadian and Catholic Confederation of Labour. As has been mentioned, a strike and lockout of boot and shoe workers in Quebec City in 1900 was the occasion of one of the first interventions by the Catholic Church into union affairs in that province.

Later, the growth of international unions in Quebec became of increasing concern to the church authorities, who saw these as materialistic, irreligious, and foreign organizations. Educational programs were introduced in the parishes to teach workers the application of the principles of their church to industrial relations. The teaching included attacks on international unions, and it was customary at the conclusion of the course to form a purely Catholic union. In situations where an international union posed an immediate threat, the educational program was dispensed with. There were some extremely bitter conflicts between the Catholic unions and the internationals, carried over into communities and resulting in neighbourhood squabbles.

Priests were attached as chaplains to each unit of the Catholic unions. They had the right to attend all meetings and take part in the discussions, though not to vote. Their influence was considerable. In its initial stages the Catholic union movement was entirely church-inspired, and it was in no sense a spontaneous

---

* The Progressive Party had been formed in 1920 in opposition to high tariff policies. Its strongest support came from western farmers, and in the 1921 election it won 64 seats. Breakaways followed in 1924, and six members formed an alliance with Woodsworth and Irvine.

workers' movement. It came under attack from other unions —
'neutral' organizations as the Church called them — as being
little more than company unionism. Many employers showed a
preference for the Catholic unions, and the friendliness between
the Church and the Quebec government was to their advantage.

These were serious handicaps, but the Catholic unions still
provided some form of organization, and as the years went by,
the nature of the movement altered radically. There was a
marked growth in militancy, and the ties with the Church were
gradually loosened. The confessional nature of the organization
was abandoned and membership thrown open to all, regardless
of their faith. With the dropping of the word 'Catholic' from the
name it became the Confederation of National Trade Unions,
and now the CNTU ranks with the most active and militant
labour organizations in the country.

The labour movement in Canada was taking on a new form,
but it was going to need all the strength it could muster to meet
the catastrophic economic conditions that were fast approaching.

15 The Terrible Thirties

This was the time of the Great Depression. Human suffering surpassed description. There was widespread industrial strife, and outbreaks of violence were frequent. The existing structure of the labour movement proved as incapable as other sectors of society of coping with the near-disaster conditions. The turmoil which spread across the country provided fertile ground for the Communists' efforts to capitalize on discontent. They succeeded not only in this but in extending their organization at a time when most unions were losing members.

Canadians were searching for political solutions to the stupendous social and economic problems confronting them. It was during the 1930s that the Co-operative Commonwealth Federation came into being, an event of considerable importance to labour's future political activities. Others turned to a very different political solution. In Alberta the evangelist William Aberhart was swept into office as the leader of a Social Credit government. For many Albertans the monetary theories of that party offered the only hope of escape from the depths of the Depression.

The Depression left indelible marks on an entire generation. Decades later the thinking and attitudes of much of labour's leadership, and some of the membership, still reflected the impact of those difficult years. While the Depression was worldwide, it struck Canada with particular force because of the country's dependence on export trade. The situation was further complicated by the failure of governments to cope with what were extraordinary situations.

The seriousness of economic trends was becoming apparent in 1929, but faced with an election, Prime Minister King did his best to sweep the problems under the rug. He maintained that the responsibility of looking after people in need rested with the provinces and added that no province under a Conservative administration could expect a nickel from federal coffers to help them meet these needs.

King went down to defeat, and the Conservative leader, R. B. Bennett, took office. He had made economic conditions a major election issue, but once in power he showed little imagination in doing something about them. Funds were made available for welfare and for make-work projects, and tariffs were raised sharply in an effort to protect Canadian industry. The measures were insufficient, and unemployment continued to climb.

Even before the Depression struck, most Canadian working-class families were in a precarious financial position. In 1930 about 60 per cent of the male wage-earners and 82 per cent of the female labour force were earning less than $1,000 a year. Government figures placed the minimum standard of decency for a family at $1,200 to $1,500. As jobs disappeared, people were forced to dip into what savings they had and then to pawn or sell their possessions. Finally there was public welfare — relief. This was before the days of unemployment insurance, and destitution was a prerequisite to obtaining public assistance. Relief carried a stigma that left many psychological scars.

The scales of assistance varied from province to province. The lowest was in Saskatchewan, which was also beset by drought. There, a family of five received $10 a month and a 98-pound sack of flour. In Ontario's industrial communities, people lined up at warehouses to get their bags of beans, flour, and macaroni. Some of them took the handouts home in baby carriages in an attempt to hide the fact that they were dependent on public support for their groceries.

Some communities applied pressure on federal authorities to deport families which had become public charges. Speaking in the House of Commons in November 1932 Woodsworth pointed out that of the 15,368 deportations which had been recorded in the previous eighteen months, 9,446 had been for this reason. Many undoubtedly involved people who had been enticed to Canada under the country's immigration schemes.

By the Spring of 1933 there were a million and a half Canadians on relief — 15 per cent of the population. Estimates of unemployment were as high as 32 per cent of the labour force, yet even these figures fell short of revealing the actual number of jobless. There were the young people who had never had a job — who had finished their formal education and found themselves rejected by society. They became a particular problem for authorities, as more and more wandered the country looking for work.

In 1932 the situation reached such a state that relief camps were set up under the supervision of the Department of National Defence to accommodate single men. Whether the men went to these camps by choice or by compulsion is a purely theoretical question. Municipal authorities in most centres refused them assistance, and they had nowhere else to go. Most of the camps were in isolated locations, and once there the men were put to some form of work and paid at the rate of 20 cents a day, supplemented by a tobacco allowance of 10 cents a week.

The camps were operated under strict military discipline, and there was a blanket ban on any kind of organization or representative committee to air grievances or discuss problems with camp officials. The official policy was made quite clear in a statement which declared:

> The Department will not countenance any steps to bring accusations before the tribunal of public opinion, either by speeches or letters inserted in newspapers, by men actively employed on relief work. Such a proceeding is a glaring violation of the rules and shows a contempt for properly constituted authority.[117]

Later this highly autocratic policy was modified to allow individuals to file complaints, but the prohibition of any form of organization remained in effect.

Vancouver became the most popular gathering place for transients, many attracted by the moderate climate. As early as 1929 a

Vancouver Unemployed Workers' Association had been formed. There had been a raid on a relief office and clashes with the police. The British Columbia government had anticipated trouble and opened relief camps before the federal program was started.

The men in the camps became increasingly restless, and in December 1934 some 1,500 staged a strike and trekked to Vancouver. Their demonstration had little effect, and they were forced to return to the camps. By Spring, conditions had worsened, and 4,000 men gathered in Vancouver, demanding work at 50 cents an hour, an end to military control of the camps, and recognition of camp committees. They roamed the streets and staged tag days, soliciting help by 'tin canning' — asking for cash donations and using cans to hold the contributions.

All this was not entirely spontaneous. The restrictions had not prevented the Workers' Unity League from promoting undergound organizations in the camps. As part of an international plan, the Communist Party in the United States had established the Trade Union Unity League in 1929, and the Workers' Unity League was the Canadian counterpart. Its purpose was to work within established unions and undertake new organization, including the unemployed. The League's objective was

> . . . a program and policy of revolutionary struggle for the complete overthrow of capitalism and its institutions of exploitation, and the setting up of the State power of the workers and poor farmers through a workers' and farmers' government.[118]

Vancouver was in a state of turmoil for weeks. Then the unemployed decided to organize a trek to Ottawa to place their complaints directly before the federal government. On 3 June 1935, about 1,000 men climbed aboard a freight train and headed east. Others joined them along the way.

Ottawa viewed the trek with growing alarm, and instructions were issued to the RCMP to stop the men at Regina. By the time they reached that city, they numbered about 2,000, and it was reported another 1,000 were waiting to join them at Winnipeg. Representatives of the federal Cabinet met them and suggested they would arrange for a small delegation to go to Ottawa to meet with the Prime Minister; the others were to wait in Regina. A committee went, headed by Arthur Evans, one of the trek leaders. The meeting turned out to be nothing more than a shouting match between Evans and Bennett, with no discussion of the men's problems at all.

The committee returned to Regina with the intention of having the trek resumed; but the authorities intended otherwise, and when several truckloads of men pulled out of Regina, the trucks were promptly stopped and the men placed under arrest.

This led to the Regina Riot. Arrangements had been made for a meeting to be held in the Market Square on Dominion Day, the first of July. Several hundred strikers turned up, but they were far outnumbered by the estimated 3,000 to 4,000 spectators and sympathizers. This was the time the police chose to enforce an order which had come from Ottawa for the arrest of the strike leaders. As police pushed their way through the crowd to the platform, fighting broke out. It raged for three hours. The police used tear gas, clubs, and revolvers; the civilians used their fists and anything they could lay their hands on. Fighting spread to downtown streets, where store windows were smashed. When it was all over, a city detective was dead and more than a hundred people were injured. Eight strike leaders and seventy-five others were arrested. The strikers returned to their camp at the Regina Exhibition Grounds, where they were surrounded by police armed with machine guns.

There was a dispute about responsibility for the riot. The Saskatchewan government had been trying to arrange to have the men disperse, and it accused the federal authorities of interfering at a most inopportune time. The provincial government did, in fact, end the matter by arranging special trains to send the men back west. A commission which conducted an inquiry into the affair directed blame at the Workers' Unity League and the Communist Party.

The Regina violence was symbolic of the bitterness of the times. In 1938 some 1,200 men occupied the Vancouver Art Gallery, the Georgia Hotel, and Vancouver's main post office. There was considerable trouble when police used force to evict the men, whose sit-in at the post office had lasted almost six weeks.

The Workers' Unity League was active in all these demonstrations and was in most instances the chief instigator. But the League was also active in union organization. They established associations for the unemployed in various areas. As to activity in the relief camps, Jamieson has commented that the WUL

> . . . played a dual role as agitator and propagandist for the Communist Party, and the more limited role of campworkers' organization.[119]

The Communist Party had suffered a setback in 1931, when the federal government, alarmed at what it regarded as a serious threat, used the broad-axe terms of Section 98 of the Criminal Code, which had proven useful in the Winnipeg General Strike. Immediately after his election, Bennett had announced that Communism would be crushed by the iron heel of ruthlessness. When the heel descended, the party was declared illegal, and eight of its top leaders were taken into custody, most receiving jail terms.

At a time when many regarded new union organization as impossible, the Workers' Unity League was making strides. It established organization in the needle trades, among woods workers, miners, longshoremen, and fishermen, and in the boot and shoe industry. Later the WUL spread to textiles, the furniture industry, and to some extent into steel, auto, and rubber. As a result of the League's efforts, union membership on an industrial basis was put within the reach of thousands of workers who until then had been largely ignored.

Then in 1935, again in line with official Communist Party policy, the WUL began promoting a 'United Front', abandoning its independent organizational efforts and turning over groups it controlled to the newly-formed CIO. Communists have always been extremely agile in performing this sort of somersault.

The earlier stance had been demonstrated in the western coalfields, where there was bitter competition between the United Mine Workers and a national organization, the Mine Workers'

Union of Canada. The WUL entered the picture and in 1930 declared its intention

> . . . to unite the miners of all camps into the Mine Workers' Union of Canada on the basis of the struggle against the operators, to smash the United Mine Workers and to smash the leadership of the MWUC, to transform the MWUC into a militant union fighting for the local of the MWUC. [120]

One of the most serious strikes of the decade was at Estevan, Saskatchewan, where the miners had affiliated to the WUL. Recognition of the union was a primary issue, as it was in many other disputes at that time. There were also complaints about low rates, violations of the Mines Act, short-selling practices, and discrimination.

When the men went on strike in 1931, strikebreakers were imported, but mass picketing kept the mines idle. The strikers, with their wives, planned a parade in Estevan for 29 September. Police reinforcements were sent to the area, and the Mayor issued an order forbidding the parade. This information reached the strike headquarters, but there is some dispute as to whether or not it was passed on to the strikers.

In any event the parade took place, and fighting broke out, lasting for almost an hour. Three miners were killed, and a number of strikers, police, and bystanders were injured. Eight strike leaders were later given jail sentences. A commission, which drafted the agreement that ended the strike, made a number of recommendations for improvements in conditions.

Estevan was one of a series of strikes in the West, many of them accompanied by violence. At Corbin, B.C., there were injuries when police drove a bulldozer into a picket line of coal-miners' wives.

Longshoremen, seamen, and others in allied occupations were involved in a hard-fought dispute on the Pacific coast, and the WUL's organization of fishermen and fish-cannery workers brought about work stoppages. On Vancouver Island 2,300 woods workers staged a four-month strike in their struggle for recognition of the Lumber Workers' International Union, a WUL affiliate. At Flin Flon, Manitoba, another WUL union struck over recognition. In Ontario there was trouble at the Lakehead, Nipigon, and Sault Ste Marie.

In Montreal, jurisdictional struggles between unions complicated the conflict between employees and employers. The United Clothing Workers of Canada, a left-wing organization, was battling with the Amalgamated Clothing Workers for the loyalty of some 3,000 to 4,000 workers. The UCW won the first round after a strike, but a year later there was a second strike, and the Amalgamated came out on top. The growing strength and militancy of the Canadian and Catholic Confederation of Labour provided an additional challenge to international unions in Quebec.

By no means all the violence of the period could be laid on the doorstep of the Communist Party. With the new fighting spirit in the CCL, there was resentment not only concerning wages and working conditions but also over control of Quebec industry by English-speaking management, much of it American. In some instances church authorities, largely in the hope of maintaining peace, entered into new agreements with management on behalf of the union without consulting the membership. This undercut the strength of the CCL and created divisions between some of the union members and the Roman Catholic Church.

Unrest became general throughout the country. Strikes during 1937 reached a record exceeded only by that of 1919. The trouble centre shifted from parts of the country where such primary industries as mining and logging were dominant to Central Canada, where the manufacturing industries of Ontario and Quebec were expanding and where the idea of industrial unionism was taking hold.

The most significant industrial struggle of the 1930s was the auto workers' strike at the General Motors plant in Oshawa, Ontario, which is part of the story of the rise of the CIO (see Chapter 16).

Politically, the outstanding event of the decade was the founding of the Co-operative Commonwealth Federation. The Ginger Group had made an impact on the House of Commons out of all proportion to its numbers. As early as 1926 Woodsworth had taken advantage of a balance of power position to push Mackenzie King into the introduction of Canada's first old age pension plan.

Within the little parliamentary group and elsewhere, there was recognition of the need for a more structured approach, uniting those who shared generally similar political views. A group of faculty members at McGill and the University of Toronto had been instrumental in starting the League for Social Reconstruction, which arranged lectures and discussions on economic and political subjects. There was a new political interest and, in western Canada, another effort to establish farmer-labour co-operation.

In August 1932 about a hundred delegates representing various bodies, most of them from the West, met in the Calgary Labour Temple and decided to form a political party to be known by the somewhat awesome name, 'Co-operative Commonwealth Federation; Farmer-Labour, Socialist'. Little wonder that its identification soon boiled down to CCF. The only trade unionist of any stature attending was Mosher of the Canadian Brotherhood of Railway Employees. A list of objectives was prepared as the basis for study and discussion and for consideration at the founding convention, which was to be held in Regina in mid-July 1933.

The declaration of principles then adopted became known as the 'Regina Manifesto'. It included the statement that:

> No CCF government will rest content until it has eradicated capitalism and put into operation the full program of socialized planning which will lead to the establishment in Canada of the Co-operative Commonwealth. [121]

This led to charges that the CCF was Communist-dominated. Woodsworth, who was the party's leader, made his position clear with the statement that:

> The CCF advocates peaceful and orderly methods. In this we distinguish ourselves sharply from the Communist Party which envisages the new social order as being ushered in by violent upheaval and the establishment of a dictatorship. The decision as to how capitalism will be overthrown may of course not lie in our hands. Continued bungling and exploitation, callous disregard of

the needs and sufferings of the people, and the exercise of repressive measures, may bring either the collapse or riots, or both. But in Canada we believe it is possible to avoid chaos and bloodshed which in some countries have characterized economic and social revolutions.[122]

The following year there were serious disruptions in the Ontario branch of the party as a result of Communist infiltrations. The public airing of this conflict frightened off a number of prospective supporters, particularly farmers.

Organized labour's reaction to the new party was slow. Woodsworth had recognized labour's political role in his Regina address when he said:

> The CCF is essentially a drawing together of the common people. The more intelligent and aggressive members of the labour movement have rather prided themselves as being 'class conscious', but too often they have been only group conscious and even then their ideas were projected from a mental background quite divorced from Canadian realities. In a country not predominantly industrial a labour party could not, unaided, hope to obtain power. Further, the technological and financial developments demand the adoption of new ideas, new types of organization and a new technique.[123]

Within the Trades and Labour Congress there was an undercurrent of support for the CCF, but it was a minority opinion. The majority adhered to the traditional policy of political independence. The Communists in the Congress wanted to support only parties which followed the Communist Party line.

It was not until 1938 that the Nova Scotia District of the United Mine Workers became the first union to affiliate to the CCF. Only then was a formal link established with organized labour; the relationship was, however, one which was to continue and to grow.

16 Craft *vs* Industrial Unions

The conflict between craft and industrial unionism, which harked back to the days of the Knights of Labour, the Industrial Workers of the World, and the One Big Union, was never-ending. Beyond the strictly practical aspects, it involved basic philosophic differences. At one extreme were the business unionists, who saw their responsibility as protection of the craft and the obtaining of periodic improvements in wages and conditions. At the other extreme were those who regarded the labour movement as a social force striving for the betterment of all mankind. It was essential to the second purpose that union organization should be extended to the hundreds of thousands of employees in the mass-production industries, most of whom were not craftsmen in the accepted sense.

While it was in the United States that the new drive for indus-trial unionism first surfaced, the sentiments of those behind it were shared by many Canadians. As has been seen, repeated efforts to have the Trades and Labour Congress move in that direction had failed, but the desire remained.

Union organization in United States factories had been ac-tively encouraged by President Franklin D. Roosevelt. Under his administration the National Labor Relations Act, more com-monly known as the Wagner Act, required employers to bargain in good faith and to refrain from discriminating against em-ployees because of union activity.

Impatience of the workers with the American Federation of Labor was mounting. In 1935 John L. Lewis, president of the United Mine Workers, openly attacked the AFL leadership for its failure to respond to the demands for organizational expansion, but the policy remained unchanged. The promoters of industrial unionism pressed on, and soon new unions began appearing in such industries as auto, steel, and rubber. Within the AFL some unions which were already rather more industrial than craft joined the campaign.

By November 1935 the Committee for Industrial Organization — later the Congress of Industrial Organizations — had been formed, and the CIO was in business. Its purpose was 'to encourage and promote organization of workers in the mass-production and unorganized industries', and it was intended to be affiliated to the AFL.

The first big test came in Akron, Ohio, when the Goodyear Corporation refused to recognize the new Rubber Workers' Union. A strike lasted five weeks before the company gave in.

Management resistance to this new wave of unionism was strong. The Steel Workers' Organizing Committee, forerunner of the United Steelworkers, organized employees of Republic Steel at South Chicago and obtained a National Labor Relations Board order for recognition, but the company refused to have anything to do with the union.

A strike followed, and as a demonstration of the union's strength, a parade was arranged for Memorial Day. A force of 150 police showed up and broke up the demonstration, using firearms. Ten of the strikers were killed, seven of them shot in the back, apparently while they were trying to escape. More than a hundred were injured. A Senate inquiry found that the strikers had been quite within their rights in holding the parade and the attack by the police was unprovoked. The Memorial Day Massacre has a permanent place in the history of North American union organization.

Such opposition failed to dampen the ardour of those who saw the dawn of a new day. The letters 'CIO' took on a magic aura and offered new hopes to those whose wages were low and working conditions poor; and the wave of enthusiasm which was sweeping the United States soon spread into Canada.

But the attitude of the craft unions toward the new organizations toughened, and in 1936 the American Federation of

Labor suspended several unions on charges of dual unionism —
the promotion of organizations in jurisdictional conflict with AFL
affiliates. State federations of labour and local labour councils
were ordered to refuse recognition to delegates from these organizations. Then in 1938, charters of the offending unions were
revoked.

This created an extremely difficult situation for the Trades and
Labour Congress in Canada, where there were strong demands
for recognition of the new groups, regardless of the AFL policy.
The TLC's president, P. M. Draper, tried to provide a middle
course by giving an interpretation of the constitution which, he
said, accommodated both craft and industrial unions. He maintained that it was the intention of the constitution to allow union
members to decide the type of organization they wanted and
that either was acceptable to the Congress.

It proved not quite as simple as that, and by the time the TLC's
1937 convention rolled around, the reality of the AFL's orders
had to be faced. The TLC was not anxious to unseat delegates
from the unions which were in trouble with the AFL, but neither
had it any desire to arouse the anger of the AFL by allowing them
to remain in the Congress, a position which it was feared might
lead to the withdrawal of international unions.

The TLC executive was instructed to meet with AFL officers in
an attempt to clarify the situation. Desire among Canadian
unionists for a healing of the differences was strong, and there
were even suggestions that the TLC might act as a mediator. But
events had gone far beyond that point, and when the TLC
officers went to Washington they were given a message that was
crystal clear.

They returned home to report that they had been made fully
aware of the consequences if they failed to expel the unions
which were in bad grace with the AFL. It would 'lead to almost
complete disorganization of the Congress as it has been established since 1902'.

The executive was polled, and seven organizations were suspended, the final action to rest with the next convention. The
unions affected were: United Mine Workers, Amalgamated Clothing Workers, International Union of Fur and Leather Workers,

International Union of Quarry Workers, United Automobile Workers, Steel Workers' Organizing Committee, and Mine, Mill and Smelter Workers. Altogether they had about 22,000 members.

The 1939 convention upheld the executive's action and ordered the unions expelled, but only after a lengthy debate. The desire for unity was much stronger in Canada than in the United States, but the AFL's ultimatum carried the day for the craft group.

Draper was not at the convention; he was ill and intended retiring. R. J. Tallon, the secretary-treasurer, spoke for the executive and was frank in explaining the position the Congress was in:

> They [the CIO] set up a definite movement, dual and in opposition to the AFL. We had already been notified by some of our affiliated international unions that they refused to remit tax on their Canadian membership if affiliation of CIO unions was continued; and others had instructed their executive officers to take similar action. . . .
>
> The question for you as delegates to decide is whether you are going to be inside this Congress, or on the outside watching other organizations than your own constituting its membership. You might as well know right now where you fit in.[124]

Tallon rejected suggestions that the AFL had applied pressure on the TLC; rather, he said, the message had come from individual international unions. The distinction was a fine one. There was a roll-call vote on the expulsion resolution, and it was adopted, 231-98. The split between craft and industrial unions had separated the Canadian labour movement into two parts.

A CIO office had been opened in Toronto in 1937, with Silby Barrett of the United Mine Workers in charge. Even before this there had been some organizational activity, including a tragic experience at the Holmes Foundry at Sarnia, Ontario. This was a plant with about 375 employees. The Steel Workers' Organizing Committee had been approached for help, and an organizer, Milton Montgomery, was sent to Sarnia. From the outset there seemed little chance of success, but Montgomery signed up about a quarter of the employees, most of them Europeans. Within the plant there was hostility between the native Canadians and those they called 'hunkies'.

The new union members, becoming impatient, decided to call a sit-down strike, a method which had been used with some success in the United States. Employees simply sat down at their work places and stayed there indefinitely. The theory was that this reduced the possibility of violence and made it difficult for the employer to use strikebreakers. That was not the way it worked at the Holmes Foundry.

A group of non-striking employees, armed with clubs, invaded the factory, beating the strikers and chasing them out. A number were injured, some seriously. Sarnia police refused to intervene, explaining that the foundry was on a side of the street outside their jurisdiction and that by crossing the street they would jeopardize their insurance protection. Several of the sit-down strikers were charged with trespassing, but no charges were laid against those who had made the attack.

Canada's first sit-down strike had failed, and so had efforts to establish a CIO union at the Holmes Foundry. Elsewhere SWOC was more successful, establishing itself at an early stage in Nova Scotia and later in several Ontario and Quebec communities.

The most dramatic CIO success was in the organization of automobile workers at the General Motors plant at Oshawa. The American Federation of Labor had started a craft union among a group of trimmers in 1927, but it lasted only a few months. In 1936 pieceworkers were making from ninety cents to a dollar an hour and day workers only forty-five cents an hour. A fifty-nine hour week was usual, and at peak periods it might be sixty-five hours, all at straight rates with no overtime paid. Discontent was high.

In April 1937 some 4,000 employees struck for recognition of their new CIO union and a number of improvements in wages and conditions. The situation quickly developed into much more than an ordinary strike. Ontario's premier was Mitchell Hepburn, a man who held some strong views on labour, despite the fact that his industrial relations experience had been restricted to his onion farm at St Thomas.

At the time of the Holmes Foundry strike Hepburn had declared:

> My sympathies are with those who fought the strikers. Those who participate in sit-down strikes are trespassers, and trespassing is illegal in this province. This government is going to maintain law and order. [125]

He saw a threat far more serious at Oshawa and said he was prepared to use the province's entire resources to smash the CIO:

> The issue is not wages. The issue is whether or not agitators are to be allowed in Ontario to defy our laws. This is part of a Communist plot to smash our economy and we will not tolerate it. [126]

Behind all this was a close personal friendship between Hepburn and the owners of some of the province's largest mines, an influence which was apparent in his warning: 'Let me tell Lewis and his gang here and now that they'll never get their greedy paws on the mines of Northern Ontario'. The management of two of the largest mines — McIntyre Porcupine and Hollinger — said they would close down the operations before they would deal with a CIO union.

Hepburn decided the way to break the Oshawa strike was by a show of strength, and he asked the federal government to send in a detachment of a hundred RCMP. When this force had no immediate effect, he asked for another hundred, and those the federal authorities refused. Hepburn then told Ottawa to take the RCMP out, and he proceeded to recruit a special police force of his own, mainly veterans and university students, numbering about 400. Toronto's Eglinton Hunt Club made sixty horses available to them. The amateur policemen became the subject of a good deal of humour, being referred to as 'Hepburn's Hussars' and 'The Sons of Mitch's'.

There had not been a single act of violence, and throughout the strike there was not one arrest. Oshawa's Mayor, Alex Hall, was not amused by the Premier's actions. He wired him an invitation to visit Oshawa 'to see first hand the behaviour of the men and the remarkable condition of law and order existing'.

The political repercussions were sizable. Two members of Hepburn's cabinet resigned — Arthur Roebuck, the Attorney-General, and David Croll, Minister of Labour. In his letter of resignation Croll said he would 'rather walk with the workers than ride with General Motors'. George Drew, then the Conservative Party's director of organization in Ontario, split with his leader, Earl Rowe, who supported the right of the workers to have their union. Drew ran as an independent in the next election.

General Motors had signed an agreement with the United Auto Workers in the United States but refused to deal with it in Canada because of its international nature. Eventually the union modified its demands, and the strike was ended. The company had maintained its position concerning formal recognition of the UAW, though the negotiations which led to a settlement involved a committee from the union.

George Burt, then a worker in the Oshawa plant and later Canadian director of the UAW, recalled:

> We struck for recognition, an agreement, wage increases, and adjustment of piece work rates, seniority and a grievance procedure. We won everything, except we failed to gain recognition of the union. The name of the UAW was not mentioned at all in the contract, although the company knew with whom they were bargaining; and they did meet with an international representative. The first contract was signed in Hepburn's office in Toronto. Charlie Millard was there, along with the Local 222 (UAW) committee.[127]

Millard was the first president of the Oshawa local; he was later to become the CIO representative in Canada and then Canadian director of the United Steelworkers. He saw the Oshawa experience as having important political implications, explaining:

> In those days we were long on enthusiasm and short on experience. At Oshawa we certainly had a baptism of political fire; and since I have often wondered if Mr Hepburn and the old parties he represented ever realized what they were doing by putting the unions into politics, whether or not they wanted to be.[128]

The Oshawa settlement was followed by similar agreements at General Motors plants in St Catharines and Windsor; but it was not until 1942, when Ford signed an agreement, that any of the Big Three auto manufacturers gave formal recognition to the UAW. Labour regarded Oshawa as a great victory, but the immediate aftereffects were anticlimactic. Several smaller strikes were lost, and the momentum of organization slowed down. The CIO was short on both funds and experience. Hepburn's success at the polls in an election which followed a short time later indicated that he, rather than the union, had public support.

Nevertheless there was progress, particularly in the rubber, meat-packing, and steel industries. The United Rubber Workers opened an educational and social centre at Kitchener, Ontario, and after a month-long strike won recognition and contracts with two companies — Merchants' and Dominion. A seven-week strike against Kaufman Rubber at Kitchener failed, and the union has never been able to organize the Kaufman workers, despite several attempts. By 1939 the Rubber Workers' Union had contracts with Goodyear, including one with a large plant at New Toronto.

In British Columbia the AFL-CIO differences renewed a jurisdictional struggle in the organization of woods and sawmill workers. When the Workers' Unity League tried to get its woodworkers' union to affiliate with the Carpenters, a new organization, called the Federation of Woodworkers, was created on both sides of the border. This group joined the CIO and changed its name to the International Woodworkers of America. It was soon involved in an unusually rough strike at Blubber Bay, lasting eleven months and marked by outbreaks of violence and eviction of employees from company-owned houses.

Co-ordination of the new industrial unions in Canada was through a CIO committee which by 1939 claimed to represent 55,000 workers in sixteen different unions. The following year representatives of the CIO unions in Canada and the All-Canadian Congress of Labour met in Toronto to found a new central body, the Canadian Congress of Labour.

It is not only politics that makes strange bedfellows. The ACCL had been a sharp critic of international unions; but Mosher, who was elected president of the new Congress, was apparently satisfied that the CIO unions in Canada would enjoy a much higher degree of autonomy than had the international unions in the Trades and Labour Congress. Throughout its history the CCL's relationship with its American counterpart, the CIO, would differ from that existing between the TLC and the AFL. At no time did the CIO try to dominate Canadian affairs, and the individual CIO unions in Canada operated with much greater independence than those affiliated with the AFL. The new Congress had a keener interest in political matters than the TLC and was more active in promoting union organization.

The unions which joined in forming the Canadian Congress of Labour in 1940 included: Canadian Brotherhood of Railway Employees; United Mine Workers; Amalgamated Clothing Workers; Steel Workers' Organizing Committee; United Rubber Workers; United Auto Workers; United Electrical Workers; United Packinghouse Workers; International Union of Mine, Mill and Smelter Workers; American Newspaper Guild; National Union of Operating Engineers; Canadian Association of Railwaymen; and Canadian Electrical Union.

The divisions had become more sharply defined. With the arrival of the CIO and the creation of the Canadian Congress of Labour, there was a new vehicle for those whose ambitions went beyond the restrictions of craft unionism. In the years ahead they were to use this to exert considerable influence on the course of organized labour in Canada.

17 World War II and After

The CIO unions and their new Congress were barely established when the country was plunged into another war. With it came drastic economic changes, new approaches in labour legislation, and complications for management, which, while still opposed to the new industrial unions, faced mounting demands for war production.

There had been an economic slump, but the unemployment rate of 11 per cent in 1938 was quickly replaced by a labour shortage. It was the old story — war meant work.

Canadian union membership lagged behind that in the United States — 17.5 per cent of the Canadian labour force in 1940 to 24.8 per cent in the United States. The growth of unions in the mass-production industries was proportionately slow. Employer resistance was higher in Canada than in the United States, and there was still officially no outright endorsation of collective bargaining.

In a study prepared for the Royal Commission on Dominion-Provincial Relations in 1939, A. E. Grauer commented:

> The hostile attitude of many employers to collective bargaining has defeated the chief purpose of unions in organizing to bring about greater equality in bargaining power. . . .
> A considerable number of strikes and substantial loss of working time has been occasioned by disputes over recognition of unions or dismissals for union activity; and . . . disputes from these causes have increased rather than diminished in recent years.[129]

Such statutory support as there was for the principles of organizing and bargaining was largely negative. In 1939 the Criminal Code was amended, making it an offence for an employer to employ or dismiss an employee solely because of his union membership. The explanation was that, since employees were within the law in forming unions and bargaining collectively,

> . . . it should, as a matter of public policy, be unlawful for employers to seek by overt acts of intimidation, threat or conspiracy to prevent them from belonging to such unions.[130]

This was a left-handed endorsation, and it has always been difficult to give effect to this type of legislation. It is not hard for an employer to find some excuse to fire an employee for reasons other than union activity. It was not until 1972 that the federal statutes embraced a positive statement of support for collective bargaining.

During World War II a whole series of temporary orders and regulations was introduced in an effort to keep industrial disputes to a minimum, to quickly settle those which did occur, and to maintain a high level of production. The Industrial Disputes Investigation Act was extended to cover all war industries, a term which was interpreted broadly. The government's overall policy was spelled out in an Order-in-Council — P.C. 2685 — which recommended acceptance of fair and reasonable standards of wages and working conditions. The order recognized the right to organize and favoured the settlement of disputes through negotiations or, failing that, through the government's conciliation services. It also recommended the inclusion of a grievance procedure in all collective agreements to provide a method of dealing with differences which might arise during the term of the contract.

Organized labour had initially shown much greater support for the war effort than it had at the outset of World War I, but before long there was a growing uneasiness in union circles. While there was not outright opposition to the cause, except for a time from the Communist faction, there was disillusionment with the effectiveness of regulations applying to wages and industrial relations generally.

One bone of contention was the Order-in-Council which defined the government's policy on wages — P.C. 7440. Originally this applied only in war industries, but it was later extended to almost all forms of employment. The intention was to provide a guide for conciliation boards and a buffer against rising living costs. In general, wages in the 1926-9 period were to be accepted as the base, and adjustments from that point were to be in accordance with variations in the Dominion Bureau of Statistics Cost-of-Living Index.

When the order was broadened to cover all employees, the base date was changed to November 1941, and a structure of War Labour Boards, national and regional, was established for administrative purposes. Later the wage formula was dropped, and increases were to be authorized only where there was evidence of gross injustice or in instances which would not result in price increases; in other words there was a form of wage freeze.

This meant that normal collective bargaining was suspended and unions had to argue their case before a War Labour Board rather than across the bargaining table. They were quick to accuse employers of taking advantage of the situation, and there was a flood of complaints of wages having been frozen at low levels.

Organized labour's position was complicated by the actions of the Communist Party, which had at first opposed the war effort and adopted disruptive tactics. When Germany invaded the Soviet Union, the party swung to the other extreme and attempted to force unions into no-strike pledges, and a running battle followed. In the United States, unions had adopted a no-strike policy when that country entered the war, but Canadian unions insisted on retaining greater freedom of action.

One of the first wartime strikes involved employees of Peck Rolling Mills at Montreal, who argued that if there was to be regulation of wages then national uniformity should be established. The rates being paid the steelworkers at the Montreal plant were considerably below those in steel mills at Hamilton,

Sault Ste Marie, and Sydney. The War Labour Board gave a majority decision disagreeing with the idea of uniformity, but the matter of national wage standards was an increasingly important issue.

Dissatisfaction with both conditions and the regulations was at the root of a number of strikes. The management of National Steel Car at Hamilton refused to co-operate in a government-supervised vote to determine whether or not the employees wanted to be represented by the Steel Workers' Organizing Committee. The employees struck, and the government placed the company under a controller to avoid a halt in production. The vote was held, with SWOC an easy winner, but then the government controller refused to negotiate with the union. He was replaced, and eventually the union was recognized. It was obvious that employer resistance was not only continuing, but was at times being placed above the war effort.

Another example of employer opposition involved 2,800 gold miners at Kirkland Lake, Ontario. The fears Hepburn had expressed concerning a CIO invasion of northern Ontario's gold mines were well founded. The International Union of Mine, Mill and Smelter Workers organized the miners and struck when the companies refused to have any dealings with the union. There was an effort to introduce the old Mackenzie King type of 'employees' committee'; but the men rejected the idea, and a Conciliation Board was appointed to seek a solution. The Board was unanimous in recommending that the companies recognize the union, but they still refused. The men were equally determined, and a strike went on for three months. It was lost, but not before many of the miners had learned some lessons. Kirkland Lake's picket lines were a breeding ground for an unusual number of union leaders, by no means the least of whom was Larry Sefton, who became one of the top officers of the United Steelworkers.

The war placed union leaders in a delicate position, and they were keenly aware of it. They shared in the prevailing spirit of patriotism and support for the forces fighting overseas; but at the same time they felt a responsibility to protect the interests of their members and prevent exploitation under the waving of flags. Participation was essential at the level where policies governing industrial relations were made. Labour representatives were placed on some boards and commissions, but they were subject to continual sniping from the Communists on the one hand and the autocratic pronouncements of wartime bureaucrats on the other.

Complaints built up, causing more work stoppages. In 1943 some 21,000 Montreal aircraft workers left their jobs in the largest strike since Winnipeg in 1919. There was more trouble in the coalfields, a matter of vital concern because of the importance of coal in the war effort.

Government concern mounted, and the National War Labour Board was instructed to make a full-scale investigation of industrial relations. There was a four-month delay in the publication of the Board's report while new legislation was drafted; then the report formed the basis of a new Order-in-Council — P.C. 1003 — which gave a new degree of recognition to organization and bargaining. It also provided machinery for defining bargaining units and certifying unions as recognized bargaining agencies. When the authorized process had been followed, the employer was required to bargain in good faith. A conciliation procedure was provided for disputes. If that failed, the order affirmed the right to strike, except during the life of an agreement. In brief, the unions had gained a new status. About the same time, British Columbia amended its legislation to clarify the status of unions, providing for recognition, conciliation, and the discouragement of company unions.

With the end of the war there was an easing of pressures. Emergency controls remained in effect for some time, however, partially as a method of coping with the economic problems involved in the conversion from a war to a peacetime economy.

Fear of a postwar depression created an atmosphere of uncertainty, and unions were still suffering from a deep sense of insecurity arising from employer opposition. This was nowhere more apparent than at Windsor, Ontario, where Ford Motor Company employees went on strike in 1945 in an effort to gain security for their union. They wanted an agreement which would require all employees to hold union membership, with their dues collected by a check-off system of payroll deductions. This was a lesser form of security than the 'closed shop' common in many agreements with craft unions. Under the closed shop arrangement an employer could hire only people who were already members of the union. A 'union shop' contract left the employer free to hire at will but required union membership once the employee had become established. It was the Ford strike that brought about what became known as 'The Rand Formula', which established principles of union security.

Ford had signed a union shop agreement with the United Auto Workers at its Detroit operations just across the river from Windsor. Rates there were also considerably higher. In Canada the company refused similar security to the same union, with the explanation that the Canadian union leadership was 'irresponsible'.

The strike started on 12 September 1945 and lasted ninety-nine days. From the outset the union adopted a hard line. Pickets prevented supervisory personnel from entering the company property, and later a motor blockade was set up, cutting off several streets and keeping hundreds of cars, buses, and trucks trapped for days on end.

Both federal and provincial authorities intervened, but they were unable to move either side. The Canadian Congress of Labour tried to find a settlement formula, but there was internal dissension when some left-wing UAW members tried to call a national sympathy strike, a tactic which the CCL leaders strongly opposed.

The final solution was acceptance of an arbitrator, whose finding was to be final and binding on both parties. Mr Justice Ivan Rand, a member of the Supreme Court of Canada, was chosen for the difficult task. His report did not go as far as the UAW wished, but it was considerably beyond the company position. Rand proposed a moderate form of union security which, sometimes with variations, was to become a part of hundreds of union contracts. In essence the Rand Formula gave the union security through the compulsory payment of dues by all employees in the unit concerned, but left the individuals free to decide whether or not they would actually become union members. The collection of dues was to be made by the company through a check-off. A government-supervised vote of all employees was required before there could be a strike, and penalties were specified for unauthorized, or wildcat, strikes.

The principles involved in the Rand report are fundamental to labour-management relations; seldom has there been a comparable treatise. Rand's concern was with 'social justice in the area of industrial mass production', and his objective was 'to secure industrial civilization . . . based on a rational economic and social doctrine'.

His premise was that the organization of employees into unions and the practice of collective bargaining were socially desirable; and it followed that 'unions should become strong in order to carry on the functions for which they are intended'.

There was, however, need for counterchecks to establish a balance between capital and labour and some form of law to accommodate the relationship. Rand continued:

> The organization of labour must in a civilized manner be elaborated and strengthened for its essential function in an economy of private enterprise. For this there must be an enlightened leadership at the top and democratic control at the bottom. The absolutist notion of property like national sovereignty must be modified and the social involvement of industry must be in the setting in which reconciliation with the interests of labour and public takes place. This means the rationalization of the individual industrial organism. . . . Hitherto the tendency has been to treat labour as making demands quite unwarranted on any basis of democratic freedom in relation to property and business, and the ordinary mode of settling labour disputes, a piecemeal concession in appeasement.[131]

He was critical of both the company and the union in the Ford dispute, speaking of labour being purchased as a commodity and of an arm's-length relationship which engendered tension and hostility. The union was criticized for its illegal picketing. Preventing access to the plant had been 'a supreme stupidity' and the motor blockade, 'an insolent flouting of civil order'. On the other hand the judge showed some understanding of the motivation:

> There was exasperation and provocation, and these actions seem to indicate the intensity of conviction on the part of the men that fair demands were being met only by stolid negativism. No one attempts to justify these actions, but a strike is not a tea party and when passions are deeply aroused civilized restraints go by the board unless the powers of order are summoned to vindicate them. Illegal action is for the civil authorities to deal with.[132]

He rejected the allegations of irresponsible leadership and suggested that those within the union who opposed Communist methods were deserving of support.

Union security was defined as 'simply security in the maintenance of the strength and integrity of the union'. While not prepared to go as far as supporting a straight union shop, Rand held that all employees were beneficiaries of the union's effort and had an obligation to share the responsibility. He elaborated:

> I doubt if any circumstance provokes more resentment in a plant than this sharing of the fruits of unionist work and courage by the non-union member. . . .
> The company in this case admits that substantial benefits for the employees have been obtained by the union, some in negotiation and some over the opposition of the company. . . .
> I consider it entirely equitable then that all employees should be required to shoulder their portion of the burden of expense for administering the law of their employment, the union contract; that they must take the burden along with the benefit.[133]

He argued further that the payment of dues should tend to induce actual membership in the union and this, in turn, to widen interest and participation. The union would be spurred to justify itself to the dues-paying employees.

The timing of the Ford case was important to labour. The postwar uncertainties had led to a get-it-while-you-can attitude. The Canadian Congress of Labour had broken some new ground by establishing a Wage Co-ordinating Committee among its affiliates. Recognizing the complete autonomy of each union in its bargaining relationships, the committee was purely consultative, but it provided a valuable means of exchanging information which might be useful in the formulation of bargaining strategy.

A 1946 province-wide strike by the International Woodworkers of America in British Columbia was seen by many as an attempt on the part of the Canadian Congress of Labour to establish a national wage pattern. There were also strikes in rubber, electrical appliances, meat packing, and newspaper publishing. An unsuccessful strike by the International Typographical Union in an attempt to establish chain-wide bargaining with the Southam newspapers lasted almost three years.

There was considerable union activity in the basic steel industry. At the Dominion Steel and Coal Corporation's Sydney mill the success of the Steel Workers' Organizing Committee ranked as one of the union's first major victories, and dues paid by the Sydney workers helped organization in other steel towns in both the United States and Canada. The company had at first rejected the union, and the dispute which followed resulted in the adoption of the Nova Scotia Trade Union Act, which provided a greater degree of recognition for unions.

At the Algoma Mill in Sault Ste Marie, SWOC displaced an independent employees' organization; but at the Steel Company of Canada at Hamilton the union ran into greater difficulty. When a national basic steel strike was called in 1946, seeking wage increases and the establishment of uniform rates, there was considerable resistance among Stelco employees. Those who refused to join the strike stayed on the job and were housed in the mill. Airplanes and boats were involved in spectacular picket-line activity, as the strikers tried to make life difficult for those who were still working. The outcome of the strike was substantial wage increases, which applied in all three centres.

Union efforts in the meat-packing industry were also on a national scale, culminating in a national strike in 1947. This dispute pointed up the difficulties arising from the divided provincial jurisdictions in cases in which both the companies and the union were national entities.

But one of the most significant labour struggles of the decade was at the small Quebec community of Asbestos. A strike there by the Canadian and Catholic Confederation of Labour demonstrated more than any other event the new spirit within the CCCL. The National Federation of Asbestos Employees of Quebec, a CCCL affiliate, had been in existence for a number of years but was docile and relatively ineffective. In 1949 the company showed an unusually good profit position, and the time seemed ripe to go after substantial wage increases. The employer was the Johns-Manville Company, a large international corporation which was much in the favour of Maurice Duplessis, the Quebec Premier who governed the province with the characteristics of a dictator and who looked with disfavour on the changing attitude of the CCCL.

No sooner had the strike been called than the government declared it to be illegal and decertified the union, ruling that it was no longer entitled to represent the employees. Ties between the Church and the Duplessis government were close, but in this instance the Church aligned itself with the strikers. Although there had been no violence, special squads of police were sent to the area. The Asbestos Town Council later condemned the Quebec Provincial Police for episodes of drunkenness, indecent behaviour, and unprovoked attacks on the strikers.

Prominent among the union leaders was Jean Marchand, a CCCL official who later became a member of the Cabinet in the Trudeau government. The provincial Minister of Labour offered to meet a delegation of strikers, but only on condition that Marchand be excluded. The strikers refused the invitation. The company recruited strikebreakers and announced a general wage increase. Strikers were invited to return to work at the higher rates and were told that when the strike was over those who had crossed picket lines would get preferential treatment.

Still the strikers remained solid, and sympathy for them spread. In an unusual demonstration of unity the Trades and Labour Congress and the Canadian Congress of Labour joined in supporting the strikers.

As feelings mounted, there was violence, and a mass riot was averted only by the intervention of church and union officials. On one occasion police broke into a church hall and arrested strikers who were sleeping there; others were arrested at their homes or on the streets. This inspired still greater support from outside.

The strike lasted five months, until it was finally brought to an end through mediation efforts initiated by the Church. There was a wage increase of ten cents an hour and a guarantee that strikers would be taken back without discrimination. The mere fact that they had survived so long against the odds of the large international corporation and the autocratic Duplessis government was in itself a major victory. The Canadian and Catholic Confederation of Labour had won new prestige and respect.

A strike of non-operating railway employees in 1950 was the first national stoppage involving both the Canadian National and Canadian Pacific railways. It followed negotiations which had lasted for a year. Prime Minister Louis St Laurent hastily summoned Parliament, and special legislation was passed ordering the men back to work. The legislation imposed arbitration for the settlement of issues which could not be agreed upon in further negotiations.

The St Laurent government adopted a policy which was to be followed by other administrations. It was made clear that the legislation was to be considered an emergency measure and not a precedent for such disputes as might occur in the future. The laws did, however, establish a pattern which has become firmly established insofar as the railways and their employees are concerned and which has also had a bearing on disputes in other essential services.

The role of government as an intervener between employees and employers was coming more to the fore. Of more immediate concern to many unionists, however, was the rising political pressure of differences within their movement.

18 The Power Struggle

Political differences within the labour movement sharpened, and there was a no-holds-barred drive by the Communists to gain control of both the Canadian Congress of Labour and the Trades and Labour Congress. The influence of left-wing elements in some unions justified their being considered Communist-controlled, and these unions provided a base of operations within both central labour bodies. The power struggle pushed other differences into the background and resulted in some seemingly contradictory situations. For example, the Communists were far more successful in gaining power in the conservative TLC than in the CCL, which was considered to lean to the left.

The political positions of the two congresses remained poles apart. The TLC stuck to its hands-off attitude toward politics, while the CCL was becoming more involved with the CCF. Neither position gave immunity from the Communist problem. Within each congress there were varying outlooks, which were reflected in the personalities of some of the union leaders of the time.

The TLC's president, Percy Bengough, was believed to personally favour the Liberal Party, though officially he adhered to the Gompers line and carefully avoided open association with any party. This was highly satisfactory to the Communist elements in the TLC. This was not the only occasion on which the

Communists showed concern that a party moderately to the left, such as the CCF, might attract support from some who might otherwise be enticed into the Communist Party. Knowing that outright endorsation of their own party was beyond reach, they favoured a non-partisan position, or even qualified support for the Liberals or Conservatives, rather than endorsation of a party which they considered a closer rival.

The Communists' greatest strength was in the Canadian Seamen's Union, though they were also influential in the Machinists' and Textile unions. The seamen's organization was headed by Pat Sullivan, a prominent Communist who later became secretary-treasurer of the Trades and Labour Congress. Opposition to the TLC's Communist faction was led by Frank Hall, top Canadian officer of the Brotherhood of Railway and Steamship Clerks, Freight Handlers and Express and Station Employees. The success of the non-Communists was not helped by a running disagreement which existed between Hall and Bengough.

In the Canadian Congress of Labour the president, A. R. Mosher, and the secretary-treasurer, Pat Conroy, were both vehemently anti-Communist. Mosher was still in office as president of the Canadian Brotherhood of Railway Employees, and it fell largely to Conroy to be the front-line spokesman for the CCL. Charles Millard, Canadian director of the United Steelworkers, was also prominent in the anti-Communist group, but there was little love lost between him and Conroy.

Millard, it will be recalled, had been the first president of the Oshawa local of the Auto Workers. He was soon displaced by George Burt, who won his election with Communist support. Millard was one of the CCF's most ardent supporters, and combining missionary zeal with aggressive militancy, he pursued a course in which he saw the objectives of the CCL and those of the CCF as being one and the same.

Millard recruited staff from among young CCFers, many of whom were later prominent in the labour movement. The list included Eamon Park, Eileen Tallman, and Murray Cotterill of the United Steelworkers; Joseph MacKenzie in the Rubber Workers; Fred Dowling in Packinghouse Workers; and David

Archer, who became president of the Ontario Federation of Labour. In their formative years these and other unions frequently received much-needed assistance from the United Steelworkers of America.

Conroy was a pragmatic trade unionist. He had come from the Alberta coalfields, and as far as he was concerned, if the CCF could be helpful to the union cause, then it was deserving of support; but the union came first, and there was to be no doubt about that. He viewed Millard as an opportunist who not only had political ambitions but wanted to build his own empire within the labour movement to a degree which challenged Conroy's control of the CCL. This clash of personalities eventually brought about Conroy's resignation. He was later labour attaché at the Canadian Embassy in Washington for some years.

Within the CCL the most effective Communist spokesmen were Clarence Jackson and George Harris of the United Electrical Workers and Harvey Murphy of the International Union of Mine, Mill and Smelter Workers. Within the TLC there were fewer Communist Party members and less control of individual unions but far greater influence at the executive level. In the CCL the executive remained tightly in the hands of CCF supporters. In the early stages of World War II several unionists from both congresses were interned as Communists whose activities might be detrimental to the war effort.

As far as the bulk of the union membership was concerned, the complexities of this political in-fighting were not of very great interest. Many considered the quarrels to be little more than a clash of personalities, which they were; but they were also much more.

At the nub of the TLC's difficulties was the Canadian Seamen's Union, which had been founded in 1936 and which a few years later had 7,000 members on lake and deep-sea ships. Although a tool of the Communist Party, the CSU unquestionably did a great deal to improve the lot of sailors. It was finally killed by a combination of anti-Communist forces — labour, management, and government — and it was replaced by the Seafarers' International Union. Sullivan, president of the CSU, and Gerry McManus, secretary-treasurer, defected from the Communist

Party and publicly admitted that, acting under instructions, they had used the Seamen's Union for the party's purposes.

The TLC's Frank Hall had clashed with the CSU when he found some leaders of that organization attempting to induce his members to stage an illegal strike. Hall was a man who fought hard for his membership, but once a contract was signed, he was meticulous about its observance. He was furious at the CSU interference and determined to get rid of the organization.

Hall had considerable influence in international union circles, and he turned to Washington for help. The American Federation of Labor, without bothering to consult the TLC, ruled that the Seafarers' International Union should be given jurisdiction over all North American waters, making the CSU open to charges of dual unionism. At that time the SIU had a bare toehold in Canada, with 300 members at Vancouver. Bengough, resentful at the AFL's interference in a Canadian situation, threw his support behind the CSU, and his differences with Hall deepened.

Attempting to institute a system of three eight-hour watches instead of two watches of twelve hours, the CSU called a strike on the Great Lakes in 1946. The companies refused to negotiate and, under the terms of the wartime emergency measures which were still in effect, the government placed twenty-nine shipping companies under controllership. The National War Labour Board then ordered the introduction of eight-hour watches, and the companies signed agreements.

These agreements covered the 1947 shipping season but also included an undertaking to negotiate new agreements for 1948 if a vote showed that a majority of the sailors supported the CSU. The union won sweeping victories in votes on the Colonial and Sarnia line ships. No vote was conducted among employees of Canada Steamship Lines. But the agreements and the votes meant little, for pressure to kill the CSU was building.

When Sullivan resigned as president in 1947, he formed a new organization, the Canadian Lake Seamen's Union, and a few months later several of the companies announced they had severed their relations with the CSU and signed agreements with the new organization.

Two of the companies — Sarnia and Colonial — were sharply criticized by an Industrial Inquiry Commission, which investigated the whole affair. The commissioners accused the companies of breaking 'the admirable, long-established and beneficial practice' of negotiation. The TLC, still supporting the CSU, had offered to negotiate on behalf of the union, with three of the senior Congress officers acting as the bargaining committee, but the companies refused. The commissioners said the companies' attitude was intransigent, in defiance of the law, and a breach of existing agreements.

Canada Steamships had objected to a union which it said was under Communist control. The Commission commented:

> Although a company might see fit to take objection to the personal qualities or political opinions of officers or members of the union, until the law of the land made the public holding or expression of any political opinion illegal, no company could legally take upon itself the right to refuse to negotiate on these grounds.[134]

Nevertheless the Canada Labour Relations Board later revoked a certification of the Canadian Seamen's Union on the ground that, being Communist controlled and directed, it was no longer a trade union within the meaning of the Industrial Relations and Disputes Act.

With the opening of the 1948 navigation season the CSU did its best to prevent the sailing of ships manned by rival union crews. There were attacks on ships along the Welland Canal and at other points.

The CSU, which still had a few members on deep-sea ships, called a strike and enlisted support from dockworkers in Britain and other overseas ports. There were charges of a Communist plot to interfere with the shipment of goods being sent to Europe under the Marshall Plan to help war-ravaged countries. Again the CSU was defeated, and the Seafarers' International Union picked up its agreements. The SIU, which succeeded the CSU, fell into bad grace for other reasons, but that is a later story (see page 209).

In the summer of 1948 Sullivan had vacated the office of president of the new union (the Canadian Lake Seamen's Union) and departed for the Gatineau Hills outside Ottawa, where he purchased a hunting and fishing resort. Before disappearing into obscurity, he wrote a book giving an account of his experiences with the CSU and the Communist Party.

McManus left the labour scene to become a real estate agent in Toronto. In a magazine article written shortly after his defection from the Communist Party, he gave an insight into the relationship between the CSU and the party:

> I was also a member of the Communist Party which dictated — at every step and in every particular — the events which led to the union's bitter, inglorious ruin . . .
>
> In every one of a series of strikes from 1946 through 1949 which culminated in the CSU's downfall I obeyed the Communist Party's direct and specific orders, both in helping to call strikes and in helping to run them. . . .
>
> In strict accuracy there is no such thing as a Communist-dominated union. Once it falls under Communist domination a union ceases to be a union. It becomes a branch of the Communist Party.[135]

McManus estimated that fewer than 10 per cent of the members of the CSU were Communists but that the others were content to leave the running of the union to this minority. The scattered membership, difficulties of communication, and the complacency of the membership from which most unions suffer made the CSU's structure ideal for control by any well-organized faction.

After Sullivan's withdrawal, the Canadian Lake Seamen's Union merged with the Seafarers' International Union, and there was no difficulty in completing contracts with the shipping companies.

While the TLC was having its difficulties, things were also hectic within the CCL, though the pattern differed. There was continual sniping between the administration and the Communists. The Wage Co-ordinating Committee had collapsed, and Conroy blamed its failure on the disrupting tactics of left-wingers.

All that was needed for a clash of opinions was a platform. At conventions both sides held back-room caucuses to map strategy. Speakers were assigned and dutifully took their places at microphones to expound their particular viewpoints. In closed-door executive and committee meetings there was a continuous exchange of insults.

The CCF was making progress, and many of the arguments revolved around politics. In British Columbia the CCF became the official opposition in 1941; and the next year the party scored an important victory in the Toronto riding of York South, defeating one of the Conservative Party's leaders, Arthur Meighen. By 1943 the CCF had become the official opposition in Ontario, and of the thirty-four members elected to the Legislature, nineteen were trade unionists. The first CCF government was formed in Saskatchewan in 1944.

The CCFers who were part of the CCL hierarchy were anxious to use their influence to advance the party's cause, but they were nervous about pushing their luck too far. Regardless of the staunch party loyalty of those at the top, the vast majority of union membership had no more than a passing interest in political matters, and it was feared they might revolt against efforts to line them up behind a particular party. The Communists were well aware of this and used every opportunity to beat the non-partisan drum and warn against the dangers of political alliances. Beyond this, the CCL had no desire to promote an open clash with the TLC on political grounds.

Union membership was expanding rapidly, doubling between 1940 and 1944. Proportionately, growth was faster in the CCL, which had the advantage of heavy concentration in mass-production industries and which was more aggressive in seeking new members. Some TLC unions were sensitive to this trend and broadened their membership categories by loosening the craft restrictions. Competition for members became keen, and it was not at all uncommon for workers to find representatives from two different unions handing out literature at the plant gate and seeking their support. The exchange of insults between competing organizers must have been confusing to workers who were being bombarded with messages about labour unity.

In the political arena the CCL moved toward a more formal relationship with the CCF. In 1942 efforts were made to have individual unions affiliate to the party, and the CCF sponsored a trade union conference, which attracted delegates from sixty-nine local unions, most of them CCL. The conference endorsed the CCF as 'the political arm of labour', a phrase which was to be heard with increasing frequency.

It was not only the labour leaders who were hesitant about becoming too openly and too deeply involved. There was recognition that labour alone could not ensure success for the CCF, and within the party's ranks there was fear that too close and obvious an alliance with labour would frighten off other potential supporters, particularly among farmers.

However, at its 1943 convention the Canadian Congress of Labour took the plunge, adopting a resolution which said:

> Whereas in the opinion of this Congress, the policy and program of the CCF more adequately expresses the viewpoint of organized labour than any other party.
> Be it therefore resolved that this convention . . . endorse the CCF as the political arm of labour in Canada and recommend to all affiliated unions that they affiliate with the CCF.[136]

There was strong opposition from the Communists, who wanted a purely labour party which would accept the Communist Party as an affiliate. The CCF's policy remained firmly anti-Communist. To avoid Communist infiltration and control, delegates to CCF conventions were required to declare themselves not to be members of any other party. The initial results of the new CCL-CCF alliance were not as successful as the promoters had hoped. Response to the invitation to affiliate was slow. A peak was reached in 1944, when unions with a combined membership of 50,000 were affiliated. This later dropped off, and by 1952 it was down to 16,500.

There was little communication between the CCF and its new affiliates, and a good deal of suspicion lurked on both sides. Within the CCL the differences between Millard and Conroy continued. Some CCFers thought Conroy's support for the party was lukewarm and subject to serious qualifications.

The Communist Party created a new vehicle, the Labour Progressive Party of Canada, in 1943, and during the period in which it supported the war effort, the LPP backed the Liberals and attacked the 'struggle and conflict' policies of the CCF. The LPP said that the Liberals 'represent those of the capitalists who understand that they can and must co-operate with labour'. In the 1945 federal election, Mackenzie King's government was re-elected, and the Communists swung back to an anti-capitalist line and called for a CCF-Communist united front.

The CCL had formed a Political Action Committee to implement its political policy. One of its functions was the preparation of a legislative program, which was to be circulated to all political parties, seeking their endorsation. This was largely a political ploy which, it was hoped, would win new support for the CCF. The program called for:

> Government acceptance of responsibility for a full employment program.
> Social ownership of banking, insurance companies, war plants, coal mines, and transportation.
> Adoption of national policies for food and fuel.
> A comprehensive social security program.
> Severance pay for members of the armed forces, payable on their discharge.

The program was promptly endorsed by the CCF; the Liberals and Conservatives merely acknowledged receipt of the document; the Labour Progressive and Social Credit parties ignored it. Meanwhile, at the TLC's 1944 convention, Bengough said his Congress would not 'become the dog running after the wagon of any political party'; and the convention adopted a resolution reaffirming non-partisanship. The west coast Communist paper *The Pacific Advance* headlined its report 'TLC Achieves Unity and Makes Progress' and went on to say that the TLC's deliberations were 'a refreshing contrast' to those of the CCL.

In the CCL the lines were more clearly drawn. It was estimated that almost a third of the CCL's membership was under Communist control, with several major unions following the party line with absolute loyalty regardless of the twists and turns involved. These included the United Electrical Workers; Mine, Mill and Smelter Workers; and Fur and Leather Workers. The position of the United Auto Workers was less clearly defined. The UAW had a strong Communist element, which exerted considerable influence on Burt, the Canadian director. The election of Walter Reuther as international president of the UAW in 1947, however, marked a change. Reuther was an avowed socialist and was personally anxious for the success of the CCF. He made his views known to Burt, reportedly with some force, and from that point on there was greater UAW support for the CCF.

By 1946 Conroy was tiring of his efforts to work with all factions, and he was smarting under the action of the left-wing UAW leaders who had tried to short-circuit the CCL during the Ford strike. A showdown was drawing near.

Born in Scotland of Irish parents and a graduate of the Alberta coalfields, this once-red-headed, short, stocky labour leader was not one to back away from a fight. It had become the custom at CCL conventions to delegate to him the job of delivering what it was hoped would be the knockout punch in debates involving the Communists. There was almost a ritual. Conroy would pace up and down at the back of the platform, sorting out his arguments and getting up steam. Then, taking off his jacket and carefully draping it over the back of a chair, he would go to the platform microphone in his shirtsleeves as the final speaker in the debate. Mosher, as chairman, was skilful in controlling the conventions, and no matter how uproarious they became, he saw to it that Conroy got the floor at the right time. Then the ex-coalminer would deliver his message, loud and clear.

Conroy told the delegates to the 1946 convention:

> The issue in this convention is whether the LPP will dominate the CCL, or whether the CCL shall remain in the hands of the membership. . . .
> I say let's speak up for Canada now. Let's develop a political party that will inspire the whole Canadian people. We have but one choice to make.[137]

The next year the line was harder. There was a resolution condemning 'Communist Imperialism' and another denouncing

Communist Party activity in the labour movement. In a show of strength the CCL administration exerted pressure to have Burt defeated as an elected member of the CCL executive and replaced by a little-known member of the UAW. Following a short time in purgatory Burt was returned to favour and again given a place on the executive.

The west coast remained a Communist stronghold, dominated by the International Woodworkers of America. The IWA, the Shipyard and General Workers' Union, and the Mine, Mill and Smelter Workers were all in the Communist camp. CCF progress had been effectively blocked. Millard decided to take an active role from his headquarters in the East, and he sent out several of his staff to tackle the job of revitalizing the CCF and taking control of the unions out of the hands of the Communists. Conroy was at first suspicious that this was another move in Millard's drive for power, but he later agreed to co-operate.

The Communist hold on the IWA was weakening. At the international union level, left-wing candidates for office had been defeated. While the party held on in British Columbia, with Harold Pritchett as district president, there were rumbles of discontent among the membership. William Mahoney, an upcoming Steelworkers' representative who later became national director of the union, had been sent out with the CCL's blessing to fan the flames of revolt. With the help of a group of disillusioned IWA members he adopted a favourite Communist technique, organizing cells within the union. At the same time he prompted curiosity about the union's financial affairs. The members forced an audit, which revealed some $100,000 not properly accounted for; in particular there were no vouchers to cover union funds which had been provided to Nigel Morgan, provincial leader of the Labour Progressive Party.

Defeat of the Communist executive was inevitable. In desperation they tried to lead the membership out of the IWA and into a new union, the Woodworkers' Industrial Union of Canada, which had been created to cope with the emergency of an anticipated defeat in the union election. The breakaway failed, and after a short but hard-fought struggle the new union was wiped out. The IWA emerged under new leadership, stronger than ever.

The anti-Communist forces were making headway in other quarters. In 1948 they gained control of the British Columbia Federation of Labour by a bare majority. George Home, a pack-inghouse worker who later became political education director of the Canadian Labour Congress, won the critical position of secretary-treasurer by a single vote.

The extreme left-wing unionists were coming under fire from all sides, and the developments in Canada were not unrelated to what was happening in the United States. In both countries the pace of battle was accelerated.

One of the first targets in the CCL was the Mine-Mill union. Murphy, its west coast leader, had attacked Mosher in terms so lurid that the newspapers refrained from actual quotations. This was but one of a series of attacks on the CCL leadership, and eventually the union was suspended from the CCL. At the 1948 convention, Mine-Mill asked for a lifting of the suspension, apologizing and withdrawing allegations that both Mosher and Millard had sold the workers out in negotiations in which they were involved. That was not good enough, and the convention voted to continue the suspension. The Mine-Mill supporters accused the CCL officers of operating 'a school for red-baiting', and Conroy replied: 'We can't fight the Communists with one hand and the bosses with the other. To fight the boss we must get rid of the Communists.'

That was the administration line. By the time the next conven-tion was held, Mine-Mill was in deep difficulty in the field. A large Port Colborne, Ontario, local had transferred to the Steel-workers. In northern Ontario the Mine-Mill organization among hard-rock miners was falling apart, and the Steelworkers were fighting for control. The CCL suggested that both unions withdraw and agree to have the Congress undertake reorganiza-tion and the negotiation of new contracts. Mine-Mill refused and was subsequently expelled from the Congress.

The United Electrical Workers' union was also in trouble. The union's paper had published what was considered to be 'a slan-derous attack' on officers of the Ontario Federation of Labour, accusing them of being 'in complete alignment with every anti-union and union-busting individual and organization in Canada'. The UE was suspended and then later expelled on a technicality concerning non-payment of dues.

Left-wing unions were having a rough time in the United States. There, union officers were required by the Taft-Hartley Act to take an affidavit declaring themselves not to be members of the Communist Party. The CIO moved against a number of its affiliates, conducting intensive investigations into their activities and policies and relating them to those of the Communist Party. In the 1949-50 period the CIO expelled eleven unions which it found to be Communist-dominated. Included were the United Electrical Workers, Mine-Mill, and the Fur and Leather Workers.

The CIO convention resolution calling for the expulsion of the Electrical Workers took four printed pages, commencing with the statement: 'We can no longer tolerate within the family of the CIO the Communist Party masquerading as a labour union.' An entirely new union — the International Union of Electrical, Radio and Machine Workers — was immediately chartered to operate in the jurisdiction which UE had occupied.

The Canadian Congress of Labour adopted a constitutional prohibition on Communist and other totalitarian organizations in 1950 and the next year used it to expel the Fur and Leather Workers' Union. The Trades and Labour Congress had adopted similar constitutional provisions earlier and in 1953 expelled the United Fishermen under that clause.

Differences in opinion, forcefully expressed, have always been characteristic of labour conventions, but never since has there been the vehemence of the 1940s and early 1950s. Some of the expelled unions were returned to favour in the Canadian Labour Congress in 1974, but the speeches of their representatives, some of them veterans of the earlier days, were a pale echo of the past. Nevertheless, the struggle for power continues.

19   The Merger

Canada's dominant labour body, the Canadian Labour Congress, came into being in 1956 as a result of the merging of the Trades and Labour Congress and the Canadian Congress of Labour. To those concerned with the inner working of the labour movement in Canada, this was unquestionably the most important event since the founding of the TLC in 1886. Divisions within the movement, as has been apparent, have always been one of its most serious handicaps. The 1956 merger represented a healing of old wounds and the creation of a new spirit of unity. Whether this new cohesion was to prove strong enough to withstand strains which refused to disappear is still an open question.

Such uncertainty as there is in this regard in no way detracts from the significance of the melding of two competing central labour bodies into one. This feat became possible only through a combination of circumstances, a very essential one being a similar development in the United States.

Regardless of the differences between craft and industrial unions, there was a desire for unity and the creation of one central body, a sentiment which was stronger in Canada than in the United States. This had been apparent in the reluctance of Canadian unionists to expel the CIO unions which were being thrown out of the American Federation of Labor.

In Canada the demands for one central body were most apparent in the Canadian Congress of Labour, though the feelings were shared by an impressive minority in the TLC. The CCL leadership was strongly pro-merger, while the TLC leadership showed little inclination in that direction.

At the very founding of the CCL the officers were instructed to seek 'a complete consolidation of Canadian labour' and thus a healing of the division which had made the formation of the CCL necessary. This desire persisted, despite the lack of interest of the TLC. Delegates to CCL conventions consistently passed resolutions directed to bringing the two groups together. They were encouraged in 1944 when a TLC convention told the officers to give serious study to the possibility of establishing one trade union centre, but added the rider, 'with proper safeguards for all unions with regard to their jurisdictional rights'. This was a milestone, but it pointed up the difficult hurdle of union jurisdictions.

Wartime travel restrictions caused cancellation of the national labour conventions in 1945, but the next year talk was revived, with CCL people discussing the immediate urgency of action. Bengough remained cool to the whole idea; others in his Congress were favourably inclined but hesitant to press for specific action.

The two organizations were extremely different in character. The Trades and Labour Congress, long-established, regarded itself as the official spokesman for organized labour in Canada. It conducted its affairs with a carefully maintained dignity and nurtured its connections with government. To some extent it had a stand-pat attitude. The Canadian Congress of Labour was young and bombastic, speaking for the downtrodden and chafing at the bit to spread the gospel of unionism and take the unorganized into its fold. The CCL's views on social and economic matters were strong and frequently expressed through slashing attacks on any government which failed to follow what was thought to be the proper course.

Those controlling the TLC's affairs thought they had little to gain and much to lose by allowing themselves to be associated with the younger group. Certainly the CCL had much to gain and little to lose.

But the unity sentiment was building even in the TLC, and in some areas of mutual interest there was the development of a gradual, but extremely cautious, form of co-operation. In 1948 the two congresses joined with some railway unions in protesting Prince Edward Island's labour legislation. Both congresses joined with the Canadian and Catholic Confederation in publicly objecting to Quebec legislation. In 1950 there was a joint TLC-CCL statement of support for the United Nations stand on the Korean situation. Later the two congresses jointly filed objection to the imposition of compulsory arbitration in a railway dispute.

In retrospect such activity seems only common sense, but at the time it was highly significant and marked real progress. Some of those seeking unity thought the most practical path was through the cultivation of co-operative action in areas where there was little, if any, difference of opinion. The problems facing the two congresses, and their objectives, were almost identical. They shared concern and had very similar policies with regard to housing, health insurance, labour legislation, unemployment insurance, immigration, taxation, and pensions.

Pursuing this line, the CCL at its 1950 convention proposed a Joint National Consultative and Co-operative Council to facilitate and promote common policies. Such a committee, composed of senior officers and including also the CCCL, was formed. High living costs were much to the fore, and there was agreement on a program seeking rent control and the reimposition of price controls. But a year later this hopeful beginning collapsed when the TLC executive accused the CCL of trying to use its association with the older congress to gain prestige.

This was only a temporary setback. Efforts to close the gap continued, and even Bengough admitted that merger was inevitable. It was becoming largely a matter of time. Union leaders in both congresses were worried by the slowing down of new organization, and it was realized that something had to be done to reduce the jurisdictional fights which were so damaging to the movement. Pressure was building up among members, who were more concerned with their day-to-day problems than with the technicalities of an alliance. Plain logic was demanding that the groups get together; thus, in 1953, a Unity Committee was formed. It was composed of four top officers from each congress and charged with exploring the possibility of organic union.

Jurisdictional problems received first attention, and the committee recommended a pact against raiding in the hope of curbing union efforts to steal members from each other. In this and other respects, developments in Canada closely paralleled those in the United States. Actually, because of the influence of international unions, eventual merger would not have been possible had there not been a similar move in the United States.

The American Federation of Labor had looked with some disdain on the Congress of Industrial Organizations. William Green, the AFL president, suggested there was one way to achieve unity in the labour movement and that was for the CIO to return to 'the House of Labour' on terms laid down by the AFL.

But, as in Canada, union leadership in the United States was alarmed at the failure of membership drives. It was estimated that between 1951 and 1953 a total of $11,400,000 was spent on organization, with barely any increase in the total number of members. Largely all that was accomplished was a shuffling of members from one union to another through jurisdictional raids. By 1953 the situation had become so serious that there was agreement on the establishment of a joint committee. The committee's solution was a no-raid pact.

When the Unity Committee in Canada adopted a similar approach in 1954, it said that this 'removed a serious barrier to ultimate unity'. The building trades unions in the TLC, always jealous of their jurisdictions, were hesitant; so was the Steelworkers' Union in the CCL, because of a particular situation at Kitimat, B.C. But both congresses approved the pact in principle, and it was left to individual unions to subscribe to the terms.

The signators undertook not to interfere with the collective bargaining relationship of other unions. H. Carl Goldenberg, a Montreal lawyer with considerable industrial relations experience, was appointed as permanent arbitrator to deal with any disputes which might arise. The principles of the original document were carried over into the Canadian Labour Congress and, while by no means eliminating jurisdictional problems, proved useful in meeting some difficult situations.

Adoption of the no-raid pact opened the way for further progress toward the unity goal, and by 1955 the Unity Committee was able to issue a statement announcing that agreement had been reached 'on all the basic principles of the merger'.

Once again events south of the border had been helpful. Green, the AFL president, and Philip Murray, president of the CIO, had both died within a short period, removing the possible difficulty of accommodating two well-entrenched officers. The leadership situation in Canada had been eased by the resignation of Bengough and the impending resignation of Mosher, who was seventy-three. Bengough had been succeeded by Claude Jodoin, a member of the International Ladies' Garment Workers' Union who had been prominent in Quebec labour circles and who was a popular choice for president of the new Congress.* Donald MacDonald, secretary-treasurer of the CCL, was a natural choice to continue in that position.

It was in Canada that the first delegate group considered actual merger. This was at the convention of the Trades and Labour Congress, and if there was to be serious opposition, that was where it was expected. The AFL convention was scheduled to follow immediately. The debate at the TLC meeting was opened by Frank Hall, the railway union leader who had been primarily responsible for the expulsion of Mosher's railway union from the TLC many years before. Recalling the battles of the past and the money and energy that had gone into them, Hall told the delegates: 'Someone else has been benefiting from that. The time has come to call a halt.' Some of the delegates had their reservations, but the merger resolution passed without a dissenting vote.

The proposal to create a new labour body which would have a million members aroused widespread public interest. Cartoonists had a field day with the theme of a labour marriage. In company board rooms there was more serious discussion. A

---

* Jodoin had been a victim of the Depression. His previously wealthy family had lost all, and after a stint on government road work, Jodoin found employment with the ILGWU. He liked to recall that his first responsibility was sweeping the floor of the union hall.

spokesman for the Canadian Manufacturers' Association, in a somewhat hysterical outburst, termed the merger 'a threat to our democratic liberties' and went on to gloomily predict, 'out goes [sic] our freedom and our industrial liberties'. Fears were expressed that an organization representing 80 per cent of the unionized employees would prove to be a colossus that would seize control of the country's economy.

Jodoin attempted to set these fears at rest when, in his address at the opening of the founding convention, he said:

> Our purpose is not to control. Our purpose, as it has always been, is to obtain the greatest measure of social and economic security for ourselves and for all Canadians, as far as humanly possible.[138]

Despite the spirit of optimism prevalent in both congresses, there were those who forecast a short life for the new organization. In particular there were predictions it would founder on political differences; next to the protection of union jurisdictions this was the most sensitive area. Many CCFers in the CCL had always used the labour conventions as a platform to expound the CCF philosophy with great vigour. But when they met in 1955, with the merger around the corner, they exercised extreme moderation and performed with the skill of high-wire artists. The convention, with little fuss or rhetoric, simply reaffirmed its support for the CCF. Jodoin, who was a guest speaker, took the position that the political policies of the new congress were a matter for the future. The CCL convention endorsed the merger proposal.

The actual merger, creating the Canadian Labour Congress, took place on 23-7 April 1956 at a convention held in the Coliseum on the Canadian National Exhibition grounds, Toronto. It was attended by 1,620 delegates and attracted more attention than any labour gathering before or since.

There were some differences between the mergers in Canada and the U.S. The rather clumsy hyphenated name, American Federation of Labor — Congress of Industrial Organizations, was indicative of a reluctance in the U.S. to adopt an entirely new approach. Even within the new AFL-CIO there was to be an Industrial Union Department to maintain a relationship among industrial unions. This was once described as an escape hatch, should the merger become unstuck. In Canada a new name, the Canadian Labour Congress, proved quite acceptable to both groups, and there was no special treatment for either industrial or craft unions.

The TLC had the larger membership — 600,000 to the CCL's 400,000; but the CCL had the stronger staff structure, including technical specialists. Financing presented a bit of a problem. The CCL with its more extensive service program collected a monthly per capita tax of ten cents per member from affiliated unions, while the TLC's per capita levy was only four cents. A compromise was reached at seven cents.

The final agreement to create 'one completely autonomous labour centre' set forth a number of principles:

> This new Congress shall embrace as equals all affiliated and chartered unions and organizations which are presently in either the Trades and Labour Congress of Canada or the Canadian Congress of Labour who wish to join and will accept the policies and principles that will govern its affairs and activities. . . .
> This new Congress shall be dedicated to the principle of promoting and advancing the best interests of its membership in the economic, social and legislative fields. . . . The objective . . . is the eventual unification of all sections of bona fide organized labour in Canada.
> The principles of both industrial and craft concepts of organization are recognized as equally necessary, and the new Congress will endeavour to organize all Canadian workers into the appropriate type of union.[139]

The first item of business for the newly-formed Congress was the adoption of a constitution, including a preamble setting forth the objectives. Organized labour has always been inclined to somewhat flamboyant language, and this document was no exception. The preamble declared:

> Dedicated to the proposition that Canadian workers as free citizens are entitled to secure and protect their mutual welfare and that of their families by all legitimate means, this autonomous Canadian labour centre is brought into being.
> Inherent in this proposition is the attainment of its economic, social and legislative objectives through the organization of Canadian workers into free trade unions, and the promotion and

advancement of their interests in all fields of common endeavour by the utilization of their collective strength, abilities and resources.

Founded to contribute to the realization of the legitimate aspirations of those who toil for a living, this organization will not deviate from the pursuit of the cause of peace, freedom and security for all people. It will at all times hold true to the high ideals and principles of social justice on which the labour movement was founded.

Unalterably opposed to corruption and totalitarian ideologies in all forms, it will utilize every resource at its command to combat these evils, wherever they may be found. It will seek to eliminate tyranny, oppression, exploitation, hunger and fear, as well as discrimination on the basis of race, colour, creed or national origin. With a keen appreciation of the tremendous responsibilities which it has assumed, this organization accepts the challenge of the future to foster and defend the principles of democracy in the economic, social and political life of the nation. [140]

One of the most prominent guests at the convention was George Meany, the AFL-CIO president. Because of past experience there was a good deal of speculation about the probable relationship of the central labour bodies in the two countries. Meany indicated that the birth of the CLC marked a new era:

Let there be no misunderstanding as to the relationship between the AFL-CIO and the newly-founded Canadian Labour Congress. This organization that you are forming is a free independent trade union centre for Canada, just as the AFL-CIO is a free independent trade union centre for the United States. . . . We expect to co-operate with this newly-merged organization in the international field, just as we co-operate with the British and German trade unionists, the Scandinavians and others. [141]

His reference to the similarity between the AFL-CIO's relationship with trade union centres abroad and those in Canada ignored the important fact that a large part of the CLC's membership was in unions also affiliated to the AFL-CIO and subject to its influence. He went on in his address to announce that the AFL-CIO would no longer maintain staff in Canada, as the AFL had, nor would it charter unions in Canada. The intent of Meany's message seemed clear, but there were to be occasions in the future when he would seem to have forgotten its implications.

The matter of political policy was even more touchy. After a great deal of soul-searching in the inner circles it had been decided to put the subject before the convention in the form of two resolutions. One outlined a program of political education and possible action, and the other dealt with co-operation with other organizations, particularly in the legislative field.

The first resolution spoke of labour's political responsibilities and recognized the existence of two different approaches. The resolution continued:

> The overriding need now is to go forward in a spirit of unity to achieve the basic objectives we hold in common, while at the same time ensuring to affiliated organizations maximum freedom of action as to the specific methods they will use in pursuing these objectives.[142]

Machinery in the form of a Political Education Department and a Political Education Committee was proposed, to institute programs and provide assistance where it was desired. Affiliates were urged to 'take the utmost interest in political affairs'; but the form such interest was to take was a matter for decision by each union.

The second resolution, without so stating, heralded the birth of a new political party. It drew attention to labour's traditional interest in legislative matters and pointed out that this was shared by others. The executive was instructed

> . . . to initiate discussions with free trade unions not affiliated with the Congress, with the principal farm organizations in Canada, with the co-operative movement and with the Co-operative Commonwealth Federation or other political parties pledged to support the legislative program of the Canadian Labour Congress, excluding Communist and fascist-dominated parties, and to explore and develop co-ordination of action in the legislative and political field.[143]

The resolutions had been masterpieces in compromise, accommodating widely divergent viewpoints. The debate was surprisingly brief. There were just twelve speakers, and only one was in opposition, that on the ground that there was not outright endorsation of the CCF.

Apart from politics, there was hope that the creation of a new congress might result in the unification of the labour movement in Canada. The immediate affiliation of the remaining vestige of the One Big Union was a step in that direction. Of much greater importance was the position of the Canadian and Catholic Confederation of Labour. There had been discussions, and the CLC officers were told to pursue them in the hope the CCCL might join.

A series of meetings followed, but there were insurmountable obstacles. The CCCL wanted to retain its identity and freedom to operate as it wished within the province of Quebec. The CLC already faced substantial jurisdictional problems, and these would be compounded if the CCCL's proposal were accepted.

While the CCCL's leadership adopted the unassailable position of voicing support for the principle of labour unity, they had little enthusiasm for a melding of organizations. Gérard Picard, the president, had expressed the opinion that the formation of the CLC would mean greater domination of unions in Canada from the United States. Jean Marchand, the CCCL's secretary-treasurer, was among those who were convinced the CLC would not survive. It became apparent that agreement was impossible, and the talks were broken off. Jurisdictional clashes between the two bodies were intensified and have continued ever since.

There was more success with two railway unions which were outside the Congress. The Brotherhood of Locomotive Firemen and Enginemen affiliated later in 1956, and the Brotherhood of Railroad Trainmen joined the following year.

A new central body, representing the vast majority of union members in Canada, was firmly established. There were expectations that the example would be followed by the merger of unions in overlapping jurisdictions and that the creation of a stronger labour movement would mean expansion of organization and progress toward labour's objectives. All this was going to take considerably more time than was realized in the enthusiasm of 1956.

20 Troubled Times

If there were any illusions that the founding of a million-member congress would be the answer to unions' problems, they were rudely shattered by the Newfoundland loggers' strike of 1959 and a wave of industrial unrest that followed in the 1960s.

The Newfoundland strike divided communities, caused a political uproar and created serious jurisdictional trouble, as well as leading to what was probably the most stridently anti-labour legislation in the country's history. Organized labour rallied behind the strikers to a degree seldom equalled, but this was insufficient to offset the combined opposition of management and government. All this was a bitter experience for a labour movement just emerging from a time of jubilation, and it strengthened the argument of those who maintained that unions still had to fight for their existence.

Earlier attempts to organize Newfoundland woods workers had not been notably successful, and in 1956 the International Woodworkers of America launched a new and ambitious campaign. At the same time, some activity was being shown by the United Carpenters and Joiners, but nothing to match the aggressiveness of the IWA.

Two companies were involved — Anglo-Newfoundland Development and Bowaters Pulp and Paper Mills — though attention centred on the AND company. Both firms were adamantly opposed to the IWA and did their best to prevent union organizers from getting into the isolated camps where most of the AND's 6,700 woods employees were housed. Wages and working conditions were established by a Woods Labour Board. The IWA complained that the loggers lacked proper representation on the Board and that wages were low, hours long, and living conditions in the camps intolerable. Despite the difficulties, the IWA was able to sign up a sufficient number of the employees to file an application with the Newfoundland Labour Relations Board, seeking certification as the bargaining agent. The application was rejected on the technical ground that the union had not established its status in the province.

A second organizing campaign was undertaken and a new application filed, resulting in a government-supervised vote in November 1957. After some delay the Board announced that 87 per cent of the men had been in favour of the IWA as their bargaining representatives. The union was officially certified in May 1958, and the companies were then in the position of being required by law to enter into negotiations with the union.

Negotiations went on from June to September, without any progress. The union was asking a wage increase of five cents an hour, a very moderate proposal designed to facilitate the completion of a first contract. There were also requests for a reduction in the prevailing sixty-hour week and improvements in camp conditions. When the stalemate became obvious, a Conciliation Board was appointed. It recommended a five-cent increase, payable in two instalments, and reduction of the work week to fifty-four hours the following year. As far as camp conditions were concerned, the Board took note of AND's declared intention to make improvements.

The IWA quickly accepted the Board's recommendations. The company rejected them, claiming the cost would be prohibitive. The union then conducted a vote in which 98 per cent favoured a strike.

Work stopped 31 December 1958. Police reinforcements were immediately sent to the logging areas, although there had been very little trouble. Soon scores of strikers were arrested and charged with violence, damaging company property, and interfering with traffic. At first the union paid the fines, but before long the financial squeeze became too great, and the men went to jail, their wives taking their places on the picket lines.

The company recruited fishermen to work in the woods, and there was some violence when the strikers reacted. A bunkhouse was raided, and the strikebreakers in their nightclothes were chased out in sub-zero temperatures. About a hundred strikers were taken into custody and marched ten miles through the woods before being taken by buses to an armoury, as the jails were not large enough to accommodate them.

An atmosphere of hysteria was building in the province, fanned by Premier Joseph Smallwood, whose opposition to the IWA had become fanatical. Smallwood was then at the height of his career, and there is reason to believe he saw the IWA as a threat to his previously unchallenged one-man rule. Smallwood aligned himself with the company and used his considerable radio and television skill to paint the IWA as a foreign, racket-controlled force which had invaded the province and would sweep it with violence and disregard for law and order. The IWA had a good record, but this was unfamiliar to the people of Newfoundland, to whom Smallwood's word was gospel.

The Premier moved on both the organizational and legislative fronts. He arranged a province-wide radio network to announce that he was personally undertaking the formation of a new union to replace the IWA. Free taxi rides and meals were offered those attending a founding meeting at Grand Falls. He summoned a special session of the Legislature to pass emergency legislation outlawing the IWA in Newfoundland. Meantime the companies refused any contact with the IWA and were threatening to shut down their paper mills — the largest source of employment in the province — rather than deal with the union.

The Legislature gave hurried approval to bills giving the government authority to 'dissolve' any union in which

> . . . it appears . . . that a substantial number of officers, agents or representatives of a trade union or body, group or organization of trade unions outside the province have been convicted of any heinous crime such as trafficking in narcotics, manslaughter, extortion, embezzlement or perjury.[144]

Such unions were forbidden to hold meetings, collect dues, or in any other way function as a union. Organizations and individuals found in violation were subject to heavy fines and imprisonment. The government could seize and dispose of all the assets of offending unions. The IWA and the International Brotherhood of Teamsters were immediately brought under the new legislation.

Smallwood's suggestions of improper conduct had been entirely by innuendo. At no time did he name any individual, except through some references to the Teamster president, James Hoffa, in the United States. The IWA had its main strength in British Columbia, where the Vancouver *Province* commented editorially: 'British Columbia knows from long experience that there is no gangster, racketeering or hoodlum control of the IWA.'

A week after the first meeting of Smallwood's new Brotherhood of Woods' Workers, the AND company announced that negotiations were taking place, and five days later an agreement was signed. It provided an immediate five-cent wage increase but no reduction in hours.

But it was at the little woods community of Badger that the IWA would suffer its fatal blow. There were different accounts of what led to the scuffle in which a policeman was fatally injured. The provincial Attorney-General's office reported that a party of seventy police was attacked by some 300 strikers. There were only two witnesses whose impartiality was unquestioned; they were Ray Timson, a veteran Toronto *Star* reporter, and a photographer accompanying him. Timson had no hesitation in placing the blame. His account to the *Star* began:

> Badger, March 11 — Marching three abreast and carrying nightsticks a column of 66 policemen waded into a throng of striking loggers last night, clubbed two of them unconscious, flattened dozens more, while their wives and children screamed for them to stop.
> I watched the attack on mainly defenseless men for about an hour. One Newfoundland policeman was hit with a two-foot long piece of birchwood in the face and is in hospital at Grand Falls in critical condition. One Mountie was punched in the face. Both blows were struck after the police started wielding billies.

Nine of the loggers were arrested; most beaten to the ground, handcuffed and dragged to their feet. One unconscious logger was dragged to a patrol car by four officers.
It was a dark hour for Canada's finest. . . . [145]

The constable fatally injured was William Moss, a member of the Newfoundland Constabulary. Smallwood, a showman at heart, made the most of it to discredit the IWA. A train carrying Moss's body from Grand Falls to St John's stopped at every way-station, so that people could pay their respects. Public buildings in St John's were draped in black. A vigilante group, carrying clubs, appeared on Grand Falls streets, hunting IWA representatives, smashing the IWA office, and threatening mainland newspapermen.

Smallwood asked Ottawa for additional RCMP reinforcements. Justice Minister Davie Fulton authorized the mobilization of an additional fifty men but gave instructions that they should stand by at Moncton, N.B., until it was clear that they were required. Smallwood protested the delay, claiming it to be a violation of the province's contract for RCMP services. The RCMP Commissioner, L. H. Nicholson, agreed with Smallwood and resigned.

In the House of Commons, Prime Minister John Diefenbaker, explaining the government's action, accused Smallwood of having aggravated the situation 'by intervening in a labour dispute in a way which apparently goes beyond the usual role of government'. Even Smallwood's fellow Liberal, Lester Pearson, Leader of the Opposition, was critical, saying he was unable to agree with some of the procedures followed or with the new laws.

Justice Minister Fulton was more specific:

> The activities of the Newfoundland government take on the character of an intervention in a dispute actually in progress, on the side of one of the parties and against the union which up to that time had been chosen as the bargaining agent by the workers and certified as such under the terms of the appropriate legislation. This is an abnormal role for a government, and certainly has the elements of an attempt to extinguish from the province a trade union national in character and hitherto chosen by the workers in that industry, in that province, as their bargaining agent. [146]

Fulton added that he considered Smallwood's request to be one for help in 'a project to extinguish a union'.

But the strike had already been lost and the organizational efforts of the International Woodworkers thwarted. Labour across Canada, and from some places in the United States, had raised more than $850,000 for the strikers. In addition there were donations of food and clothing. Newspaper editorials had been largely sympathetic to the strikers and critical of Smallwood, though this attitude changed somewhat after the constable's death.

The Canadian Labour Congress petitioned for disallowance of the special legislation as a violation of civil rights, and the International Labour Organization was asked to intervene, but the efforts were unavailing. Later the provincial government modified the legislation.

Within the Canadian Labour Congress there were serious jurisdictional repercussions. At an early stage the IWA had accused the Carpenters' Union of interfering in its campaign, and the Carpenters' activity had accelerated when the IWA found itself in trouble. A few months after the strike the Smallwood union became part of the Carpenters' organization.

CLC officers had done their best to have the Carpenters withdraw from what was a very nasty situation, but they had refused. The CLC then found itself in conflict with the AFL-CIO, with threats from international union headquarters of retaliatory action if the CLC tried to penalize the Carpenters. The CLC suggested the matter be settled by both unions withdrawing for a year and allowing the Congress itself to maintain a loggers' union. At the end of the year the members would decide which union they wanted. The IWA accepted the proposal, but the Carpenters turned it down and announced they were withdrawing from the CLC.

In 1964, paying back dues to the time of their withdrawal, the Carpenters returned to the Congress, but they retained bargaining rights for the Newfoundland loggers. Since the strike, conditions in the Newfoundland woods have changed drastically. There has been extensive mechanization, and there are more skilled tradesmen and fewer casual employees. Improvements in camp conditions have been forthcoming, and revised work schedules mean shorter periods in the woods.

The Newfoundland loggers' strike had been spectacular, as well as unusual in the degree of involvement of those not directly concerned, including even church authorities. But there were other major disruptions. Organized labour was entering a troublesome period, one which was to bring to the surface some problems which continue to bedevil the movement.

Before the Newfoundland trouble there had been a vicious struggle between the United Steelworkers and the Gaspé Copper Company at Murdochville, Quebec. Despite company opposition the union had signed a number of members, but it claimed it had been the victim of discrimination when the Quebec Labour Relations Board refused recognition. The company fired several employees who were known union activists, and a strike vote was taken, with 98 per cent favouring a walkout.

As soon as picket lines were set up, the company obtained an injunction and started civil damage actions against union leaders. That was the beginning of a legal battle unprecedented in Canadian labour jurisprudence. There were charges and countercharges of violence. A striker was killed in a dynamite explosion, and there was heavy damage to company property.

Organized labour in Quebec and Ontario, including the CNTU, rallied behind the strikers. Several hundred supporters gathered at Quebec City, and a cavalcade of cars went to the little Quebec community in an expression of support. As the demonstrators drove by, strikebreakers, under the protection of the Quebec Provincial Police, rolled boulders down a cliff onto their cars. The strikebreakers also wrecked the Steelworkers' office.

The strike lasted almost seven months and ended in defeat for the union. The company refused to rehire many of the strikers and in an action against the Steelworkers claimed $5,000,000 damages. The court case continued for nearly thirteen years, until the union settled by payment of damages amounting to

$2,660,749 plus legal costs. It had been the largest and longest such case in legal records. The union later had the satisfaction of gaining certification, and it has since had a contract covering the Gaspé Copper employees.

Employer resistance to union organization was not geographically limited. In Brandon, Manitoba, there was a serious strike in a meat-packing plant in 1960. New owners, claiming financial difficulties, attempted to widen the differential between rates paid in Brandon and those in effect in Winnipeg. Nine months of negotiations ended with a strike. The company dismissed the strikers and took steps to have the union decertified. There was considerable violence before a settlement was negotiated between company officials in Toronto and the union's national officers. The local manager at Brandon was resentful, resigning and accusing the company of publishing false financial information. The strike attracted wide attention and was the subject of a Royal Commission inquiry. The report accused the union of being party to a 'conspiracy' against the company.

Fluctuating economic conditions affected industrial relations in the earlier 1960s. From a low point at the start of the decade, conditions improved fairly rapidly, with per capita income reaching new heights. Unemployment, which had been high, declined; but there were new inflationary pressures. A period of relative peace on the industrial front was succeeded by a number of serious strikes. Symbolic of spreading restlessness was the 1966 strike of 3,500 Montreal longshoremen. The dispute was attributed to disagreement over parking regulations; in fact, delays in negotiations had aroused resentment. The stoppage had serious effects — 150 ships tied up for a month — and was only ended with the personal intervention of Prime Minister Pearson.

These were difficult days for union leadership. The pace of growth in union membership had slowed. In 1950 total membership represented 28.4 per cent of the non-agricultural labour force. By 1955 this had risen to 33.7 per cent, but then it slipped back to 29.7 per cent in 1965. The increasing proportion of employees in service industries and the so-called white collar occupations was becoming recognized as a serious organizational problem for the labour movement.

Membership demands for job and income security, as well as sizable wage increases and various fringe benefits, were complicating negotiations. Illegal strikes, in defiance of contract provisions or the law, and wildcat strikes, contrary to the advice of union leadership, were becoming more common. In 1966 about a third of the work stoppages were in this category.

An unusually large number of young people were entering the work force. Free of the inhibitions which many older workers had inherited from Depression days, they wanted action, and fast. What organized labour had done in the past was of little significance. They asked what labour was doing now. Many of those in leadership positions had reached middle age, and they were being accused both of complacency and of creating pressures which threatened the country's economy.

In some regions there were special circumstances. Wage levels in Montreal were affected by construction work provided by Expo 67 and various spin-off projects, which created a great deal of activity and strong demand for tradesmen. When Montreal union leaders were able to get construction companies to agree to an almost unprecedented wage increase of a dollar an hour in 1965, they had great difficulty in getting the membership to agree to ratify the new contract.

At Sudbury, Ontario, the United Steelworkers emerged victors in a jurisdictional battle with the International Union of Mine, Mill and Smelter Workers, but almost immediately Steel was confronted with a ticklish contract situation affecting 15,000 employees. There had been resentment at Mine-Mill's performance in a nearly disastrous strike in 1958, and this had been a contributing factor in the Steel victory, though even with that advantage its margin was only fifteen votes.

During conciliation hearings for a new contract there was a wildcat strike, during which access to company property was blocked. The strike lasted three weeks before union officials could induce those taking part to go back to work so negotiations could be resumed. Three weeks later, when there had still been no settlement, there was a 91 per cent vote for a legal strike. It lasted only three days and ended with an agreement which established the highest rates in any Steelworkers' contract, but even then only 57 per cent voted for acceptance.

A short time later the same union was in trouble at the Steel Company of Canada, Hamilton. Again there was a wildcat strike and clashes between pickets and police. The strike lasted four days before the strikers responded to union officials' urging to go back to work and get back to bargaining. Conciliation followed, with a report recommending an increase which would make the Stelco employees the highest-paid steelworkers in the world, but the membership turned it down. It took a cooling-off period and the addition of a few more cents before the offer was eventually accepted.

Obviously there was a strong undercurrent of unrest. Two observers, J. H. Crispo and H. W. Arthurs, had this assessment:

> Most of this unrest is characterized by militancy that is less the product of labour leadership than the spontaneous outbreak of rank-and-file restlessness. . . . In some cases the rank-and-file have been rebelling against the 'union establishment' as much as against the 'business establishment'.[147]

Those in union administrative positions were inclined to attribute the turmoil to a small and unrepresentative splinter section of the movement. It was an effective splinter.

The times were also characterized by violence. At Kapuskasing, Ontario, there was an unusual episode in which three striking woods workers were shot and killed. Some settlers in the area had continued cutting during the strike, and when strikers upset piles of their wood they opened fire on both strikers and police. The union later complained that the fines imposed for shooting the strikers were less than those applicable in the shooting of a moose.

Other violent occurrences provided ammunition for those critical of the labour movement, with the International Brotherhood of Teamsters one of the most popular targets. The name of the union's president, James Hoffa, had become synonymous with labour racketeering. In the United States Hoffa had been given a thirteen-year sentence for jury tampering and mail fraud. The incalculable damage Hoffa did to the labour movement spread into Canada. Personal injuries and property damage in a Teamsters' strike in Ontario and Quebec in 1965-6 further harmed the union's reputation.

With few exceptions the labour movement in Canada has been remarkably free from racketeering and other improper practices. The notable exceptions have been in the construction industry in both Ontario and Quebec and in the Seafarers' International Union.

The SIU, it will be recalled, was encouraged by government, management, and labour to come to Canada as an alternative to the Communist-dominated Canadian Seamen's Union. The SIU's operations were under the direction of Harold Banks, sent from the United States for this purpose. Under Banks's supervision a 'Do Not Ship' list was compiled, denying employment to any who for one reason or another lost favour with the union's officials. High dues were collected from people for whom there was little or no chance of employment. There were numerous cases of individuals being threatened and beaten. Finally, protests by the Canadian Labour Congress and the Canadian Brotherhood of Railway, Transport and General Workers led to a government inquiry. An extensive investigation by Mr Justice T. G. Norris brought to light a variety of offences, and Banks, facing a charge of perjury, forfeited $25,000 bail and left hurriedly for the United States.

With considerable reluctance the CLC agreed to the SIU's being placed under a government trusteeship. This was a tactic which, it was feared, once introduced, might be later used in unjustified circumstances, but there seemed to be no alternative. The international union objected vehemently, and it had the backing of both the AFL-CIO and the United States government. This became another of the instances in which the AFL-CIO attempted to interject itself into Canadian affairs. Jodoin, the CLC president, told his United States counterpart, Meany, that what happened in Canada was none of his business, and the AFL-CIO's objections subsided.

The economic effects of labour-management relations, as well as the spread of violence and the SIU affair, caused government to take a more active role in industrial relations. Jamieson has suggested that this expansion of government activity, particularly in recommending and even influencing wage rates and other contract provisions, became an inducement to public employees to seek comparable gains. Whatever the cause, there was a new spirit among government employees' organizations, far removed from the docility often associated with the civil service.

A strike of British Columbia government employees in 1959 showed that such work stoppages were not beyond the realm of possibility, even though in this instance the strike lasted only a few hours. In 1964 Quebec Liquor Board employees stopped work for several weeks in the first of a series of stoppages by provincial employees in that province.

Public employees, who had always been told that job security was compensation for their below-average earnings, were becoming discontented and militant. At the same time there was mounting evidence that the country could survive strikes affecting services which had previously been regarded as absolutely essential.

This was apparent in the 1965 strike of postal employees. Two unions were involved, one representing the mail carriers and the other the inside workers. When a strike was threatened, there were dire predictions about the collapse of the economy should the mail not go through. But the strike occurred, nationwide in scope; it lasted more than two weeks, and the nation managed to come through intact.

The government and the unions were going through a new experience in hard-nosed bargaining, and both were showing their inexperience. The union originally asked for an annual increase of $600. The settlement was for increases ranging from $510 to $550. Jamieson, in a study for the federal Task Force on Industrial Relations, said the union leadership 'exhibited weakness, confusion and indecision'; but this was 'more than matched by the divisions, weaknesses and inconsistencies on the part of the federal government'. There had been heavy pressure from editorial writers and other quarters for the imposition of compulsory arbitration, but the government had shown unexpected patience in riding the situation out.

Less than a year later the federal government faced another difficult situation with its employees on the St Lawrence Seaway. They had been seeking a wage increase, one of their claims being that they were entitled to equality with American employees doing the same work on the Seaway. The increases won by Montreal longshoremen brought the situation to a head, and faced with a strike which would have been extremely costly, the government appointed a Conciliation Board, which recommended an almost unheard-of-increase of 30 per cent. The employees were quick to grasp it, and the government found itself burdened with what became known as 'The Pearson 30 per cent Formula'. Employers complained that it encouraged others to seek equal increases.

Employees of the Canadian National and Canadian Pacific railways, who had been involved in drawn-out negotiations, were certainly aware of the terms of the Seaway settlement. There had been wildcat strikes on the railways on a local basis, but in August 1966 Canada faced its second national railway strike. The pattern had been established in 1957, and this time the government had emergency legislation ready before the strike started. Parliament was summoned, but it took four days of debate before the bill was adopted. Initially the government had recommended an increase of 8 per cent, to be followed by conciliation and, if necessary, arbitration to determine anything beyond this. When union leaders said this proposal was totally unacceptable and would be ignored by the membership, the government upped the ante to 18 per cent; but even then the union leaders, who accepted that proposal, had difficulty getting the workers back on the job.

Not all the disputes of the late 1950s and early 1960s were on such basic issues as wages. Automation, a word loosely used to cover various forms of technological change and mechanization, was becoming a major concern. This had been the cause of the 1957 strike of the Brotherhood of Locomotive Firemen and Enginemen on the Canadian Pacific Railway. The coal-burning locomotives had been replaced by oil-burning diesels, and the company said firemen were no longer required and it proposed to phase them out. The union maintained the men were still necessary for safety of operations. Fewer than 3,000 men were directly involved, but 65,000 were affected when a strike was called. It lasted nine days and ended with the appointment of a commission to investigate the situation. The commission's finding was basically in agreement with the company's position and provided for reduction of the staff through attrition. Threats of a second strike collapsed when other railway unions said they were not prepared to give support. The union had lost one of Canada's first technological change cases.

Other occupations were also being affected. In Toronto, newspaper employees who belonged to the International Typographical Union were involved in negotiations which continued for almost two years. Differences had narrowed down to the right of the employers to make technological changes in composing-room practices. The union considered the proposed changes to be a threat to jobs and to the very existence of the union.

Management decided to proceed nevertheless, and a strike followed. The mailers joined the typographical workers on the picket lines, but most other employees crossed the lines, prepared to continue working. Careful preparations had been made by the managements of the papers, and publication continued. The international union headquarters saw the strike as being likely to affect decisions which would have an impact on its members throughout the continent, and this led to a toughening of its attitude.

The constitution of the International Typographical Union gives the international officers considerably more authority than in most unions. In the Toronto case this was used to refuse approval to settlement terms which might have been acceptable to the Toronto membership. The union has a very generous scale of strike pay benefits, and this reduced local pressure for a settlement. Because of the nature of a newspaper's operation, picketing of the premises is less effective than in many other types of business. The sting of the strike began to wear off, and the newspapers started hiring permanent replacements for the strikers. The strike started in 1964, but it was not until 1972 that the ITU formally declared it ended. Actually the union had lost long before then.

It was another railway dispute that got to the root of the technological change issue. Improvements in rail equipment made it possible for trains to lengthen their runs, resulting in less frequent changes of train crews. The revised schedules were known as 'run-throughs', and trouble came when stops at Nakina, Ontario, and Wainwright, Alberta, were eliminated. The objecting employees were backed by their fellow employees, and 2,800 CNR workers booked off sick; a national tie-up of Canadian National service was threatened.

Other forms of improved mechanization had already reduced employment on the railways. There had been a drop of 19 per cent between 1952 and 1959, and it was continuing. Those who had once been considered the aristocracy of the labour movement felt their jobs were in jeopardy.

It was only when the federal government agreed to have a comprehensive study made that the employees returned operations to normal. Mr Justice Samuel Freedman of the Manitoba Court of Appeal was appointed Commissioner, and his report became a classic on the problems of automation. It is discussed in more detail in Chapter 22.

It should be noted that a corollary to automation is a lessening of the effectiveness of strikes. Increased mechanization means fewer people, and often supervisory personnel who are outside the union are able to carry on. An example of this was a 1965 strike in a number of oil refineries. One of the issues was a union demand for prior notice of equipment changes which might affect jobs and for protection for the status of employees. While a number of places were involved, the key situation was in British Columbia. Although the workers stayed out almost three months, the company claimed that through the use of supervisory people and mechanized equipment they were able to maintain at least 80 per cent of normal output. Included in the terms of settlement was agreement to establish a labour-management committee to attempt to cope with problems related to technological change.

Yet, while labour seeks to cope with new and different conditions, it sometimes seems to find history repeating itself. A wave of Quebec strikes in 1972 revived memories of Winnipeg in 1919. Never since then had Canada been as close to a general strike.

The Quebec disputes involved 200,000 provincial government employees, including teachers and hospital workers. There were a number of issues, but most prominent was the demand for a minimum wage of $100 a week for provincial employees. More than 70 per cent of Montreal's 12,000 hospital workers were below that standard. The drive was considered so important that for a time the three central labour bodies in the province — the CLC's Quebec Federation of Labour, the Confederation of National Trade Unions, and the Quebec Teachers' Federation — put aside their considerable differences and joined in what became The Common Front. Provincial government employees were represented in all three.

In late March 1972 there was a one-day stoppage, which had little effect except to alarm the authorities sufficiently to have injunctions issued compelling hospital employees and some hydro workers to stay at their posts in the event of a strike.

Then on 11 April a province-wide strike began in earnest. The union leaders advised their members to ignore the injunctions but to maintain skeleton essential services. The strike was highly effective. There were conflicting reports about the extent of suffering that resulted, but there was no question about the disruption of services being widespread. Schools were closed and various public services were reduced to a minimum. Public concern throughout the country was intensified by the fact that municipal employees in a number of communities outside Quebec were already on strike.

Contempt-of-court citations were promptly issued against a number of unions and their leaders for disregard of the injunctions. The Quebec courts moved quickly. Fines of up to $50,000 were imposed on unions and up to $5,000 with six-month jail terms on individuals. The three top leaders were Louis Laberge, president of the Quebec Federation of Labour, Marcel Pepin, president of the Confederation of National Trade Unions, and

Yvon Charbonneau, president of the Quebec Teachers' Federation. They were tried at a later date. All three freely admitted they had counselled strikers to defy court orders, and they were sentenced to a year's imprisonment but were given conditional releases after four months.

Ten days after the strike started, the Quebec Assembly rushed through emergency legislation ordering all employees back to work. This time the leaders recommended the employees comply. Gradually work was resumed and conditions returned to normal.

The effort to establish more equitable wage rates for hospital workers was not peculiar to Quebec. It was later pursued in Ontario and other parts of the country, with considerable success. The Canadian Union of Public Employees conducted a campaign appropriately entitled 'Catch Up'. Despite the supposedly essential nature of the work, hospital wage rates had for years been substandard.

It was not only the non-professional employees whose interest was aroused. Many professional and semi-professional groups were being attracted by the idea of bargaining collectively. Nurses and teachers, for example, were turning to union-like organization and bargaining, often prepared if necessary to go as far as striking.

The profile of Canada's labour force was changing. The rapid growth of white collar occupations created a new situation for a labour movement which had its base among blue collar production and craft workers. The number of working women was soaring, and there was an unusually heavy inflow of young people into the working force. The potentials of union organization changed drastically during the 1960s, and a decade later the labour movement was still struggling with the difficult task of coping with the new conditions.

Labour's difficulties were becoming more complex, and episodes of industrial conflict were having wider effect. There was obviously a necessity for improvement in labour-management relations, a subject that is explored in Chapter 22.

21 Labour and the NDP

While collective bargaining remains the primary concern of organized labour, political affairs have continued to attract attention from a large part of the union membership. Hopes expressed by delegates to the founding convention of the Canadian Labour Congress for greater co-operation among groups with common political interests developed faster than most expected.

The idea of such co-operation, involving farm organizations, co-operatives, and others, as well as the CCF, had been expressed at an unpublicized caucus of about fifty labour CCF supporters at London, Ontario, shortly before the 1956 merger convention. There was considerable disagreement between those who wanted to use the opportunity to drive for endorsation of the CCF by the new congress and those who thought it more politic to take a moderate position and let time provide new converts. In retrospect it seems likely that a resolution of endorsation would have passed the convention, but it would also have led to unfortunate divisions at a time when unity was the theme.

Following the merger there were still those who had been in the TLC, particularly from craft unions, who thought the labour movement should remain non-partisan. But they had become a minority in the new Congress and no longer pressed their view as they had in the Trades and Labour Congress. While their position is often compared to that of most trade unionists in the United States, as it has been in previous chapters, there is an essential difference. Gad Horowitz points this out in his impressive study *Canadian Labour in Politics*. In the United States the American Federation of Labor, and later the AFL-CIO, supported the capitalist system and 'American free enterprise'. The non-partisans in the TLC were neither for nor against any particular system; they were simply opposed to becoming politically involved.

Once the new Canadian Labour Congress was established, its political education program was launched with a burst of zeal, much of it originating with Howard Conquergood, director of the department responsible. Conquergood, a one-time football player and former YMCA worker, had an enthusiasm that was contagious. This was reflected in CLC political literature, which declared:

> Never before in the affairs of labour has there been the opportunity for a comprehensive program of political education and action as has now been achieved with the merger. Perhaps never before has there been greater need for labour to play its full part in the political life of the nation.[148]

But even Conquergood recognized that it would be unwise to press too hard. The emphasis was to be on education rather than direct action. This meant promoting studies of the parliamentary system, including election techniques; and there was to be a flow of information on current issues. The assumption was that this would more or less automatically lead to support for the CCF.

The issues in which the Congress was interested were spelled out in the *Platform of Principles* which had been adopted at the founding convention. These issues included: 'a comprehensive national social security system', embracing unemployment insurance, family allowances, and old age pensions; a new system of industrial pensions (the Canada Pension Plan); health insurance with sickness benefits; a minimum wage of $1 an hour; the forty-hour week; uniformity of labour and social legislation in Canada; and improved mothers' and widows' allowances.

An election in 1957 came on the heels of the founding of the Canadian Labour Congress, too early for labour's new political approach to have much effect. The CLC's Executive Council issued a low-key statement urging union members to become familiar with the issues and support candidates who were prepared to 'initiate programs of health care and who will support the legislative program of the Canadian Labour Congress'.

The Ontario Federation of Labour was more forthright, declaring its support for CCF candidates and becoming actively involved in the campaign. This was also the position of the United Steelworkers, but most other unions stayed on the sidelines.

Meanwhile quiet discussions were going on between top-level officers of the CLC and CCF. The Congress had made a deliberate attempt to better its relationship with the farm community, but there had been little response. It was decided to seek approval from the CLC 1958 convention for the creation of a joint CLC-CCF committee to work on the development of 'an effective political instrument, somewhat along the lines of the British Labour Party'.

Before that convention was held, the CCF came near disaster. In a 1958 election the party's representation in the House of Commons was slashed from twenty-five to eight. Among the casualties were the party leader, M. J. Coldwell, and Stanley Knowles, one of its most effective parliamentarians. It was in this atmosphere that the CLC considered its future political policy.

Major changes were also pending in the CLC leadership. Gordon Cushing, former TLC secretary-treasurer who was an executive vice-president, was resigning to take a government position. Cushing had been cool to political involvement. Knowles, at a loose end with the loss of his seat, was elected to succeed Cushing, qualifying through his membership in the Typographical Union. A second executive vice-president was considered necessary, and William Dodge, a Montreal unionist who was an active CCF supporter and former candidate, was the choice for that position.

The CCF forces in the Congress were being strengthened, and there was no doubt of the success of a carefully prepared resolution on politics. After recognizing the 'tremendous contribution' of the CCF, the 1958 convention resolution went on:

> The time has come for a fundamental re-alignment of political forces in Canada. There is need for a broadly based people's political movement, which embraces the CCF, the labour movement, farm organizations, professional people and other liberally minded persons interested in basic social reform and reconstruction through our parliamentary system of government.
>
> Such a broadly based political instrument should provide that labour and other peoples' organizations may, together with the CCF, participate directly in the establishment of such a movement, its organizational structure and basic philosophy and progress, as well as in its financing and choice of candidates for public office. The experience of labour and social democratic parties elsewhere should be studied for whatever their history and structure may contribute, while recognizing that any effective political instrument in Canada must be Canadian in character and structure.
>
> In participating in and initiating the creation of a new political movement, labour emphasizes that not only is there no wish to dominate such a development, but there is the fullest desire for the broadest possible participation of all individuals and groups genuinely interested in basic democratic social reform and the democratic planning necessary to such reform.
>
> This convention, therefore, instructs the Executive Council to give urgent and immediate attention to this matter by initiating discussions with the CCF, interested farm organizations and other like-minded individuals and groups, to formulate a constitution and program for such political instrument of the Canadian people; and to report on such a plan, draft constitution and program to the next convention of this Congress for action.[149]

The CCF's election defeat had created a sense of urgency. The legislative accomplishments of the CCF had been considerable, but they had been achieved indirectly and with little public recognition. Success at the polls had been less notable.

While the resolution passed the CLC's convention without difficulty, it soon became apparent that the path was not going to be an easy one. Farm organizations in Alberta, Saskatchewan, and Manitoba were considered the groups most likely to respond to the proposal for joint political action, and they were the first approached. All three rejected the invitation to become involved, and this non-partisan position was reaffirmed at subsequent conventions of all three organizations.

The CLC faced a problem within its own ranks from government employees who were union members but who felt that because of their position they should not be involved in any way in political matters. They were fearful that political action by the CLC might prove embarrassing to them. The CLC was sensitive to the situation and defined its policy in a statement by Jodoin:

> There are, within the CLC, a number of affiliated unions consisting almost entirely of government employees. The Congress recognizes that these unions must maintain . . . a position of strict [political] neutrality. It was not anticipated that this position would be changed by the Congress decision, nor would the Congress want this to happen.[150]

This was, however, not sufficient for some of the organizations, and they withdrew from the Congress.

There were also reservations in the CCF's ranks. Some party members doubted the wisdom of a closer relationship with organized labour, fearing that the party's image might suffer and that there would be an attempt by the unionists to take control of the party. Others thought the party's ideology might be watered down to accommodate labour. However, the majority favoured establishing a new party, and when the CCF convention was held in August 1958, a resolution to that end received unanimous support.

That resolution restated the principles on which the CCF was based as a 'people's political movement' and reaffirmed support for public ownership and control. The position adopted by the CLC was welcomed as recognizing the common social objectives of labour, the CCF, and farmers and offering new hope for progress.

With that approval the way was clear for action, and both the CLC and the CCF plunged into a series of meetings, conferences, and seminars, trying to involve as many people as possible in the formulation of policies for the new political vehicle. No name had been chosen, but it became known, almost spontaneously, as The New Party, and New Party Clubs were formed to accommodate those who would not normally have contact through established organizations.

When the CLC next met in convention, in Montreal in April 1960, the time had come to take another step. In his opening address Jodoin outlined what the executive had accepted as political policy. It was in line with the tradition of the old Canadian Congress of Labour rather than the Trades and Labour Congress:

> For the unions that make up this Congress to associate themselves freely with the party of their choice is consistent with the role that unions, as a social force working for the betterment of all mankind, have to play. I would go further and say that not only have unions a right to undertake political activities and try to elect a government of their liking; but they have a responsibility to help provide the people of their country with an opportunity to exercise a meaningful choice as to their representatives in Parliament and the legislatures and municipal councils. I am not suggesting that the Canadian Labour Congress should itself become an appendage of any political party. . . . Our position in this regard is identical with that of the British Trades Union Congress in relation to the British Labour Party. As in the case of the British TUC and labour organizations in other countries, so we will most certainly remain first of all a trade union organization. We shall retain our rights as trade unionists regardless of what party happens to be in power.[151]

The policy received overwhelming endorsation, and a supplementary resolution emphasized the voluntary nature of support for the New Party.

In April 1960 the CCF held what was to be its last convention and gave approval to the drafting of specific proposals for the formation of the New Party.

The founding convention of the New Democratic Party was held in Ottawa, 31 July — 4 August 1961. In a carnival-like atmosphere, quite different from that of the usually austere CCF gatherings, the NDP was born. There had been speculation that the convention might be dominated by unionists. Official figures showed the division of delegates: CCF, 710; unions, 613;

New Party Clubs, 318; others, 142. There was considerable overlapping but no evidence of union blanketing. In a leadership contest between T. C. Douglas and Hazen Argue, the labour vote went almost solidly for Douglas, who won 1,291 to 380.

Strongest labour support for the party continued to come from the larger industrial-type unions, though there was an increase in interest in some craft unions from the former TLC. A few of the international unions were barred by their constitutions from political activity, the constitutions being patterned to meet United States circumstances. This restriction on the Canadian membership was later removed in most cases.

Within three years of the founding of the New Democratic Party some 220,000 members of CLC unions were involved in a plan which provided regular financial contributions to the New Democratic Party. This has continued to be a major source of stable income for the party, though participation in the plan has not increased in proportion to the growth in union membership.

22 A Search for Answers

Through the 1960s and into the early 1970s there was a spate of probes, inquiries, and investigations into all aspects of organized labour and labour-management relations. These had been spurred by the turbulence of immediately preceding years. They were largely fact-finding exercises, conducted in the hope of providing information and recommendations which would be useful in the drafting of new legislation. Legislative changes followed, but few were fundamental.

Introduction of the Corporations and Labour Unions Returns Act in 1962 followed somewhat similar legislation in the United States. The Canadian Act was designed primarily to gather information on the activities of international unions and corporations. The Act has been under continual fire from labour, which alleges the annual reports issued under its provisions to be incomplete, misleading, and the basis for misrepresentation of international unions. The government, at both cabinet and departmental levels, has admitted weaknesses in the Act, and in 1975 it was under review.

A development of considerably greater consequence was the Freedman Report, following the inquiry into the Canadian National run-through dispute (see page 213). On the specific issue, Freedman found the company had the legal right to institute changes, but he strongly recommended further negotiations in an effort to overcome the problems created for the employees and communities involved.

But Freedman's terms of reference went far beyond Nakina and Wainwright, for he had been directed to consider 'other related matters'. This was an invitation to consider technological change at large, and Freedman accepted. He found that programs which had been introduced to cushion the impact of change were inadequate and that there was a need for legislation. He also called on both management and labour to demonstrate greater co-operation.

Some of Freedman's conclusions were very basic: management should not have the unbridled right to institute changes which might affect both individuals and communities; the cost of providing protection should be regarded as part of the cost of making changes and should be borne by those who would benefit rather than those who would lose; management had a responsibility to take employees into its confidence when important changes were contemplated.

While Freedman's inquiry focused on technological change, that of a federal Task Force on Industrial Relations covered an extremely wide field. The subsequent report, with a number of related studies, constitutes the most detailed work of its kind.

The Task Force was composed of academics, all with some experience in labour-management affairs. Dean H. D. Woods of McGill University was chairman, and the members were Dean A. W. R. Carrothers, University of Western Ontario, Professor John Crispo, University of Toronto, and Abbé Gérard Dion, Laval University. They were appointed in 1966, and their findings were published two years later.

The Task Force was cognizant of mounting criticism of collective bargaining amounting to 'a crisis of confidence in the present industrial relations system'. But members of the group were emphatic in the opinion that, despite its weaknesses, collective bargaining remained not only the best, but the only, democratic method of dealing with the inevitable differences between employees and employers.

They further concluded that strikes and lockouts, expensive as they might seem, 'play an indispensable part in the collective bargaining process'. The Task Force was firmly opposed to compulsory arbitration and favoured flexibility in legislative approaches to meet varying circumstances.

Strikes affecting services generally considered to be essential were receiving a good deal of public attention. The Task Force proposed a three-member Public Interests Disputes Commission, with power to investigate and mediate but not to impose a settlement. That step, the Task Force maintained, should remain the prerogative of the government or Parliament.

About the same time that the Task Force was engaged in its investigations, Justice Rand, author of the Rand Formula, following the Ford strike of 1945 (see page 170), was making a somewhat more restricted inquiry on behalf of the Ontario government. A number of unionists had been arrested in connection with a demonstration at a strike in Peterborough, Ontario, and Rand had been asked to direct his attention particularly to picketing, boycotts, demonstrations, and other such activities, as well as to the more general aspects of labour-management relations.

Rand's approach was more along judicial lines than was that of the Task Force. He thought the time had come for both labour and management to accept limitations on actions, including strikes, which might affect the public. He was favourable to compulsory arbitration and foresaw the creation of something along the lines of labour courts. The heart of his proposals was a powerful Industrial Tribunal, backed by a support staff of experts. The Tribunal would have authority to terminate strikes and impose arbitration. Rand wanted tighter restrictions on picketing and boycotts; but he also put forward a plan to restrict the operation of struck plants. The idea of strikes in the public service was completely unacceptable to Rand.

Reaction to the Task Force report was mixed; both management and unions were able to find some points of agreement and others of disagreement. Labour's reaction to the Rand report was vigorous opposition, and while management was less vocal it was far from enthusiastic. The academics had shown a much greater awareness of the facts of industrial life than had the judge. The Task Force report was more realistic, especially in displaying the flexibility necessary to meet very different and complex situations.

British Columbia was also considering amendments to its labour legislation, and in 1967 it enlisted the assistance of Mr Justice Nathaniel Nemetz, a jurist who had met with some success as a mediator in major west coast disputes. Nemetz was asked to study labour law and practices in Sweden, a country with a good reputation in industrial relations.

British Columbia's experience with labour legislation demonstrates the limitations of legislative approaches to the human problems of labour-management relations. In 1947 the province adopted an Industrial Conciliation and Arbitration Act, which followed the provisions of the federal government's wartime labour regulations but added new restrictions on strikes. Government-supervised votes were required, and there were severe penalties for illegal strikes or lockouts.

The Act proved ineffective; there was an increase in strikes, leading to new demands for more effective laws. This became an issue in the 1952 election, in which the Social Credit government gained power. New legislation followed in the form of a Labour Relations Act, which was intended to curb illegal strikes. The Minister of Labour was empowered to deprive offending unions of their bargaining rights and such other benefits as the check-off of union dues. Although strikes again increased, this somewhat sweeping section was never used.

It was against this background that Nemetz was sent to seek new answers abroad. There are major differences between Sweden and Canada, and Nemetz was careful to point them out. Sweden has a unitary rather than a federal system of government. The extent of organization among both employees and employers is far greater in Sweden. Bargaining is generally centralized in Sweden, while it is largely on an individual operation basis in Canada. The general social climates, including attitudes toward organized labour, differ widely.

Nemetz did, however, make a number of recommendations for change in British Columbia. He urged a strengthening of a labour-management committee; compilation of research material, to be available in negotiations; a program to develop more qualified mediators; improved machinery for settling disputes over the interpretation of collective agreements; and the creation of an Industrial Inquiry Commission on a permanent basis to hear disputes referred by the Minister of Labour.

The government used his report for terms of reference in new legislation identified as Bill 33. This created a permanent Mediation Commission, which could impose terms of settlement in disputes referred by the government. This was, of course, a form of compulsory arbitration, and it aroused strong objections from labour.

Bill 33 proved a dismal failure. The Commission was largely ignored by both labour and management and, on occasion, by the government itself. The legislation was repealed as soon as the New Democratic Party gained power in 1972.

There were several inquiries into the construction industry in Canada in the 1960s and early 1970s. In a number of ways, employment in construction differs from other occupations. The employees are divided into fairly well-defined trades, with a tendency toward self-preservation which leads to numerous jurisdictional disputes. Employment is temporary, ending with the completion of a project, and there is not the permanent employee-employer relationship usually found elsewhere.

In 1962 Carl Goldenberg conducted an investigation into conditions in Toronto housing construction, and later he joined with John Crispo in a more extensive study for the Canadian Construction Association. In 1970 Dean H. D. Woods looked into conditions in the industry in Nova Scotia, where there had been serious effects from frequent strikes. In both Ontario and Quebec there have been public inquiries which have disclosed improper practices by both management and labour in the construction industry. These and other investigations made it clear that special provisions are required to meet conditions peculiar to the industry. But, as elsewhere, legislation falls far short of providing a complete solution to difficulties.

One of the more recent provincial investigations was that conducted for the Province of Newfoundland by Dean Maxwell Cohen of McGill University in 1972. Cohen's report covered a wide range and included suggestions for a number of legislative changes. He favoured the use of compulsory arbitration in so-called essential disputes. He also proposed strengthening the authority of the Labour Relations Board by allowing it to issue 'cease and desist' orders in strikes found to be illegal.

The most significant changes in labour legislation are found in amendments to the Canada Labour Code adopted in 1972. These constituted, in effect, a consolidation, replacing the former Industrial Relations and Disputes Act. For the first time, the federal government enshrined in legislation a positive statement of support for freedom of association and free collective bargaining 'as the bases of effective industrial relations for the determination of good working conditions and sound labour-management relations'.

Before it was adopted, the bill was the subject of numerous representations, including objection from some management spokesmen to such outright endorsation of collective bargaining. Submissions made by labour resulted in some important revisions, including the removal of a section which would have imposed severe restrictions on picketing.

The most novel feature of the 1972 legislation was an entirely new section applicable to situations created by technological changes. Employers were required to give notice, and if a substantial number of workers were likely to be affected, the union could have the contract reopened. If no agreement was reached, they could strike. This was an answer to union complaints that the introduction of new working conditions during the term of an agreement — when strikes were prohibited — amounted to changing the rules in the middle of the game.

But not all the inquiries and probing of labour originated outside the movement. The Canadian Labour Congress itself became involved in a unique looking-glass experiment. In 1966 the Congress was coming under increasing criticism from within its own ranks, and a Commission on Constitution and Structure was set up to look into Congress operations and the general performance of organized labour in Canada. The Commission was to report in two years, but it became a permanent body; the problems with which it was dealing refused to go away.

The Commission has been worried by the multiplicity of unions and has sought ways of encouraging mergers. It has dealt in some detail with the activities of international unions and the growing demands for Canadian autonomy. Improved methods of dealing with jurisdictional disputes between unions have also received a good deal of attention.

The CLC is the only central labour body known to be engaged in such a process of continual self-examination. The Commission's findings have led to constitutional and policy changes, in a slow but deliberate trend toward greater authority for the central body in controlling its affiliates. International unions have been made subject to standards intended to assure reasonable autonomy for the Canadian membership. New pressures have been applied to affiliates to assure the provision of satisfactory standards of service to members. Just how far the Congress will be able to go in exercising tighter control of its affiliates remains an open question.

Improvement of wages and conditions is the primary motivation for unionization, but many also regard the movement in more idealistic terms. Labour's function as a social force is seen by some to be especially important in its appeal to white collar groups. Confinement to the business unionism of more dollars and cents would deprive the movement of much of the attraction it now holds.

Organized labour regards itself as a spokesman for all wage and salary earners, regardless of whether or not they hold union cards. In its broader responsibilities it is conscious of a need to become increasingly involved in social issues at the national, provincial, and community levels. It is unfortunate that a human tendency to centre attention on matters of conflict results in little attention being paid to a variety of union activities which have very positive social values.

Originally unions tried to protect their members against adverse circumstances by creating special union funds to help meet such emergencies as funeral expenses and short periods of unemployment and pay modest pensions. These plans were common in the craft unions, and some still exist, but they proved inadequate, particularly in times of high unemployment when the needs were greatest. It was not at all uncommon for unemployment to destroy a union.

Gradually collective bargaining came to be used in an effort to gain protection against many of life's uncertainties. Negotiations were broadened to seek inclusion in collective agreements of life insurance, hospital plans, medical care, and pensions.

Going beyond its own membership the union movement has throughout its existence been a leading proponent of social security legislation applicable to all. While organized labour cannot claim exclusive responsibility, it can justifiably take some credit for contributions to the development of a system of social security enjoyed by all Canadians. Some of the legislative objectives have been directly related to work situations, such as workmen's compensation and unemployment insurance; others have been more general.

The first Workmen's Compensation Act in Canada was adopted in Manitoba in 1910, patterned after English legislation. Employers were required to pay injured employees 55 per cent of their normal earnings during the time they were off work as the result of an industrial accident. There was no provision for medical service.

Other provinces followed Manitoba's example. Present workmen's compensation plans are largely based on that adopted by Ontario in 1914. There has been a constant effort on the part of unions to have the benefits increased and to ensure the provision of adequate services, such as rehabilitation. In most provinces there is a good working relationship between unions and the Compensation Boards, and fairly extensive rehabilitation services have been introduced.

Labour lobbied long and arduously for unemployment insurance, overcoming strong opposition from employer groups. Since unemployment insurance was introduced in 1940, labour has been involved in an advisory capacity and in some aspects of administration.

Many of labour's legislative interests go beyond matters related to employment. Pensions have been of continuing concern, and as early as 1905 organized labour was urging the adoption of a national pension plan. In 1914 the Trades and Labour Congress made a formal presentation, entitled *Labour's Case for Old Age Pensions*, to a House of Commons committee.

There is a close relationship between labour's interest in pensions and its political programs. The first Old Age Security Act became law largely through the efforts of J. S. Woodsworth, leader of the CCF. The first pensions were payable at age seventy and were subject to a means test. The labour movement conducted nationwide campaigns to have the means test removed, pensions increased, and the pensionable age lowered. Improvement of the existing plan is one of labour's present objectives.

Hospital and medical insurance on a national scale was another high-priority objective. Labour's political activists like to point out that it was a CCF government in Saskatchewan that introduced hospital insurance in 1946 and medical care insurance in 1962. Later the Canadian Labour Congress initiated a program of co-operation among a number of groups interested in the introduction of national medicare.

Labour's lobbying technique includes the annual meetings which are held with the federal Cabinet by the Canadian Labour Congress, the Confederation of National Trade Unions, and a group of railway unions. The CLC's memorandum, in addition to dealing with purely labour matters, expresses opinions on broad social issues and on international affairs. Somewhat similar representations are made at other levels of government by provincial federations of labour and community labour councils.

Labour has always had a keen interest in education and, from its inception, has pressed for the availability of educational facilities without regard to financial means. An extensive educational program has also been developed within the movement. Each year some 25,000 unionists take part in institutes, seminars, and summer schools conducted by the CLC, and many thousands more are involved in the educational projects of their own unions. The Confederation of National Trade Unions is also active in union education.

As a method of developing better leadership, the CLC promoted the Labour College of Canada, which is operated in co-operation with McGill and the University of Montreal. There, young trade unionists take residential short courses in general subjects, at a level roughly equivalent to second-year university.

There is increasing recognition of the responsibility of labour to become more involved in community situations if it is to fulfil its social role. The Canadian Labour Congress established a Social Action and Community Programs Department in 1970 to encourage such activity. Labour groups have become involved in co-operative housing and the promotion of community health centres. The Ontario Federation of Labour has shown a special interest in the needs of the aged and of workers employed in farm labour. Some sections of the movement have given assistance in programs directed to combatting the misuse of alcohol and drugs.

Usually little is known of such activities as these, but even less is known of labour's international relationships. There is a continuing effort to arouse membership interest in international affairs, and frequent representations are made to government, putting forward labour's viewpoint on specific issues.

Frequently, the policy of the Canadian Labour Congress has been directly opposite to that of the AFL-CIO, which has adhered closely to the foreign policy line of the United States government. For many years the CLC argued for the recognition of the Republic of China and the admission of that country to the United Nations. The CLC was strongly opposed to United States policy in Vietnam, though this policy was consistently supported by the AFL-CIO. The CLC was among the first to propose expulsion of South Africa from the Commonwealth because of her apartheid policies.

Labour has been internationally involved, through active participation, in a number of world organizations. The CLC was one of the founders and leading supporters of the International Confederation of Free Trade Unions, a worldwide organization of central labour bodies. It has also been prominent in the International Labour Organization, where Joseph Morris, now CLC president, headed the workers' delegations for some years. A number of Canadian union leaders have spent time abroad, assisting in educational programs for workers in less developed countries.

Labour's interests, both at home and elsewhere, continue to expand. The tortuous course that has led the movement from a few small groups of workers attempting desperately to maintain a shaky organization to a complex structure involving well over two million men and women continues.

By the mid-1970s the labour movement was still struggling with some of the basic difficulties which confronted its pioneers. Simultaneously it was attempting to cope with the challenges of a new age. The essential principles and purposes remained little changed; but the time had come for new approaches and greater flexibility if the movement was to maintain its hard-earned place in society and fulfil its possibilities in a future which is as uncertain as its past.

References

(Secondary references in brackets)

1   Nova Scotia, Act 27, Statutes of 1816. (Charles Bruce Fergusson, *The Labour Movement in Nova Scotia before Confederation*, Public Archives of N.S.; quoted by Eugene Forsey, 'Insights Into Labour History in Canada', *Laval Industrial Relations Quarterly*, Vol. 20, 1965)

2   Records, International Typographical Union, No. 91, Toronto. (H.A. Logan, *Trade Unions in Canada*, 1948)

3   Lord Byron, House of Lords. (Labour Scrap Book, United Rubber Workers)

4   Hamilton *Spectator*, 1854. (Muriel Clements, unpublished study for Ontario Educational Communications Authority)

5   *The Colonial Advocate*, 9 September 1830

6   Montreal *Gazette*, 1834. (Margaret Mackintosh, *An Outline of Trade Union History*, Canada Department of Labour, 1938)

7   *Victoria Gazette*, 1859. (Paul Phillips, *No Power Greater*, B.C. Federation of Labour, 1967)

8   Minutes, York Printers, 1848. (H.A. Logan, *Trade Unions in Canada*, 1948)

9   Records, National Typographical Union, 1860. (Margaret Mackintosh, *An Outline of Trade Union History*, Canada Department of Labour, 1938)

10   Margaret Mackintosh, *An Outline of Trade Union History*, Canada Department of Labour, 1938

11   Constitution, Knights of St Crispin. (Don D. Lescohier, *Knights of St Crispin*, University of Wisconsin, 1910; quoted by Eugene Forsey, 'Insights Into Labour History in Canada', *Laval Industrial Relations Quarterly*, Vol. 20, 1965)

12   *See* reference no. 8.

13   Toronto *Globe*, 21 September 1871. (Doris French, *Faith, Sweat and Politics*, McClelland & Stewart, 1962)

14   *Ontario Workman*, 18 April 1872. (Leslie Wismer, *Workers' Way to a Fair Share*, Trades and Labour Congress, 1951)

15   Toronto *Globe*, 17 April 1872. (Leslie Wismer, *Workers' Way to a Fair Share*, Trades and Labour Congress, 1951)

16   Montreal *Star*, 1872. (Leslie Wismer, *Workers' Way to a Fair Share*, Trades and Labour Congress, 1951)

17   Toronto *Globe*, 8 July 1872. (Doris French, *Faith, Sweat and Politics*, McClelland & Stewart, 1962)

18   *See* reference no. 17.

19   *See* reference no. 17.

20   Toronto *Globe*, 16 July 1872. (Doris French, *Faith, Sweat and Politics*, McClelland & Stewart, 1962)

21   *Ontario Workman*, 18 July 1872. (Doris French, *Faith, Sweat and Politics*, McClelland & Stewart, 1962)

22   Proceedings, Canadian Labour Union. (Canada Department of Labour Library)

23   *See* reference no. 22.

24   *See* reference no. 22.

25   Toronto *Mail*. (Canadian Labour Union Records, Department of Labour)

26   *See* reference no. 22.

27   *See* reference no. 22.

28   Toronto *Leader*. (Canadian Labour Union Records, Department of Labour)

29   *Labour Movement of Canada – Canada and Its Provinces*, Vol. IX. (H.A. Logan, *Trade Unions in Canada*, 1948)

30   Ottawa *Daily Citizen*. (Doris French, *Faith, Sweat and Politics*, McClelland & Stewart, 1962)

31   *See* reference no. 30.

32   *Beldon's Atlas of Ottawa and Carleton*. (Doris French, *Faith, Sweat and Politics*, McClelland & Stewart, 1962)

33   Toronto *Globe*. (Doris French, *Faith, Sweat and Politics*, McClelland & Stewart, 1962)

34   Toronto Trades and Labour Council Minutes. (Doris French, *Faith, Sweat and Politics*, McClelland & Stewart, 1962)

35   Toronto *Globe*, 20 November 1886. (Doris French, *Faith, Sweat and Politics*, McClelland & Stewart, 1962)

36   Doris French, *Faith, Sweat and Politics*, McClelland & Stewart, 1962.

37   *See* reference no. 34.

38   Trades and Labour Congress Proceedings, 1907. (Leslie Wismer, *Workers' Way to a Fair Share*, Trades and Labour Congress, 1951)

39   'Canadian Labour Interests and Movements', *Encyclopedia of Canada*, 1900.

40   Knights of Labour Constitution. (D.R. Kennedy, *The Knights of Labour in Canada*, University of Western Ontario, 1956; quoted

by Eugene Forsey, 'Insights Into Labour History in Canada', *Laval Industrial Relations Quarterly*, Vol. 20, 1965)

41   Terence V. Powderly, *The Path I Trod*, Columbia University Press, 1940. (Doris French, *Faith, Sweat and Politics*, McClelland and Stewart, 1962)

42   *See* reference no. 41.

43   Ontario Bureau of Statistics Report, 1886. (Doris French, *Faith, Sweat and Politics*, McClelland & Stewart, 1962)

44   *Palladium of Labour*, 15 December 1883. (Martin Robin, *Radical Politics and Canadian Labour*, Industrial Relations Centre, Queen's University, 1968)

45   A. Andras, *Labour Unions in Canada*, Woodsworth House.

46   Margaret Mackintosh, *An Outline of Trade Union History*, Canada Department of Labour, 1938.

47   Report, Royal Commission on Capital and Labour, 1889.

48   *See* reference no. 47.

49   Report, Ontario Bureau of Industries, 1890. (Martin Robin, *Radical Politics and Canadian Labour*, Industrial Relations Centre, Queen's University, 1968)

50   *See* reference no. 10.

51   Minutes, Provincial Workmen's Association. (H.A. Logan, *Trade Unions in Canada*, 1948)

52   H.A. Logan, *Trade Unions in Canada*, 1948.

53   Proceedings, Trades and Labour Congress Convention, 1892. (H.A. Logan, *Trade Unions in Canada*, 1948)

54   Leslie Wismer, *Workers' Way to a Fair Share*, Trades and Labour Congress, 1951.

55   *See* reference no. 54.

56   *See* reference no. 52.

57   Proceedings, TLC Convention, 1894. (H.A. Logan, *Trade Unions in Canada*, 1948)

58   *See* reference no. 57.

59   Eugene Forsey, 'Compulsory Arbitration', *Canadian Labour*, January 1965.

60   Report, Ontario Bureau of Industries, 1886. (Doris French, *Faith, Sweat and Politics*, McClelland & Stewart, 1962)

61   Eugene Forsey, *Canadian Labour*, January 1965.

62   Conciliation Act, 1900. (*The Labour Gazette*, Vol. I, 1900)

63   *See* reference no. 61.

64   Proceedings, TLC Convention, 1902.

65   *See* reference no. 62.

66   *The Labour Gazette*, September 1909.

67   Stuart Jamieson, *Times of Trouble: Labour Unrest and Industrial Conflict in Canada, 1900-66*, Study No. 22, Task Force on Industrial Relations, 1968.

68 *See* reference no. 67.

69 Proceedings, TLC Convention, 1905. (H.A. Logan, *Trade Unions in Canada*, 1948)

70 *See* reference no. 69.

71 Martin Robin, *Radical Politics and Canadian Labour*, Industrial Relations Centre, Queen's University, 1968.

72 Sir William Mulock to Sir Wilfrid Laurier, Laurier Papers. (Stuart Jamieson, *Times of Trouble: Labour Unrest and Industrial Conflict in Canada, 1900-66*, Study No. 22, Task Force on Industrial Relations, 1968)

73 Report, Royal Commission on Industrial Disputes, 1904. (*The Labour Gazette*, Vol. IV; quoted by H.A. Logan, *Trade Unions in Canada*, 1948)

74 Report, Royal Commission on Industrial Disputes. (Martin Robin, *Radical Politics and Canadian Labour*, Industrial Relations Centre, Queen's University, 1968)

75 *British Columbia Federationist*, 10 January 1913. (Paul Phillips, *No Power Greater*, B.C. Federation of Labour, 1967)

76 Proceedings, TLC Convention, 1901. (H.A. Logan, *Trade Unions in Canada*, 1948)

77 Samuel Gompers, *Seventy Years of Life and Labour*, 1925. (Martin Robin, *Radical Politics and Canadian Labour*, Industrial Relations Centre, Queen's University, 1968)

78 Proceedings, TLC Convention, 1887. (Martin Robin, *Radical Politics and Canadian Labour*, Industrial Relations Centre, Queen's University, 1968)

79 Lady Dufferin, *My Canadian Journal, 1872-8*. (Martin Robin, *Radical Politics and Canadian Labour*, Industrial Relations Centre, Queen's University, 1968)

80 Proceedings, TLC Convention, 1886. (Martin Robin, *Radical Politics and Canadian Labour*, Industrial Relations Centre, Queen's University, 1968)

81 *Palladium of Labour*, 25 October 1885. (Martin Robin, *Radical Politics and Canadian Labour*, Industrial Relations Centre, Queen's University, 1968)

82 Minutes, Toronto Trades and Labour Council, 6 October 1882. (Leslie Wismer, *Workers' Way to a Fair Share*, Trades and Labour Congress, 1951)

83 Proceedings, TLC Convention, 1894. (Clifford Scotton, *Canadian Labour and Politics*, Canadian Labour Congress)

84 *See* reference no. 83.

85 Clifford Scotton, *Canadian Labour and Politics*, Canadian Labour Congress.

86 *See* reference no. 85.

87 *The Voice*, 17 October 1896. (Martin Robin, *Radical Politics and Canadian Labour*, Industrial Relations Centre, Queen's University, 1968)

88   *The Voice*, 7 March 1896. (Martin Robin, *Radical Politics and Canadian Labour*, Industrial Relations Centre, Queen's University, 1968)

89   *The Voice*, 14 November 1902. (Martin Robin, *Radical Politics and Canadian Labour*, Industrial Relations Centre, Queen's University, 1968)

90   Proceedings, TLC Convention, 1906. (Martin Robin, *Radical Politics and Canadian Labour*, Industrial Relations Centre, Queen's University, 1968)

91   *Western Clarion*, 24 June 1905. (Martin Robin, *Radical Politics and Canadian Labour*, Industrial Relations Centre, Queen's University, 1968)

92   *Fourth Annual Report on Labour Organizations*, Canada Department of Labour, 1914. (Martin Robin, *Radical Politics and Canadian Labour*, Industrial Relations Centre, Queen's University, 1968)

93   *The Labour News*, 7 August 1917. (Martin Robin, *Radical Politics and Canadian Labour*, Industrial Relations Centre, Queen's University, 1968)

94   *The Labour Gazette*, 1917. (Paul Phillips, *No Power Greater*, B.C. Federation of Labour, 1967)

95   *British Columbia Federationist*, 9 November 1917. (Paul Phillips, *No Power Greater*, B.C. Federation of Labour, 1967)

96   Interim Report, C.H. Cahan, 1918, Borden Papers. (Martin Robin, *Radical Politics and Canadian Labour*, Industrial Relations Centre, Queen's University, 1968)

97   Proceedings, TLC Convention, 1919. (Martin Robin, *Radical Politics and Canadian Labour*, Industrial Relations Centre, Queen's University, 1968)

98   *British Columbia Federationist*, 25 October 1918. (Martin Robin, *Radical Politics and Canadian Labour*, Industrial Relations Centre, Queen's University, 1968)

99   *See* reference no. 52.

100   Winnipeg *Free Press*, 3 June 1919. (*Information*, May 1969)

101   Kenneth McNaught, *A Prophet in Politics*.

102   *See* reference no. 101.

103   *See* reference no. 101.

104   *See* reference no. 101.

105   Report of Royal Commission. (D.C. Masters, *The Winnipeg General Strike*)

106   *Information*, May 1969.

107   *See* reference no. 67.

108   Grace MacInnis, *J.S. Woodsworth*.

109   Proceedings, TLC Convention, 1919. (Martin Robin, *Radical Politics and Canadian Labour*, Industrial Relations Centre, Queen's University, 1968)

110   *See* reference no. 109.
111   *Western Labor News*, 13 June 1919. (Martin Robin, *Radical Politics and Canadian Labour*, Industrial Relations Centre, Queen's University, 1968)
112   *Report on Labour Organizations in Canada, 1922.* (H.A. Logan, *Trade Unions in Canada*, 1948)
113   *See* reference no. 112.
114   Proceedings, TLC Convention, 1921. (Martin Robin, *Radical Politics and Canadian Labour*, Industrial Relations Centre, Queen's University, 1968)
115   Proceedings, TLC Convention, 1922. (H.A. Logan, *Trade Unions in Canada*, 1948)
116   Francis A. Curman, 'The Labour Party in Parliament', *Dalhousie Review*, Vol. II, 1923. (Martin Robin, *Radical Politics and Canadian Labour*, Industrial Relations Centre, Queen's University, 1968)
117   Hansard, 1935. (Stuart Jamieson, *Times of Trouble: Labour Unrest and Industrial Conflict in Canada, 1900-66*, Study No. 22, Task Force on Industrial Relations, 1968)
118   *Labour Organizations in Canada, 1931.* (H.A. Logan, *Trade Unions in Canada*, 1948)
119   *See* reference no. 67.
120   *Labour Organizations in Canada, 1930.* (Stuart Jamieson, *Times of Trouble: Labour Unrest and Industrial Conflict in Canada, 1900-66*, Study No. 22, Task Force on Industrial Relations, 1968)
121   W.H. McCollum, unpublished article.
122   *See* reference no. 108.
123   *See* reference no. 108.
124   Proceedings, TLC Convention, 1939.
125   Michiel Horn, *The Dirty Thirties*, 1972.
126   Ralph Hyman, 'The Birth of UAW Power in Oshawa', Toronto, *The Globe and Mail*, 4 February 1966.
127   *Where was George Burt?* United Auto Workers' booklet.
128   Charles Millard, 'After 25 Years', *Information*, April 1962.
129   Study by A.E. Grauer, Royal Commission on Dominion-Provincial Relations, 1939. (Stuart Jamieson, *Times of Trouble: Labour Unrest and Industrial Conflict in Canada, 1900-66*, Study No. 22, Task Force on Industrial Relations, 1968)
130   *The Labour Gazette*, Vol. XXXIX. (H.D. Woods and Sylvia Ostry, *Labour Policy and Labour Economics in Canada*, 1962)
131   *The Labour Gazette*, January 1946.
132   *See* reference no. 131.
133   *See* reference no. 131.
134   Report of Industrial Inquiry Commission on the Disruption of Shipping.
135   *Maclean's* Magazine, December 1950.

136	Proceedings, Canadian Congress of Labour, 1943.
137	Proceedings, Canadian Congress of Labour, 1946.
138	Proceedings, TLC Convention, 1955.
139	Merger Documents, TLC-CCL, Public Archives, Ottawa.
140	Constitution, Canadian Labour Congress, 1956.
141	Proceedings, Canadian Labour Congress Convention, 1956.
142	*See* reference no. 141.
143	*See* reference no. 141.
144	Bill amending Labour Relations Act, Newfoundland House of Assembly, 6 March 1959.
145	Toronto *Star*, 11 March 1959.
146	Hansard, 16 March 1959.
147	J.H. Crispo and H.W. Arthurs, *Industrial Unrest in Canada*, unpublished paper, Canadian Political Science Association, Ottawa, 1967.
148	*Political Education Program*, CLC booklet.
149	Proceedings, CLC Convention, 1958.
150	News release, Canadian Labour Congress, 2 May 1958.
151	Proceedings, CLC Convention, 1960.

Index